Hidden Hands

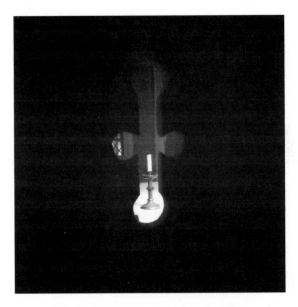

The view from the anchorite's cell at
St Nicholas' Church, Compton.

MARY WELLESLEY

Hidden Hands

The Lives of Manuscripts and Their Makers

riverrun

First published in Great Britain in 2021 by

riverrun

An imprint of

Quercus Editions Ltd
Carmelite House
50 Victoria Embankment
London EC4Y 0DZ

An Hachette UK company

Hardback ISBN 978 1 52940 093 9
Ebook ISBN 978 1 52940 095 3

10 9 8 7 6 5 4 3 2 1

Designed and typeset by EM&EN
Printed and bound in Great Britain by Clays Ltd, Elcograf S.p.A.

Papers used by Quercus are from well-managed forests
and other responsible sources.

For AW, CW and FD

god helpe minum handum

Anonymous scribe[1]

Good syster of your charyte I you pray
remember the scrybeler when that ye may

Anonymous reader[2]

If you are reading, this manuscript at least
will have survived.

Margaret Atwood[3]

Contents

List of Illustrations

Figures

p. ii – The view from the anchorite's cell at St Nicholas' Church, Compton. Courtesy of the author.

p. 1 – Elizabeth Danes' note, from John Lydgate, *Life of Our Lady; The Life of St Dorothy; The Abbey of the Holy Ghost*, c. 1475–1500. British Library Harley MS 5272, f.42r (detail). © British Library Board. All Rights Reserved/ Bridgeman Images

p. 23 – The author turned parchmenter. Courtesy of the author.

p. 36 – Incipit page to the Gospel of St John from *St Cuthbert Gospel*, 8th century. British Library Add. MS 89000, f.1r (detail). © British Library Board. All Rights Reserved/Bridgeman Images

p. 179 – Letter from John Paston III to John Paston II, 8 July 1472, from *Paston Letters and Papers*, British Library Add. MS 27445, f.59r (detail). © British Library Board. All Rights Reserved/Bridgeman Images

p. 190 – Autograph lines from Thomas Hoccleve, *Poems*, 1400-1425. The Huntington Library MS HM 111, f.19r (detail). The Huntington Library, San Marino, CA

p. 195 – *Caedmon's Hymn*, from Bede, *Historia ecclesiastica gentis anglorum* (the 'Moore Bede'), 8th century. Cambridge University Library MS Kk.5.16, f.128v (detail). Reproduced by kind permission of the Syndics of Cambridge

Plate Sections

1 Decorated capital from an Abbreviato of the *Domesday Book*, c. 1241. National Archives MS E 36/284, f.196 (detail). The National Archives, Kew

2 Aethelwine the Black (Egelwynus ye Swarte) and his wife Wynflaed, from Thomas Walsingham and William de Wylum, *Golden Book of St Albans*, 1380. British Library Cotton MS Nero D VII, f.89v (detail). © British Library Board. All Rights Reserved/Bridgeman Images

List of Illustrations

List of Illustrations

List of Illustrations

Introduction

At some point in the sixteenth century a girl named Elisabeth Danes wrote a threat into the pages of her book: 'Thys ys Elisabeth daness boke he that stelyng shall be hanged by a croke' ('*This is Elisabeth Danes's book, he that steals it shall be hanged by a crook [hook]*'). The note appears at the bottom of the manuscript page: defiant, a little naughty and full of bibliophilic feeling.

I first met Elisabeth Danes through her manuscript, when I was doing research in the British Library. I remember reading it and feeling the centuries dissolve. Here were the words of a fellow bibliophile from five hundred years ago; it is a reminder that there have been lovers of books for as long as there have been books to love. Elisabeth Danes treasured her book and the story it contained, and she wanted to protect it. But there was also something poignant in her words. From her handwriting, she appears to have been young. I wondered what power she had. She was a young woman, perhaps a child, in a patriarchal world; threatening potential book thieves might have been one of her few ways to assert herself. The note has a particular pathos – I discovered afterwards that it appears to be all that remains of her; she is otherwise hard to trace in the historical record.

Sometimes medieval manuscripts offer up names like Elisabeth Danes, but more often they allow us glimpses of anonymous figures. Some three centuries before Danes wrote her threat, a monk in Worcester Priory set about making careful notes in the margins of the manuscripts in the Priory's library. This scribe's handwriting was distinctive: shaky, outsized and left-leaning. Today he is known only as 'the Tremulous Hand', as scholars have been unable to discover his name. He was a prolific annotator – writing around 50,000 glosses (explanatory notes) in as many as twenty manuscripts. The majority of his annotations were in manuscripts containing Old English (the vernacular language of pre-Conquest England), yet he wrote his notes in Middle English (the language into which Old English had evolved) and Latin. At the time that he was working, in the thirteenth century, he was one of the last generations able to understand Old English – a Germanic vernacular which had changed dramatically after the Norman Conquest and its attendant influx of French vocabulary. He seems to have been collecting Old English words, possibly to make a glossary. We might see him as an early linguistic historian of sorts. Nineteenth-century scholars romanticised his work, suggesting that he was an elderly man, one of the last speakers of the dying language.[1] Today, scholars believe he had a neurological condition called 'essential tremor', which affects 4 per cent of adults. The work of the Tremulous Hand has much to tell us about language change, but whoever he was, I love how he encapsulates much of what I think is magical about manuscripts. He is anonymous. We know nothing about him except that his hand shook. But, as with Elisabeth Danes, it's hard for the manuscript scholar not to feel a kinship with him – he was intent on ferreting around in the past and decoding its remnants.

Sitting in the silence of a Special Collections reading room, and turning the pages of a medieval manuscript, is to have tangible, smellable, visual encounters with the past. Parchment manuscripts have a particular smell that is hard to describe: acrid with undernotes that suggest their organic origin. Their feel can be stiff and buckled, soft and faintly suede-like, or so finely worked as to be tracing-paper thin. Up close, the appearance of the parchment page contains ripples and imperfections – the traces of hair follicles, little repaired holes and places with discolouration. But the coloured inks and paints they contain are iridescent, having often been kept safely away from light damage for centuries.

When you hold a medieval manuscript, what lies in front of you is not only a text, but also a collection of human stories. A manuscript will have been made by many different hands and, in its history, it will have passed through many different hands again. It will bear the traces of the people who fashioned it and loved it, perhaps of those who disdained it and those who wished to alter it, often those who found it anew in a more recent time. Many remain anonymous – shadowy figures whose work with a quill, paintbrush or tool are all that survive of them. Sometimes they come into sharper focus.

The word 'manuscript' itself is a duet of two Latin words, *manus*, meaning 'hand', and *scribere*, meaning 'to write'. A manuscript is simply a handwritten object. Manuscripts are so compelling because they are made by hand – and because those hands tell us a great deal about the people attached to them. To this day, handwriting remains a personal expression of the self, perhaps ever more so as we ditch our pens in favour of our keypads. Scholars talk about the script in a manuscript as 'the hand'. A catalogue describing a manuscript might read, 'written in a fourteenth-century hand', and this terminology suggests that 'the hand' might extend towards us, might reach out to touch us. This is the magic of the manuscript.

In Geoffrey Chaucer's *The Parliament of Fowls* (written c. 1380), the narrator reflects on what people dream about – he describes the hunter dreaming of the wood, the judge dreaming of the court, the knight of fighting, and the alcoholic of his tipple. Had Chaucer included the manuscript scholar in his list, he would have said they dream of hands and folios, pen-lifts and page-gutters, of lacunae and palimpsests. To be a manuscript scholar is to worry about tiny, granular details, because a manuscript is like a crime scene – a tissue of minuscule clues to a forgotten history, which need to be examined with forensic care. Like forensics, the language of manuscript study can be strange and arcane. I have tried to explain terminology wherever necessary, but I have also included a glossary at the back of the book. Because I love language and language forms I have chosen, in almost all cases, to quote from original texts alongside modern translations. Consequently, readers will encounter some letters in the Old and Middle English alphabets which did not make it into the Modern English alphabet. These too are explained at the end of the glossary.

Manuscripts teem with life. They are the stuff of history, the stuff of literature, the material remains of the writerly act and the reading experience. But more than that, they are portals. They offer some of the only tangible evidence we have of entire lives, long receded. Manuscripts weren't only made and used and loved by wealthy elites, they were also made by ordinary people. Manuscripts grant access to the stories of anonymous artisans, artists, scribes and readers, as well as people who aren't always celebrated and discussed in our medieval histories – people of a lower social status, women, or people of colour. Without manuscripts, many historical figures would be lost, their voices silenced, their stories erased, and the remnants of their labours destroyed. Sometimes their stories can only be hinted at, while at other times they become more fleshed out.

A manuscript in the National Archives in London contains a marginal image, showing a man of African descent. The manuscript is a copy of the *Domesday Abbreviatio* – an condensed version of the Domesday Book, a census of land holdings in England made in 1085. The *Abbreviatio* itself dates from the thirteenth century.[2] The man appears on a page detailing royal land holdings in Derbyshire. The man's clothing – his short tunic – suggests he was not a person of elite social status. The artist perhaps intended to depict a servant or a slave. If this man was based on a real person, he may have come been forced to come to Europe during the migrations associated with the Crusades. Archaeological evidence indicates that there were people of African descent in England in this period, but it is hard to know how or why they came to be in England.[3] Why this marginal image appears we can't be sure, but it's an exciting reminder of a part of British history that is not widely understood, and, if drawn from life, a glimpse of one now long receded.

These little hints and clues are some of the allure of manuscripts. A charter from 1042–49 records a gift of land to St Alban's Minster. It reads:

Her swutelað on ðisan gewrite embe þa land þe Ægelwine swearte geuðe Gode to lofe [&] sancta Mariam & eallan Godes halgan into sancte Albanes mynstre for his sauwlan [&] for Wynflædan his wifes & for eallan his yldran saulan þam broðran to fode be Eadwardes cinges leafe.

Here is declared in this document about the estates which Æthelwine the Black granted to God in praise and to Holy Mary and all God's saints to St Alban's minster for his soul and for that of Wynflæd his wife and for the souls of all his ancestors to the brethren for their sustenance with the permission of King Edward.[4]

It is hard to know what this description of Æthelwine as 'the Black' means. It may simply have meant that he had dark hair. Names describing people by colours, like 'red' or 'golden' – colours that do not have the connotations they do today – are not uncommon in this period.[5] There is also every possibility, however, that the 'Ægelwine swearte' mentioned in this charter was of African descent.[6] A manuscript called the 'Golden Book of St Albans', from the later medieval period, recalls the great donations to St Albans Abbey over time and depicts the major benefactors. Here we find a tantalising image.

Alan Strayler – the manuscript artist – has chosen (or been instructed) to depict Æthelwine as dark-skinned, not simply dark-haired.[7] This might suggest that he had encountered people of a different ethnicity or else was familiar with images of people of colour. The image may be a fleeting glimpse of a little discussed aspect of British history – a history that is often more diverse and interesting than we give it credit for.[8]

Just as manuscripts offer glimpses of lives in the past, so too do they tell stories of oppression. In the Vatican Library there is a manuscript (MS ebr. 402), copied in the thirteenth century, which contains a series of *piyyutim* – Jewish liturgical poems.[9] In it, there is a poem, 'Put a Curse on my Enemy', which begins:

> Put a curse on my enemy, for every man supplants his
>   brother
> When will You [God] say to the house of Jacob, come let
>   us walk in the light?
> You are mighty and full of light, You turn the darkness
>   into light.
> Tear out their hearts – they who brought harm to those
>   who come in Your Name
> When I hoped for good, evil arrived, yet I will wait for
>   the light.[10]

The *piyyutim* in the manuscript are seemingly anonymous, but in one the poet has hidden a clue to his identity in an acrostic. It reads: 'I am Meir son of Rabbi Elijah of Norwich [Norgitz], which is in the land of the island England [Angleterre].' Nothing else is known of this Meir bin Elijah, but the chilling words of his *piyyut*, 'Put a Curse on my Enemy', should be read against the backdrop of the persecution of Jewish people in England in the thirteenth century, which culminated in the expulsion of the Jews in October 1290.[11] At the time that Meir was writing, Norwich had a population of fifty to sixty Jews, although it had had two hundred at its peak.[12] According to one source, the synagogue in Norwich was burned to the ground in 1286. Archaeological excavations in the nineteenth century uncovered a stone column, glazed tiles, pottery and – chillingly – a four-inch layer of charcoal at the site.[13] It is unclear how the manuscript containing Meir's poems came to be part of the Vatican Library's collection, but it could have been copied from a manuscript that was smuggled out of England by a Jewish person expelled in 1290 – perhaps this person knew Meir bin Elijah. Perhaps they wished to preserve his haunting *piyyutim* as a reminder to future generations of the experiences they had suffered. I like to imagine such a person, carrying a manuscript over the border amongst their possessions, carrying a message for us in later ages to remember the human stories contained in handwritten books.

In spite of their role as this essential tether to the past, manuscripts are some of the least accessible artefacts from the Middle Ages. They are kept in research libraries, often available only to scholars. When they are put on public display, what we see of them is so limited. Looking at a single opening of a manuscript is like only looking at one credit-card-sized corner of an Old Master painting: it is far from being the whole picture. The medievalist Michael Camille wrote that 'Medieval books are, of all historical artefacts, the least suited to public display in the modern museum. Behind glass their unfolding illuminations become static framed paintings, cut off from any of the sensations, texture or transport that one gets from turning their pages.'[14] But now, for the first time in human history, these previously inaccessible objects can be seen from anywhere in the world, in high resolution. We can now sit at home in our pyjamas and examine the *Beowulf* manuscript at a level of magnification that would be impossible even if we were in the reading room of the British Library, in clothing more suitable to scholarly study. At last, we all can meet these hidden hands.

INTRODUCTION

'In principio erat verbum' ('In the beginning was the word').
These are the opening lines of the Cuthbert Gospel, an
eighth-century manuscript made in the early days of Christianity in Britain, and where our own journey with words begins.
Eight hundred years later, the technology of the manuscript was
losing ground to the technology of print; as relics of a bygone
era, manuscripts became valuable historical curiosities. Yet for
all their value to collectors, manuscripts have often been treated
carelessly – burned, discarded or forgotten. Sometimes they
were recycled: their pages cut up and reused, often to make
bindings for new books. This story is one of survival against
the odds. The vast majority of manuscripts produced in the
medieval era perished through fire, flood, negligence or wilful
destruction. What does survive only does so through serendip-
itous chance, or because someone, somewhere, thought these
books worth saving. So the manuscripts discussed here are not
just antiquated objects, but cultural landmarks.

The word 'manuscript' – a handwritten object – has a transferred or associated meaning as a book (as opposed to a scroll
or single document), and the book is my primary interest, but
I've taken the liberty of including in my discussion below a
collection of letters. My first chapter begins in the twelfth century with the discovery of a manuscript from the eighth, and
my Afterword reflects on the emergence of antiquarians and
collectors in the sixteenth century – but the story I tell along
the way does not march straight through time. Manuscripts, by
their very nature, resist neat chronologies, because they often
tell simultaneous histories. They might have been written in
one age, but contain texts dated much earlier, and they also
incorporate the histories of their later owners or readers. So the
stories collected here are united, instead, by theme.

We begin with discovery and disaster: the survival and preservation of manuscripts have always been prey to chance. Manuscripts can be tools for remembrance, but they can also be easily forgotten and destroyed. The opening chapters focus on manuscripts as artefacts; later ones examine specific figures involved in the creation of manuscripts. Then we'll encounter patrons and artists. Patrons often left us their names – and their agendas – in their sumptuous books, but we don't memorialise these patrons equally: some are remembered, some forgotten. My first four chapters discuss single, monolithic manuscripts, but in the final three I move away from single books, to consider more complicated textual remains: multiple books or documents, and multiple versions of texts. These chapters discuss scribes and authors, looking first at scribes as people – at their devoted labours or their joyless drudgery – before moving on to the relationships *between* scribes and authors and, finally, to authors long hidden.

Why write about mansucripts? And why *these* manuscripts? Modern printed editions of texts are bald and lifeless things. Manuscripts are, by contrast, rich and messy. Sometimes they are beautifully decorated, sometimes untidy and illegible, but they speak of countless human stories. This book is not a story of manuscripts that changed the world, but about how manuscripts connect us to lives in the past. In attempting to illuminate these human lives, I ask why we value some figures from the past and forget others. *Hidden Hands* is about memory and forgetting, about forms of communication and memorialisation. This book grew out of my own research, so almost all the mansucripts here were created in England; many of them are literary. Most of the chapters range across the medieval period, with examples from the pre- and post-

Conquest era, but my concern has always been with what manuscripts tell us about their makers, rather than about broad historical narratives.

So many of the manuscripts in *Hidden Hands* were created by anonymous figures. We know nothing about these people – when exactly they were born and died, where they were from, let alone their names. But we have their work. We have the parchment or paper they processed, the shapes their letters made, the stitches they sewed, the bindings they fashioned, the places where they made textual changes or complained in notes of how their backs ached. This craftedness is what makes them so special. In one manuscript in the British Library there is the following scribal note:

> A man who knows not how to write may think this no mean feat. But only try to do it yourself and you will learn how arduous is the writer's task. It dims your eyes, makes your back ache and knits your chest and belly together – it is a terrible ordeal for the whole body. So, gentle reader, turn these pages carefully and keep your finger far from the text. For just as hail plays havoc with the fruits of spring, so a careless reader is a bane to books and writing.[15]

Manuscripts took many hours to produce. A manuscript is like a beautiful watch – lift the face, and beneath you will find a mechanism of startling intricacy. All the different parts are carefully crafted and work together coherently.

How a Manuscript was Made

Understanding how each of the different parts of a manuscript is made, and the labour required to do this, explains some of their magic. Until around the fifteenth century, when paper became more common as a writing material, manuscripts in Britain were mainly written by scribes on parchment, which is the prepared skin of a domestic animal, usually sheep or calves. (The term 'vellum' is sometimes used interchangeably with 'parchment', although it more often refers to calfskin.) The process of preparing parchment was skilled work (and my Prologue, below, contains an account of this process as it is practised today). In the early medieval period, parchment would probably have been made near to the place where the manuscript was copied, which was invariably a monastic 'scriptorium' (writing room). But, as time went on, scribal work was increasingly practised less in the monastery and more in secular, commercial contexts; parchment would have been processed in specialist workshops.[16]

Paper was made from cotton or linen rags, which were soaked and pulverised into a pulp. This pulp was placed into a vat of water and size (a glutinous substance), into which a sieve-like wooden frame, set with wires, was placed, to bring the pulp fibres to the surface. The film of sodden fibres was lifted out of the vat and then pressed between sheets of felt. The wires of the frame gave the finished paper ghostly lines in its surface which are only visible when the paper is held up to the light. From around 1300, European paper-makers began twisting patterns into the wire to identify the paper as their own. These patterns – little designs like the head of a bull or a bunch of grapes – are known as 'watermarks' and give scholars clues about the origins of particular paper stocks. Medieval and early modern paper made from rags is pretty durable, unlike modern paper made from wood pulp which tends to wither, discolour and crumble over time.

The architecture of a manuscript (or 'codex', to give it its Latin name), and how it was made, is worth understanding. Manuscripts were not complete books when they were copied by scribes. Instead, the parchment (or paper) was cut into an appropriate size and shape, and then folded in half. These folded pieces were called 'bifolia' – the Latin just means 'two leaves'; the singular is *bifolium*. When the bifolia were ready, they were then prepared for writing. To do this, the layout was planned and marked out with ruled lines. To get the lines all the in the right place, the scribe would first make little holes in the parchment, either with a knife, an awl (a small, pointed tool) or a 'pricking wheel', which was a spiked spinning wheel. In a large scriptorium, or workshop, this work might have been done by a more junior scribe. Depending on the status and quality of the manuscript, either big, generous margins were left, including spaces for illumination, or else the folios were ruled, so that there was little space for anything except text. The bifolia were then arranged such that their folded spines slotted into one another so that they could be sewn together in booklets, also called 'quires'. (Manuscripts, by and large, do not have pages, as we do, but 'folios', from the Latin for 'leaves', each of which has a single number, because a folio is a single sheet. References are therefore made not, say, to, 'pages (or pp.) 1–2', but instead to 'fol. 1r–v' – to distinguish between the 'recto' – the front of the single folio sheet – and the 'verso' – the back, or reverse, of that sheet.) After the bifolia were prepared, a scribe could begin writing. This was done with a quill, made from a feather and sharpened with a pen-knife (the origin of this modern term). The ink used by the scribe would most probably be made from oak galls – round, apple-like growths that grow on oak trees when gall-wasps (from the family *Cynipidae*) lay their eggs in an oak tree's developing leaf buds. The galls were ground, and then mixed with iron salts and tannic acids.

An ink recipe survives in the personal manuscript of a professional scribe. Oxford, Bodleian Library Tanner MS 407 was made by Robert Reynes – a churchwarden from the small Norfolk village of Acle – who lived and died in the latter years of the fifteenth century. His manuscript is an assortment of literary pieces, legal documents, useful charms, mnemonic devices, itineraries and prognostications—the medieval equivalent of the 'My Documents' folder on a person's computer. Amongst its paper folios, it instructs that 'Ffor to make blak ynke, take gallys, coporose and gumme of rabyk' ('to make black ink, take galls, copperas [iron (II) sulphite] and gum arabic'). It advises that the gum arabic should be soaked overnight and 'on the morwen take þi gumme-water and þi pouuder of gallys, and put hem togeder, and sette hem ouer the fyer, and lete hem sethen þe space of þis psalme seying, *Miserere mei, Deus*' ('in the morning, take the gum-water and the powder of galls, mix them together, and put them over a fire and let it simmer for as long as it takes to say the psalm, *Miserere mei, Deus* [i.e. Psalm 50]').[17] Lacking a pocket watch or clock of his own, Robert Reynes measured time in a highly practical, if also devout way.

The copying of a manuscript could take a long time, depending on the type of script used. The most stately and expensive were the most painstaking, requiring endless pen-lifts. Later in the medieval period, 'cursive' scripts became more common, meaning the letters of the words were joined together and scribes could work more quickly. (See p. 36 for a stately example and p. 179 for a cursive one.) Yet manuscripts were still laborious and time-consuming to copy. As an example, the *Moralia in Job* (an important and oft-copied commentary on the biblical Book of Job by Gregory the Great, c. 540–604) took some fifteen months to write out in the fifteenth century. A copy of the Bible might take years. It has been estimated that Romanesque scribes (i.e those working c. 900–1200), working approximately five to six hours a day, could copy around two hundred lines of text a day. This meant they might produce about twenty books in their lifetime.[18]

Once a scribe's copying was complete, the work would probably be checked by another scribe, and corrections might be made. After the text was corrected, then the work of decoration could begin. In manuscripts created on a budget, this might be restricted to occasional touchings in red ink, perhaps a few red initial letters (this practice is called 'rubrication'). In high-status manuscripts, however, the work of decoration was a serious enterprise. It might take decades. Other forms of extra-textual apparatus could be added, like tables of contents or marginal notes to guide the reader. Sometimes this kind of material could be presented quite beautifully, becoming a form of decoration in itself.

After copying and decorating, a manuscript might then be bound, with the quires sewn together in evenly spaced 'stations' along their spines. To make sure that everything was in order, scribes would write 'catchwords' at the bottom of the last folio in a booklet. (Such catchwords were the next few words of text appearing at the start of the next booklet. Sometimes these were simple things, but occasionally they became a decorative feature in their own right.)[19]

The top and bottom bands on the spine were given extra reinforcement. Then the covers could be added. Sometimes these were flexible and made of leather, but more often they were wooden boards, of a durable wood like oak or beech. Holes were drilled into the wood, and then the boards were laced onto the manuscript's spine before being covered with leather, with parchment inserts called 'pastedowns' affixed to the inside of the cover. Different kinds of leather could be used for the covers. Although calf- and goatskin were probably the most common, manuscripts were covered in all kinds of materials. Recent analysis has identified the furry covers of a number of manuscripts originating in the Cistercian abbey of Clairvaux as sealskin.[20]

Bindings could be considerably more elaborate than leather and wooden boards. Many had decorated covers – perhaps of carved ivory, or covered in metalwork and jewels. These jewelled covers, known as 'treasure-bindings', are extremely rare, as they were often plundered. (No treasure-bindings from England have remained intact, although there are written references to bindings once in existence.)[21] A rare survival is a stunning Gospel book in the Morgan Library in New York. It is one of four Gospel books commissioned by Judith of Flanders (died 1094/95), the wife of Tostig (the brother of King Harold II), who became Earl of Northumbria in 1055.

Beyond the covers, more elaborate structures could be added. 'Chemise bindings' are the 'medieval precursor of the modern dust jacket' – a little coat for a manuscript that could be made of leather, or textile.[22] They could be simple affairs – un-adorned parchment wrappers, or more elaborate things made from linen or from velvet and trimmed with beads, especially for expensive manuscripts. The wrappers also made the manuscripts easier to carry and, as such, they are akin to so-called 'girdle books'. Girdle books could be attached to a belt by a chain or rope. They were especially popular formats for prayer books, particularly those owned by wealthy women in the fifteenth and sixteenth centuries. The British Library holds a tiny copy of the Psalms owned by Anne Boleyn, second wife of Henry VIII (BL Stowe MS 956). It measures 3 cm by 4 cm and has a gold metalwork binding that was likely attached to a chain and hung from a belt. Girdle books were easy to carry around, but they were also easy to keep safe. For larger books, especially in monastic libraries, more forbidding security measures were used, where books were kept in chains.

Each of the figures involved in the production of manuscripts was responsible for important acts of textual creation and augmentation – marginal images could be used to enhance the meaning of a text, rich bindings would announce a work's value in unambiguous terms, while the labour of editors, correctors or annotators might create new meanings in different contexts. And after this, the books passed through generations of hands, some of whom left their traces in the pages. Frequently, the names of all these figures are lost, but they had a role in fashioning the object we behold, and in shaping the way we understand that object. There are plenty of splendid manuscripts in this book, but there are also some unassuming ones, because sometimes the unassuming manuscripts have the most interesting human stories to tell.

Why have we forgotten the names of so many of these figures? Our age values certain kinds of cultural production, forgetting the importance of others. We valorise authors and overlook the role of scribes, who were co-participants, alongside authors, in the creation of meaning. We've forgotten the work of manuscript artists, whose names – if they survive – aren't known beyond the academy. And in our digital age, we've *entirely* forgotten the time-consuming, highly skilled work involved in making parchment, grinding pigments, and stitching gatherings. Manuscripts now command a high price in the sale-room because of their cultural value, but if we consider the intrinsic value of a manuscript – the cost of replicating the object by employing skilled workers for years to reproduce it – we can reach a new appreciation of their worth.

Hidden Hands asks what it meant to be an author or an artist. Today, we often think of these figures – if we think of them at all – as people who worked alone, but manuscripts remind us repeatedly that making texts and making artefacts was a collaborative exercise, which was also necessary for transmission and preservation. In fact, innumerable figures were involved in the transmission of a text, each shaping it in ways both large and small. Sometimes manuscripts offer us a closer encounter with the scribes whose words we read than the authors whose work they copied.

History is a story written by the powerful, and the same is true of the literary and artistic canon. The energies of collectors, patrons, churchmen and regents have had a huge impact on what survives, but also – crucially – what comes to be celebrated and studied. There are ninety-two manuscripts of Geoffrey Chaucer's *Canterbury Tales* (which we will meet in Chapter Six) in varying degrees of completeness. Chaucer was a government official as well as a poet; he was well connected and had royal patrons. It is not surprising that so many manuscripts of his work should survive. And his place at the head of the English literary canon can be attributed, in part, to the fact that he wrote in a London dialect of English that is the ancestor of modern English. (He has always been more intelligible to later ages than – for example – the author of *Gawain and the Green Knight*, who was his contemporary.) By contrast, no medieval manuscript of Julian of Norwich's 'Long Text' of the *Revelations of Divine Love* – the earliest work in English written by a woman – survives. We are largely reliant on copies made by exiled Benedictine nuns in the seventeenth century. This is equally unsurprising: Julian was a female writer whose unusual theology was sometimes at odds with contemporary Church teaching.

That no medieval manuscript of Julian of Norwich's 'Long Text' (a kind of revised edition of this important work) survives is not unusual. Medieval manuscripts that have endured into the present day are survivors of war, fire, flood and disdain. Most of them were destroyed, those that are left are the exceptions – and so we cannot overstate their value. Some two-thirds of the extant corpus of Old English poetry survives in four physical books. The scholar Roy M. Liuzza called 'the surviving remains of Old English literature' the 'flotsam and jetsam of a vanished world'.[23] If later ages had only the flotsam and jetsam of our literary culture – survivals preserved as much by chance as design – how would they understand our age?

Manuscripts invite us to consider the lives of people who do not always loom large in our histories. And so they invite us, perhaps, to rethink the value we place in certain kinds of authors and particular patrons. You've almost certainly encountered Geoffrey Chaucer and Henry VIII, but have you ever heard of Queen Emma of Normandy, who was twice queen of England, or Leoba of Tauberbischofsheim, who was the first named female poet from England? Why do some names survive in the historical record, while others go unrecorded? Why are some celebrated and others confined to obscurity? Manuscripts, studied in detail, can tell us something about power and collective memory and the making of history. These are some of the richest and strangest objects made by human hands. Let's meet them, and their makers.

Prologue

The Alchemy of Parchment

Many manuscripts started with parchment. Nothing gives you an appreciation of these objects' value quite like watching the magical alchemy whereby animal hides – hairy, fatty, lumpy things – are transformed into immaculate writing surfaces. In June 2018, I saw this transformation on a visit to William Cowley's – a parchment maker near Milton Keynes.

The work of making parchment is unglamorous, and sometimes it smells like the inside of a boxing glove: like cheese and sweat and hard work. There is only one firm of parchment makers left in the UK. There are places elsewhere in the world where parchment is produced, but there the process is partially mechanised. At William Cowley's everything is still done by hand. What happens there is probably not much different from what was done in the Hellenistic city of Pergamon during the reign of Eumenes II (197–159 BCE). Eumenes was an avid bibliophile and built a library to rival that of Alexandria, containing 200,000 volumes at its peak. According to Pliny, Ptolemy of Egypt was so enraged by the acquisitive habits of his bibliophilic neighbour that he banned the sale of papyrus. Eumenes instructed his subjects to find an alternative writing material, and parchment was born. Where papyrus was fibrous, brittle and prone to breakage, parchment was flexible, durable and milky smooth. The city gave its name to the material: *pergamenum* is the Latin word for parchment.[1]

The initial stage of making parchment involves working with whole goat or calf hides, which come fresh from the abattoir, covered in hair. They still contain the suggestion of a lopped-off head and the beginnings of a tail. I saw one which had the remnants of some castrated testicles encased in a rubber band. In a store-room there was a huge pile of these hides, folded up, like furry pillowcases waiting to be laundered. After arriving at the parchment makers, the hides are soaked for around two weeks in a vat of lime (quicklime, not the citrus variety). At the end of this, they come out sodden on the hair side and slippery on the flesh side. The lime breaks down the follicles and loosens the hair. I watched as a hide was fished out and thrown over a wooden stump with a wet thwack. It lay hair-side up, liquid dripping from its brown curled ends. The stump is a smooth-topped wooden block, which the parchmenter leans over. It comes to just below chest height. Once there, the hair (known as the 'nap') is removed with a long, curved knife (called a 'scudder') which has wooden handles at both ends. I had a go at this and the hair peeled off like the skin from a potato – it was satisfying, if disconcerting. What is exposed is unmistakeably flesh: faintly translucent, with the suggestion of veins beneath. (Seeing this I thought of *The Silence of the Lambs*. There is something glaring about such a large piece of disembodied skin. I was reminded too of those statues of St Bartholomew – the saint who was flayed alive – with impassive, saintly expression, and his skin slung over his shoulder like a shawl.)

If I was struck by the 'skin-ness' of the hide in front of me, that wasn't just my modern sensibility interjecting. Several texts

The author turned parchmenter.

from the Middle Ages show a keen awareness of the materials on which they are written. The Middle English poem *The Long Charter of Christ* purports to be a legal document in which Christ grants salvation to mankind. In one version of the work in a parchment manuscript in the British Library (Harley MS 2346), Christ speaks, describing the events of the Passion. (The extract contains a characteristically medieval anti-Semitic trope):

> To a pilour y was py3t
> I-tugged and towed al a ny3t
> And washen on myn owne blode
> And strey3t y steyned on þe rode
> Streyned to drye on a tre
> As parchemyne ou3t for to be
> Hyreþ now & 3e schul wyten
> How þis chartre was wryten
> Upon my face was mad þe ynke
> Wiþ þe Jewes spotel on me to stynke
> þe penne þat þe lettres was with wryten
> Of scorges þat I was with smyten[2]

> *To a pillar I was tied*
> *All tugged and towed all the night*
> *And washed in my own blood*
> *And stretched and stained on the rod*
> *Strained to dry on a tree*
> *As parchment ought for to be*
> *Hear now and you shall know*
> *How this charter was written*
> *Upon my face was made the ink*
> *With the Jews' spittle on me to stink*

The Alchemy of Parchment

The pen used for the letters written
Was the scourge with which I was smitten.

Imagine the sensation for the devotional reader of reading a text like this, written on parchment – a parchment described as Christ's own face. Imagine the words of John 1:14, 'And the Word was made flesh and dwelt among us', thrumming in their ears.

After having their hair removed, the skins are dried and then stretched across a frame, known as a 'herse'. The word comes from the French *herse*, meaning an agricultural harrow, and ultimately from Latin *hirpex*. It is a cousin of 'hearse', which originally meant a frame for carrying lighted tapers over a coffin. The funereal connotation seems appropriate. Skins cannot be nailed to a frame because they would rip during the drying process. Instead, the skin's edge is gathered in bunches around balls of newspaper (in the medieval period, this would have been done with pebbles known as 'pippins') and tied with string to pegs at the edge of the frame. Treated in this way, the skin and frame take on the appearance of a rustic trampoline.

As the skin is stretched by twisting the pegs, hot water is applied and any remaining fat, especially from the meat-side, is removed using a knife shaped like a crescent moon called a *lunellum* or sometimes a *lunellarium* (at Cowley's they simply call it a 'luna'). The process of stretching and scraping is repeated several times before the frame is put into the 'oven', which is a large drying room. I made the mistake of venturing into the oven, which was hot and milky-smelling, in a heady way. My curiosity died in there.

Conrad de Mure (c. 1210–81) wrote that 'Pellis de carne, pelle caro removetur: tu de carne tua carnea vota trahe' ('Skin from the flesh, flesh from the skin is pulled: you pull from the flesh your fleshly desires'). The meaning is a little obscure here, as 'vota' is ambiguous, but de Mure's point seems to be that the labour of preparing parchment makes one purer and closer to God. Despite how unsexy the process was, I didn't feel my fleshly desires leaving me altogether, but I did see how this was a labour of love – the kind of labour that must have taken religious devotion to repeat with any frequency. A similar idea occurs in William Langland's late fourteenth-century dream-vision, *Piers Plowman*, which compares the cleaning of parchment to the shedding of pride: 'Of pompe and of pride þe parchemyn decourreþ' ('Of pomp and pride, the parchment denudes you').[3]

After the oven, the skins are ready for the final stage of their processing when the last layer of skin is shaved off, removing any dark patches or traces of hair, this time with a slightly larger 'luna'. Again, I had a go. Parchment holes are a common feature of medieval manuscripts. Picking up the knife, I was sure I was about to scrape too hard and break the skin. But the skin is strong; I could have hacked at it without breaking it. It's not surprising, therefore, that one of the main uses for parchment today is for drumskins.

Parchment is built to last. In this it an emblem of a pre-disposable culture. You need only look at the almost pristine, parchment pages of the Codex Sinaiticus, made nearly 1,700 years ago in c. 325–75 CE, to recognize this. Cheap, twentieth-century paperbacks, with glued spines and paper that withers like an autumn leaf, often present a greater challenge to library conservation departments than parchment manuscripts. And parchment, unlike many of the disposable materials we use today, was often recycled. It was cut up to make new bindings, fill holes or repair damage. Sometimes it was scraped clean of its writing and used again, leaving ghostly palimpsests for scholars to uncover.

Leaving Cowley's, I reflected that it is a place from a different time – not simply a place that plies an ancient trade, but also a place that disdains disposability. It prizes what is durable and recyclable. You get the sense that little there is thrown away unnecessarily. Everything shows the marks of use and re-use: the wooden handles of tools glossy and smooth from years of handling, the wooden blocks worked on again and again. I wondered what would remain of our culture in 1,700 years?

Chapter One

DISCOVERIES

[T]hey are ill discoverers that thinke there is no land when
they can see nothing but Sea.

Francis Bacon[1]

In scholarship, discoveries are rarely made in an instant. They
often happen via a painstaking process, drawn out over weeks,
months or years. The Egyptologist Flinders Petrie wrote that
'the true line' of research lay 'in the careful noting and comparison of small details'.[2] So imagine what it would be like
to discover something and realise that what you have in your
hands is going to change your field. Imagine what it would be
like to discover something by chance, by a 'fortunate series
of accidents' (as Walter Oakeshott described one of the most
important discoveries in medieval studies to be made in the
modern era).[3] Each of the stories here describes people finding
manuscripts quite by chance.

Here I tell the stories of three separate discoveries. They are
all quite different, but they all share a striking feature. In each
story, a manuscript made nearly half a millennium earlier is
discovered. The first is about a find made in the twelfth century,

while in the second two, the time of the discoveries is closer to our own. In the first, the discovery was seen as miraculous, but whether you live in the twelfth century or the twentieth, to uncover the material remains of a four-hundred-year-old past must feel like an experience of the divine, especially if – as a scholar – you know that this discovery will change your field. Writing about one of these finds, the scholar G. L. Kittredge wrote that it was like hearing 'a voice from the great deeps'.

'In the Beginning was the Word': The Saint Cuthbert Gospel

In August 1104, the coffin of Saint Cuthbert (c. 634–687) was opened by the monks of the Durham Cathedral. A new cathedral had been constructed and it was time to move the saint's body to a shrine behind the high altar at the east end of the new building.[4] On 24 August, a group of nine monks waited until nightfall, when they entered the old church and prostrated themselves before the shrine. They had prayed and fasted for several days before to prepare themselves for their task. The act of moving their community's most important relic was not to be undertaken lightly. They wept and offered further prayers as they laid their trembling hands on the coffin. Using 'instruments of iron', they prised open the lid to discover a chest covered in hides, held together by nails. They hesitated, but the prior exhorted them to continue in their task. Lifting the lid of the chest, they discovered an inner coffin, covered in linen. At this point they fell to their knees, weeping and praying, whereupon one of the monks named Leofwin (whose name in Old English meant 'dear friend' or 'dear joy', and who was considered very devout and 'dear to God'), exhorted them to continue in their task, saying, 'He who gave us the will to make the investigation, gives us the hope of discovering what we seek.'

They moved the inner coffin from behind the altar to the middle of the choir to make their investigation easier, removed its linen covering and examined it in the candlelight, hoping to see the contents of the chest through a crack between the lid and the base. Realising it was shut fast, they prised open the lid. There, on a shelf above the head of the saint, they found a Gospel book. It was a tiny red leather thing – so small it could have been held in one of the monks' trembling hands. Thrilled with terror at seeing the miraculously incorrupt body of Saint Cuthbert, the monks may not have realised how important this book was. It had been made at the start of the eighth century, in the time of Bede (672/3–735), and probably placed in Cuthbert's coffin a few decades after he died in 687. For four centuries, it had lain quietly on this shelf, while Cuthbert's body had been on a wandering course, as the members of his community fled Viking raiders. He was initially buried, in 687, on the island of Lindisfarne – a tidal islet off the Northumbrian coast. But in 793, just over a century after his death, the island was attacked by Vikings. These invaders were 'like stinging hornets, and overran the country in all directions, like fierce wolves, plundering, tearing, and killing not only sheep and oxen, but priests and choirs of monks and nuns'. When the raiders arrived in Lindisfarne, they 'laid all waste with dreadful havoc, trod with unhallowed feet the holy places, dug up the altars, and carried off all the treasures of the holy church. Some of the brethren they killed; some they carried off in chains; many they cast out, naked and loaded with insults; some they drowned in the sea.'[5]

In face of such savagery, in the spring of 875, the community left the island for the last time, taking Cuthbert's coffin with them. They travelled for seven long years, stopping off at Norham, Whithorn (on the Derwent) and Crayke. In 883 they settled in Chester-le-Street, where they remained until 995. In this year, Bishop Aldun – the leader of the community – 'was admonished by a revelation from heaven' that he should flee 'some pirates who were close at hand'. The monks moved again, to Ripon, but after three or four months of peace, they decided to return to Chester-le-Street. On their journey there, however, they reached a spot near Durham and 'the vehicle, on which the shrine containing the holy body was deposited, could not be induced to advance any further'.[6] The cart became stuck in the mud, which the monks took as a sign of divine providence: Cuthbert did not wish to move. It was decided that they should settle there. Perhaps Cuthbert approved of Durham's hill encircled by a river? Or perhaps it harked back to the island of Lindisfarne, where he had lived most of his life?[7]

The journey Cuthbert's body had taken illustrates the great destruction wreaked by the Vikings and the desperate efforts made by generations of monks to evade them. In the four hundred years that the little book had remained hidden in the coffin, these incursions had destroyed many important libraries in the north of England. This meant that the manuscript was a precious remnant of an important bibliographic culture, now devastated by marauding war-bands. Its survival over those centuries was extraordinary. And yet, more extraordinary still, it has survived into our own day. It is known as the St Cuthbert Gospel. It weighs 162 g and measures 10 cm by 14 cm, but its tiny size betrays nothing of its status as a cultural monolith: the

Cuthbert Gospel is still in its original binding, making it the earliest intact book in Europe.

The manuscript has had a tumultuous history up to the present day: it has survived interment, Viking incursions, Protestant despoilers, and a trip to Belgium. After its discovery in 1104 it was venerated by the monks of Durham Cathedral and seemingly protected by a higher power. Reginald of Durham (died c. 1190) recounts how, in the twelfth century, a monk attempted to 'grope' the book and died soon afterwards. The same author also describes how one of the Bishop of Durham's officials stole a thread from the strap on the book's satchel. Secreting it in his shoe, he was subsequently afflicted with a terrible swelling of the leg, which was only cured when the thread was returned.

In 1539 Durham Cathedral Priory was dissolved and the cult of Cuthbert suppressed as part of the Protestant Reformation.[8] Many of the cathedral's relics were destroyed or dispersed. Katherine Whittingham, the dean's wife, removed the stoups (the basins for holy water) and installed them in her kitchen, where she used them to store salted beef and fish.[9] As for the Cuthbert Gospel, what happened to it in this period is a mystery. It probably passed into the hands of an antiquarian (someone who collected the material remains of the past). It appears in the early seventeenth century in the collection of the mathematician and astrologer Thomas Allen of Gloucester Hall, and from there it entered the collection of George Henry Lee, 3rd Earl of Lichfield (1718–1772). Lee's ownership of the book was somewhat incongruous. He was a Tory politician described in one account as 'a red-faced old gentleman who had almost drunk away his senses'.[10] Lee gave the manuscript to a Catholic priest, the Reverend Thomas Philips, in 1769, who in turn presented it to the English Jesuit College in Liège (a training college for Catholic priests). In 1794, the staff and students fled the upheaval of the Napoleonic Wars and moved to Lancashire – to Stonyhurst College – just as nearly a millennium earlier the inhabitants of Lindisfarne had fled the attacks of Viking raiders.

In the nineteenth century scholars began to take an interest in the manuscript. In 1806 it was examined by Bishop John Milner, who exhibited it at the Society of Antiquaries. Milner confessed that he had found the manuscript's story outlandish: 'I own I rejected the story as a fabrication.' His description of it is largely accurate, except that he declared the binding to be 'of the time of Queen Elizabeth', which we can't really blame Milner for because the history of Western book-binding *begins* with the Cuthbert Gospel.[11] There wasn't much to compare it with. Milner returned the manuscript to Stonyhurst, but in 1808 it was lent once more to the Society in order that a facsimile of its first page might be taken. The manuscript went missing on its way back. Fr Marmaduke Stone, the college president, wrote, 'If it be lost, God's holy will be done.'[12] God's will or not, it was returned and kept by the Jesuits until it was bought by the British Library in 2012 for £9 million. It was the largest and most successful fundraising campaign the library had ever mounted.

Today you can see the Cuthbert Gospel (BL Add. MS 89000) in full online.[13] It is also often on show in the British Library's Treasures Gallery and periodically in Durham. Seeing it in person, you could almost be disappointed by it. It is so slight, and its binding design is relatively simple. The cover is made of embossed red leather, with a Celtic interlace pattern surrounding a plant motif. Some faint traces of pale yellow and blue pigment are just discernible in the grooves of the design.

But the manuscript was made some 1,300 years ago and, in subtle ways, it speaks to us across the centuries. It captures a sense of England, in the early days of Christianity in the British Isles. It tells us that although we might imagine these islands in the period as an outpost at the far edges of the known world, the truth is quite different. The Cuthbert Gospel was made in a flourishing monastery, a monastery with international connections, which was celebrated as a centre of learning with an important library.

The front cover of the manuscript shows, in a central panel, an embossed design of a vine sprouting from a chalice. This design recalls the early Christian fountain-of-life motif, which was common in the period in the Eastern Mediterranean, and the motif of the vine sprouting from the chalice can be found, amongst other places, on the doors of the fifth-to-sixth-century church of Sitt Barbara in Cairo.[14] At once the manuscript whispers clues as to its origin and contents. The vine motif recalls John 15: 5, 'I am the vine, you are the branches', hinting that the contents are the Gospel of St John. Around this vine motif, we can see interlacing patterns, characteristic of early medieval English and Irish art.

In the design of the front cover we already gain a sense of this as a book produced in early medieval England as a place with international connections. If you were able to remove the spine of the mansucript's binding, you would see that the manuscript's folios are bound together using a chain-stitch method that originated in Coptic Egypt. The booklets that make up the manuscript are not sewn onto cords, as was customary in Western Europe, but instead sewn together by two needles working in a figure of eight pattern from booklet to booklet. The effect is that the book opens easily and lies flat.

The Cuthbert Gospel's covers are of international significance, but for me the beauty of the manuscript is in its text pages. The opening words read:

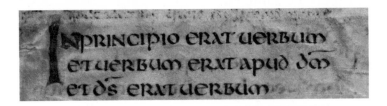

IN PRINCIPIO ERAT VERBUM
ET VERBUM ERAT APUD DEUM
ET DEUS ERAT VERBUM

In the beginning was the word
and the word was with God
And the word was God

This book – the earliest intact European book – represents the beginning of the word, or rather, a *story* of the written word, in England. It is a story that stretches from the start of the eighth century to our own day. And these opening lines are apposite because each word here has been copied out with a kind of devotional reverence. Each word here is God. The scribe has written out the text entirely in capital letters, in a script scholars call 'uncial'. The opening letters are picked out in red ink. Although punctuation was uncommon in manuscripts of this period, the scribe has divided the text using line breaks as a kind of punctuation, even though this was not the most economical use of the parchment. The words are written with crisp, clean lines; there are no traces of mistakes. In fact, the manuscript as a whole is remarkably error-free. There are only five 'erasures' (rubbings-out) and only two instances where mistakenly omitted letters have been inserted above the line in the entire manuscript.[15] The words on each folio are generously spaced apart; there are only nineteen lines per page, and the page's margins are substantial relative to the size of the text-space. These might seem like boring details, but they indicate a book produced with great care, a book whose manufacture required an investment of time and resources.

That investment of time and resources was characteristic of the scriptorium where the manuscript was made.[16] The Cuthbert Gospel was written at Wearmouth-Jarrow. This twin monastery (comprising foundations at both Wearmouth and Jarrow) once stood on the banks of the River Tyne. It was founded by Bene-dict Biscop (c. 628–690) in 672/3 (for Wearmouth) and in 681 for Jarrow. Early in its existence, Wearmouth-Jarrow became a centre of great learning. (It was to produce, a generation later, the 'Venerable' Bede – the greatest historian of the early medi-eval period in Britain.)[17] Key to this intellectual flourishing was Biscop himself. He went to Rome six times, and on three of these occasions he acquired manuscripts which he brought back with him, over the North Sea. He also recruited masters to teach liturgy and chant who likely taught the craft of writing as well. It was probably Benedict Biscop who brought back, from one of his trips to Rome, a very accurate copy of the Latin Vul-gate Bible. It was this text that would go on to be the exemplar – the source text – for the Cuthbert Gospel.

In some ways it is ironic that the manuscript should be a testament to the international reach of early medieval England because it bears the name of a saint who preferred seclusion. Cuthbert spent the latter part of his life as a monk in the mon-astery of Lindisfarne. Lindisfarne had been founded (possibly in the year of Cuthbert's birth) by Aidan (died 651), who came from the Irish monastery of Iona. Bede tells us that after 'many years' in the monastery, Cuthbert opted to live as a hermit on Inner Farne Island, where 'he joyfully entered into the remote solitudes which he had long desired'.[18] In 685, he was made Bishop of Lindisfarne, which, by all accounts, he seems to have disliked, preferring instead the splendid isolation of his cell. Bede tells us that Cuthbert built a round dwelling for himself, which he partially excavated out of the rock. It had a high wall and seemingly no windows, 'to prevent the eyes and the thoughts from wandering, that the mind might be wholly bent on heavenly things, and the pious inhabitant might behold nothing from his residence but the heavens above him'.[19]

Looking at the Cuthbert Gospel today, in the protective dimness of the British Library Treasures Gallery, the little book seems a world away from the saint after whom it was named. It seems almost impossible that it could have been made 1,300 years ago. I can understand the position of the Reverend Milner (who thought its leather cover was Elizabethan): it is miraculous that it should still be in its original binding. From our perspective today, 1104 (the year Cuthbert's coffin was opened) seems a long time ago. But when it was discovered, it was already nearly half a millennium old. The next discovery in this chapter was also a discovery of a manuscript made nearly half a millennium after it was made, but the time of discovery is closer to our own. Tantalisingly closer.

The Book of Margery Kempe

In the summer of 1934 an extraordinary, accidental find was made by a family in search of ping-pong balls.[20] A first-hand account of the event was given by Captain Maurice Butler-Bowden (1910–1984). He described how he was playing ping-pong with some friends at his family's Georgian house near Chesterfield and how 'one of us trod on the Ping Pong ball and my father went to the cupboard to get out a replacement and it was soon apparent that he was having difficulty in finding either a ball or even the tube of balls'.[21] At this point one of the Butler-Bowdens' house-guests went over to the cupboard to lend a hand with the ball-hunt. By fortuitous chance, this house-guest was a certain Charles Gibbs-Smith, who was at the time an assistant keeper at the Victoria and Albert Museum in London. The reason for the balls remaining elusive was that the cupboard contained 'an entirely undisciplined clutter of small-ish leather bound books'. Butler-Bowden recounted his father's exasperation at this pile of book-clutter: 'I am going to put this whole "——" lot on the bonfire tomorrow and then we may be able to find Ping Pong balls & bats when we want them.' Gibbs-Smith objected to this idea, asking whether he could invite 'an expert . . . acquaintance of mine who knows about these things to come and look through this cupboard, after all there may be something of real interest there which you may not at the moment realise'. Lt-Col. Butler-Bowden insisted that the books were 'all old household account books', but remarked that 'if your friend thinks his trip would be worth it', he would not mind. So the books were saved from burning and the friend was duly invited to stay.

The friend was Albert Van de Put – a medieval historian who was also on the staff of the Victoria and Albert Museum. This being 1934, he arrived 'one evening in time to change for dinner'. The next morning after breakfast Van de Put began his investigation of the cupboard's contents. Half an hour later he visited Lt-Col. Butler-Bowden in his study, saying, 'Thank you very much for your hospitality, I think I will be away now – I think I have found something more interesting than I should have hoped for in my wildest dreams.' Van de Put asked to take one of the books with him back to London. It might not have looked very exciting – it had a cover that had been repaired after being 'eaten away presumably by a mouse'. Butler-Bowden assented. Not long after this, the text in the manuscript was identified as the lost *Book of Margery Kempe*.

The Book of Margery Kempe is the first piece of autobiographical writing in English.[22] Kempe (c. 1373–1438) was an East Anglian woman who worked variously as a horse-mill operator and a brewer. She was also the mother of fourteen children. Her *Book* opens by describing how, after the difficult birth of her eldest child, she became ill and feared for her life. She called for a priest in order to make confession. When she confessed a particular transgression, which had long troubled her, he admonished her for her sinful ways – an experience which she appears to have found deeply traumatic. It induced what today we might term post-partum psychosis, which lasted for over six months. During this time, she experienced terrifying visions of devils:

And in þis tyme sche sey, as hir thowt, deuelys opyn her mowthys al inflaumyd with brenny[n]g lowys of fyr, as þei schuld a swalwyd hyr in, sum-tyme ramping at hyr, sumtyme thretyng her, sumtym pullyng hyr *and* halyng hir boþᵉ nygth *and* day duryng þe forseyd tyme.²³

And in this time she said that she thought she saw, or so it seemed to her, devils with open mouths all inflamed with burning flares of fire, who looked as though they might swallow her up. Sometimes they pawed at her, sometimes they threatened her, sometimes they pulled her, dragging her around both day and night throughout that time.

These visions occasioned suicidal thoughts – 'Sche wold a fordon hirself many a tym' ('She would have killed herself many a time') – and bouts of self-harm: she tore her own hand with her teeth, causing permanent scarring, and slashed at the skin over her heart with her fingernails. She would have done herself further damage had she had 'oþer instrumentys' and had she not been bound and forcibly restrained night and day.²⁴ She was twenty years old.

After a 'long' time had passed, Margery 'lay aloone', her 'kepars we fro hir' (i.e. there were no 'keepers' or 'warders' nearby), and she had a vision of Jesus, who came to sit at her bedside. He appeared in a gorgeous purple robe, looking 'most semly, most bewtyvows & most amyable' ('most handsome, most beautiful and most amiable'). He asked her 'why hast thow forsakyn me I forsoke neuyr þe' ('why have you forsaken me? I never forsook you'). This vision brought her great comfort, and she returned to sanity: 'stablelyd in hir wyttys *and* in hir reson' ('restored to her wits and in her reason').²⁵ This was to be the first of a series of visions of Christ, his mother and other saints which Margery experienced over the course of her eventful life.

After her early visions of Christ, and the failure of two businesses that she ran, which she interpreted as a sign of God's displeasure, she sought to live a spiritual life, despite not being attached to any religious institution. She became what is termed a 'vowess' – someone who takes unofficial religious vows. After over twenty years of marriage, she persuaded her husband to forswear sexual relations with her. (At this point in the fifteenth century, a husband had the right to have sex with his wife whenever he wished; indeed it took until 1991 for marital rape to be considered a crime in UK law.) Thereafter she took a vow of chastity, gave up eating meat and wore only white.

Margery's account of her life is beguilingly down to earth. After her first vision of Christ, she asked her husband 'þat sche might haue þe keys of þe botery to takyn hir mete & drynke' ('have the keys of the buttery so that she might have food and drink').[26] There is something so charming about a woman who can sit down to what we might imagine was a hearty meal, in the immediate aftermath of a mystical experience. It is these kinds of homely details that have captivated readers since the first edition of the text appeared in 1936.[27]

There is also something homely in Margery's expression of her devotion. It is striking that many of her visions centre on Christ as a child and the Virgin as a mother. In the work's sixth chapter, she has a vision of attending the birth of Christ in Bethlehem, in which she provides practical assistance to the Virgin Mary – finding lodgings, 'whyte clothys & kerchys for to swathyn in hir Sone whan he wer born' ('white clothes and kerchiefs for her to swaddle her son in when he was born'). Later, Margery herself 'swathyd hym [Jesus]'.[28] There is great tenderness in this, but it has the mark of a woman who has been a mother herself – a woman who knows how to be comforting as well as useful. We are left to wonder how many of Margery's fourteen children survived and why her visions sometimes focused on the experiences of motherhood. Her visions began in the immediate aftermath of the traumatic birth of her first child; we can only speculate on what psychological effect that experience had.

Margery's *Book* shows the tenderness she felt towards the person of the Christ-child, but her tenderness and compassion are discernible elsewhere. There is a moving episode in which she comforts a woman who is mentally disturbed after childbirth. In Chapter 75, Margery is praying in church when she is approached by a man in some distress. She enquires of him what is wrong, and he explains that his wife is 'newly delyueryd of a childe' and is 'owt hire mend' ('out of her mind'). You can sense his anguish when he tells her that his wife 'knowyth not me ne non of hir neyborwys. Schr roryth & cryith so þat sche makith folk euyl a-feerd. Sche wyl boþe smytyn & bityn & þerfor is sche mankyld on hir wristys' ('does not recognise me or any of her neighbours. She roars and cries, so that folk fear she is evil. She will both hit and bite and therefore her wrists are manacled'). This description is disturbing, revealing how little mental illness was understood in the fifteenth century.[29]

When Margery visits the woman, she becomes calmer, telling Margery that she is a 'ryth [truly] good woman', but later, when the woman is visited by other people, she becomes distressed again, weeping and crying and threatening to eat them. After this, the woman is taken to a room in 'þe forthest ende of þe town', where her hands and feet are shackled in 'chenys of yron' ('iron chains').[30] Margery, however, visits her every day, speaking to her and praying for her. The woman recovers, and is welcomed back into her community. Of course, it is difficult to know what to make of this story today, but what strikes me is that Margery had also been through a traumatic birth, she had also been scorned and shackled. Perhaps her gentle acceptance of the woman helped her to return to sanity.

Despite these instances of compassion, Margery often experienced derision, scorn, and even threats to her own life. She was repeatedly accused of heresy. Her tendency to weep loudly in devotion drew derision, while her willingness to admonish people on how best to live a good Christian life drew fear from some ecclesiastical authorities. The fifteenth century was an uneasy time for the Church. A muscular heretical movement, centring on the scholar and Bible translator John Wycliffe, had begun in Oxford in the late fourteenth century. By the start of the fifteenth century the Church was aggressively cracking down on anyone whom it perceived to be perpetuating unorthodox views. Unlicensed preaching was banned, and the prospect of a woman preaching was unthinkable. Margery was accused of being a heretic several times. She was interrogated by ecclesiastical authorities at Leicester and underwent trials at York, Hull, Hessle and Beverley, while travelling the country on pilgrimage, and was threatened with being burnt alive in the street.

In spite of this, Margery travelled extensively in England and abroad, going overseas on several pilgrimages. She visited Jerusalem in 1413, not returning to England until 1415. Two years later, in 1417, she travelled to Santiago de Compostela in Spain. And in 1433, after a more sedentary period at home in Lynn, she set off again, travelling to Norway, Danzig and Aachen, where she saw its four holy relics. These pilgrimages are described in vivid detail, including the scornful way she was treated by others. In Chapter 26, Margery recounts how when she was travelling to Jerusalem, she was bullied by her fellow travellers, who cut her robe so that it came just below the knee (a shockingly short length) and forbade her from eating at table with them.

Her descriptions of her travels are fascinating for what they reveal about how much the world has changed since the fifteenth century. But Margery's experiences were also timeless. In Chapter 76, she describes how she nursed her husband when he became senile and incontinent. At this point the pair had been living apart because of the vow of chastity that she had taken, but she came to live with him again and cared for him until his death. Her husband, whom she had once loved passionately, now had to be tended to like an infant. The *Book* describes how 'as a childe [he] voydyd his natural dygestion in hys lynyn clothys' ('like a child, he soiled his linen clothes') which was 'labowr meche' ('a great labour') for her, but she felt it was an appropriate divine punishment, as 'sche in hir ʒong age had ful many delectabyl thowtys, fleschly lustys & inordinate louys to hys persone' ('she, in her youth, had had delighted in many thoughts, lustful urges which centred on him, and taken great joy in his body').[31]

Margery's work is extraordinary in many ways, but in some ways its value lies in its sheer *ordinariness* – Kempe was no aristocrat or gentry woman. She was the daughter of the mayor of a prosperous East Anglian town. Too often it is the voices of a regal or ecclesiastical elite that come down to us from the Middle Ages. This is in part because so few non-elite figures in the medieval period were literate (although this began to change at the latter end of the era). Nor was Margery unusual in this. She too was illiterate. In order to record her experiences, she had to dictate the work to an 'amanuensis' – a scribe who listened to her words and wrote them down. In fact, three different amanuenses were involved in the project. The first was

'an englyschma*n*', who may have been her son, who lived in
Germany but moved to England. He 'cam in-to Yngland with
hys wife *and* hys goodys *and* dwellyd with þe foreseyd creatur'
('came to England with his wife and his goods and dwelled with
the aforesaid creature' – here, as elsewhere in the text, Margery
is referred to in the third person, as the 'creatur', to advertise
that she did not personally write the text). This Englishman
died before the work was completed and thereafter the work
was taken up by a priest who said it was 'so euel wretyn þat
he cowd lytyl skyll þeron, for it was neiþyr good Englysch ne
Dewch ne þe lettyr was not schapyn ne formyd as oþer letters
ben' ('so ill-written that he could make little sense of it, for it
was neither good English nor German and the letters were not
written as they should be').[32] At this point, Margery and the
priest began the work again from scratch. But the priest was dis-
couraged by some malicious gossip he had heard about Kempe,
and so he delayed the project for four years. He directed Kempe
to a third man, who had at one time been a correspondent of
the first amanuensis, the 'englyschma*n*'. This new scribe could
not understand the text. Subsequently, the priest began to suffer
pangs of guilt and prayed to God to be able to understand the
work, whereupon he was miraculously able to complete the
Book. Although hindered at every turn, Margery was dogged in
her efforts to preserve her story.

The manuscript itself is not the original one written down by
the last of Margery's amanuenses. But for once, we do actually
know the name of the scribe who copied it. He names himself
as 'Salthows' at the end of the text, with a conventional phrase
often used by scribes: 'Jhesu mercy quod Salthows' ('Thanks
be to Jesus says Salthouse').[33] Exactly who this 'Salthows' was
is something of a mystery. There is a village called Salthouse

on the north coast of Norfolk, about thirty-five miles northeast of Lynn, so he may have been from there. Small clues in the manuscript's physical construction tell us that it dates from c. 1440–50. It is written on paper, and in this period all paper contained watermarks. These watermarks, which simply denote a place of origin, leave ghostly clues in a manuscript's pages indicating where the paper was made. You can only see them by holding a manuscript's pages up to the light, when they shine through as paler than the rest of the paper. The watermarks in the manuscript of Kempe's *Book* show the paper was made in Holland, c. 1440–50.[34] (Much of East Anglia's prosperity in this period came from the wool trade. Part of the reason the region was so rich was that it had such good trade links with the Continent and the Low Countries in particular. It is therefore unremarkable to find an English manuscript copied on paper made in Holland.) There are further clues in the manuscript that give us a sense of its date and probable location. At the end of the manuscript we find a document called a 'faculty', which records the appointment of a certain William Buggy as vicar in Soham in Cambridgeshire, which is around thirty miles south of Lynn. The document is dated 1439, so the manuscript was likely not made before 1439 – the year after Margery probably died.[35]

The manuscript then made its way to a Carthusian priory in Yorkshire – Mount Grace. On one of its opening leaves there is an inscription that reads 'liber mon[n]te gr[ac]e. this boke is of montegrace' in a fifteenth-century hand.[36] From there – it has been conjectured – the book may have made its way to London and been acquired by an ancestor of the Butler-Bowdens, in whose untidy cupboard the manuscript was found, almost five hundred years later.[37]

The Silencing and Rediscovering of Margery

Until the discovery of the only known manuscript of the work in 1934, the text had previously only been identified in seven pages of heavily abbreviated extracts printed by Wynkyn de Worde (the successor of William Caxton, England's first printer, discussed below in the Epilogue) in 1501. The text in de Worde's edition is starkly different from the manuscript text. An editor has gone through the original and stripped out all the moments in which Christ addresses Margery in her visions and only printed these sections. In effect, the printed edition silences Margery's voice. Whereas in the manuscript version Margery is a larger-than-life character, who roars and wails and boisterously communicates her devotion, in these printed extracts she is a listener and not a speaker. The text focuses on Margery's experiences in the 1420s, thereby removing the descriptions of her pilgrimages, and harassment as a supposed heretic, and it is the voice of Christ that dominates the text.

Margery Kempe's story is, in many ways, a story of triumph over adversity, and of a woman's determination to be heard. It is appropriate, therefore, that the identification of the text in the manuscript was made by a female scholar – Hope Emily Allen. In 1934, Allen – an American scholar who had grown up in a perfectionist 'holy community' in Oneida in upstate New York, and attended Bryn Mawr and Harvard – was on a research trip to London.[38] It was at this time that Albert van de Put had brought the manuscript to the Victoria and Albert Museum. Van de Put was a historian of medieval Spain, and this piece of Middle English devotional prose was outside his area of expertise. The assistance of several scholars was sought, including

Evelyn Underhill, who suggested that her cousin, Hope Emily Allen, might be able to help. In late July 1934 Allen came to the museum, and it was there that she identified the manuscript as the only known full copy of Kempe's text.[39]

In December of that year, Allen wrote a letter to *The Times* to announce publicly that this discovery had been made.[40] (The letter appears characteristically modest, claiming no glory for herself in the identification of the text.) Allen was not interested in transcribing the manuscript or studying its language, so she suggested that her colleague, Sanford B. Meech, be appointed a joint editor alongside her for an edition for the Early English Text Society. Relations between the two quickly deteriorated and she began to suspect that Meech 'was seeking, possibly with the support of the manuscript's owner, to force her off the project'. As John. C. Hirsch notes, 'it is difficult to believe that Meech would have treated a senior male colleague with the irritation, anger and contempt he showed, over many months, to Allen.'[41] Unfortunately, much as Margery's own voice was cut down and reframed by what we can assume was a male editor in the 1501 Wynkyn de Worde edition of the text, so too was Hope Emily Allen's work sidelined by Sanford Meech, her co-editor on the first scholarly edition of the text. Allen determined to produce a second book on Kempe, placing the *Book* in the context of late medieval English mystical writers. But through ill-heath this project was never completed, and Allen died in 1960, in Oneida.

Kempe's *Book* is a powerful document, which often feels open, honest, unvarnished and unashamed. There is something so moving in the way she worked tirelessly to have her experiences recorded, overcoming social stigma, mental illness and ecclesiastical censure. The opening of the work describes how 'euyr sche was turned aȝen abak in tyme of temptacyon lech unto þe reed spyr which boweth *with* eu*er*y wynd *and* neu*er* is stable les þan no wynd bloweth' ('she was constantly rebuffed in times of trial, like the reed-spur that bows with every wind and is never still unless no wind blows').[42] In 1976, the feminist thinker Adrienne Rich wrote: 'I believe increasingly that only the willingness to share private and sometimes painful experience can enable women to create a collective description of the world which will be truly ours.'[43] Kempe's work, composed some six centuries before Rich's, and largely unknown until the twentieth, describes the world in a way that makes it just a little bit easier for women to inhabit. That it is the first piece of autobiographical writing in English makes it important, but the fact that it was composed by an illiterate woman makes it extraordinary, palpable, tangible, and it might not have come to light for even longer had it not been for that fateful ping-pong game.

Thomas Malory's *Le Morte Darthur*

The year 1934 was an exceptional one in the history of medieval English literary study. In the same year that the *Book of Margery Kempe* was found, Walter Oakeshott, a teacher at Winchester College, stumbled on something equally important. (We'll encounter Oakeshott again in Chapter Four.) At the time, Oakeshott was thirty-one years old and an 'ordinary assistant master'.[44] He had become interested in the history of book binding and had been given permission to study sixteenth-century book bindings in the College Fellows' Library. His friend Basil James Oldham suggested he examine some manuscript bindings as well. The manuscripts, however, were kept separately from the books, in a safe in the Warden's bedroom. Oakeshott wrote that this safe had

> a legendary reputation with me, since not so many years before a knowledgeable visitor who had made his way into it had recognised, in the bedside mat, a magnificent piece of Tudor tapestry probably woven for the occasion of the christening of Prince Arthur, Henry VII's eldest son, in Winchester Cathedral.[45]

So Oakeshott approached the safe 'with some excitement', but on opening it, he felt immediate 'disappointment'. There were no medieval bindings. He decided to glance at the manuscripts nonetheless. One of them caught his eye. It was 'very fat', made of paper not parchment, and the text was 'clearly about King Arthur and his Knights', but it was lacking a beginning and an end. Oakeshott 'made a vague mental note' of the manuscript and moved on to the next one.

What Oakeshott had stumbled on was the only known manuscript of Thomas Malory's great Arthurian legend, *Le Morte Darthur* – the last major piece of Arthurian literature to be produced in the Middle Ages, but also the first and only text in Middle English to recount the entire legend of Arthur from his birth to his death. In 1934 the only known copy of the work was an edition (dated to 1485) printed by William Caxton (c. 1422–c. 1491) – whom we'll meet in the Epilogue. Oakeshott might have forgotten about this 'fat' book entirely had it not been for 'a fantastic piece of good fortune' when, a few weeks later, he was preparing for a visit from the Friends of the National Libraries. He was due to bring out a few books in the school's collection printed by Wynkyn de Worde (who printed the excerpts from Kempe's *Book*). It was necessary, therefore, to do some research on this printer and his relationship with Caxton. He set out to read an article entitled 'The Introduction of Printing into England and the Early Work of the Press' by Gordon Duff. Oakeshott wrote that while reading this article he 'came across a sentence which made my heart miss a beat'.[46] It read: 'No manuscript of the work is known, and though Caxton certainly revised it, exactly to what extent has never been settled.' It transpired that what Oakeshott had discovered was a manuscript that might settle that debate.

Oakeshott decided to show the manuscript to the delegates from the Friends of the National Libraries. Their secretary, H. D. Ziman, was overawed by the discovery and insisted that Oakeshott write a column about it for the *Daily Telegraph* the next day.[47] A day or two later, Professor Eugene Vinaver – who was at the time at work on an edition of the *Morte Darthur* – arrived from Manchester on Oakeshott's doorstep. He would go on to produce an edition of the text, incorporating the manuscript version, in 1947.[48]

One of the reasons that the 'Winchester Manuscript', as it became known, caused such a stir was that, for a long time, there had been some controversy over the identity of the author. Little was known about him. Much of what could be gleaned was from a colophon – a kind of end-note to the reader – in Caxton's edition, which stated that the work was 're-duced in to englysse by Syr Thomas Malory knight'.[49] In the nineteenth century, the American scholar George Lyman Kittredge pieced together some information and identified a Thomas Malory of Newbold Revel in Warwickshire (1416–1471) as the likely author of the work. In 1928, another scholar – George Hicks – published a follow-up study in which he pointed out that Thomas Malory was something of a career criminal. He had been accused of extortion, theft, rape, cattle-rustling, robbery of an abbey, deer-theft, horse-stealing and attempted murder. This Malory had been imprisoned several times and escaped twice – once by swimming the moat of the house in which he was being detained. This image of a thug with questionable morals did not seem to tally with the nature of the text he had supposedly authored. When the Winchester Manuscript was discovered, however, the evidence that it was indeed Sir Thomas Malory of Newbold Revel who had written the *Morte* began to build. In several places in the text, in the divisions between sections, there were endnotes, which scholars call 'explicits', which did not appear in Caxton's text.[50] One, at the end of Book IV, reads:

> And this booke endyth whereas Sir Launcelot and Sir Trystrams com to courte. Who that woll make ony more, lette hym seke other bookis of Kynge Arhture or of Sir Launcelot or Sir Trystrams; for this was drawyn by a knight prisoner, Sir Thomas Malleorre, that God send hym good recover. 'Amen & c.'[51]

Here was a startling piece of information. While Caxton had simply described Malory as 'Syr Thomas Malory knyght', in this note he was described as a 'knight prisoner'. Oakeshott sent a photograph of this page in the manuscript to G. L. Kittredge – the scholar who had written so much about Thomas Malory. On 28 September 1934, Kittredge wrote back to Oakeshott, saying, 'Nothing that has crossed my path of late, has stirred me so deeply. The colophon, with its spelling of Malory's name, and its "prisoner" is like a voice from the great deeps.'[52] It confirmed Kittredge's suggestion that the Thomas Malory who wrote the work was indeed the Thomas Malory of Newbold Revel who had been imprisoned several times.

Malory appears to have lived a relatively blameless life until around 1450, when – somewhat inexplicably – he turned to a life of crime in his early thirties. He was accused of a variety of crimes. All of his biographers note, however, that although he was imprisoned several times, he never came to trial. The turbulence in Malory's own life tracks the turbulence in the realm at large. In this period, England was racked by civil war. The Lancastrian king, Henry VI (who had come to the throne in 1422 when he was only nine months old), was afflicted by bouts of mental illness and for long periods during his uneasy reign, the country was ruled by a powerful regent – Richard, Duke of York. The situation reached a crisis point in the early 1450s. Henry had failed to produce an heir, meaning his grip on power became ever more tenuous as factions circled at court. (A son was born in October 1453, but Henry was so mentally unstable he could not be made to understand what had happened.) This coincided with a breakdown in law and order in England, and open war between the Lancastrian and Yorkist factions began in 1455.

Malory was imprisoned at various prisons in London in the 1450s before being pardoned in 1462. After that he fought in a military expedition against Lancastrian strongholds in the north of England alongside the Earl of Warwick. Later, Warwick switched allegiance to the Lancastrian cause, and Malory switched with him. This turned out to be a poor decision. In 1462 he was explicitly excluded from a general pardon and, sometime after, re-arrested. The *Morte Darthur* was completed in prison at some point between 4 March 1469 and 3 March 1470. (We know this because the final endnote in the manuscript tells us that the work was completed in the ninth year of the reign of Edward IV.) He died in 1471, and his remains are buried in the ruins of Greyfriars Church – once an important establishment across the street from Newgate Gaol in London. What is left of the church is now a rose garden.

Le Morte Darthur is one of the great explorations of the culture of chivalry. It is the earliest complete coherent account of Arthurian story. In a series of individual books, it describes the story of Arthur's life from his birth to his death, but also incorporates the stories of several other famous knights of the Round Table. Malory's text includes the stories of Tristram and Isolde, Lancelot and Guinevere, and the quest for the legendary Holy Grail. It ends with Arthur's death and the downfall of the Round Table. It depicts a world of courtesy, duty and obligation, but it also exposes the dark underside of this same culture. It is tempting to look at the accusations laid against Malory and speculate that they might have shaped the way he saw the story of Arthur. Perhaps Malory – more than most – understood that chivalric deeds did not always go hand in hand with chivalric morals.

When Malory sat down to write the legendary story of King Arthur, he was only the latest writer in a tradition that had begun some three hundred years before. His great skill as a writer was his ability to blend diverse sources in a crisp and readable narrative. The *Morte* is a story with epic proportions about a pseudo-historical past, but it is also filled with timeless human stories. From the work of the Welsh writer and cleric Geoffrey of Monmouth (c. 1095–c. 1155) Malory took the story of a pseudo-historical Arthur. But he also extensively mined a tradition of French chivalric romance poetry to give us a haunting portrait of Lancelot and his adulterous love for Arthur's wife, Queen Guinevere. The moment that Malory introduces the character of Guinevere, he also introduces the fact that she and Lancelot love each other. At the start of Book III, which describes the wedding of Arthur, the king announces his intention to marry Guinevere. He tells Merlin, 'I love Gwenyvere, the Kynges doughtir of Lodegrean, of the lande of Camelerde, whyche holdyth in his house the Table Rounde this damesell is the most valyaunte and fayryst that I know lyvying, or yet that ever I coude fynde.' This is the first time that both Guinevere and the Round Table are mentioned in the narrative. But Merlin warns Arthur 'covertly that Gwenyver was nat holsom for hym to take to wyff, for he warned hym that Launcelot sscholde love hir, and sche hym agayne'.[53] Arthur, however, does not heed Merlin's warning, and instead dispatches him to the court of King Lodegrean – Guinevere's father – to ask for her hand in marriage. Lodegrean proclaims that this is the 'best tydynges that ever I herde' and resolves to 'send hym [Arthur] a gyffte that shall please hym muche more, for I shall gyff hym the Table Rounde'. Thus, the Round Table, one hundred knights and the princess Guinevere are sent to Arthur. The sense of foreboding is inescapable. Both Arthur's marriage and the Round Table seem doomed to fall.

It's hard to overstate the influence of Malory's version of the Arthurian story for us as twenty-first-century readers. Read, referenced and rewritten in the nineteenth century by Walter Scott and Alfred Tennyson, amongst others, in the twentieth century many people encountered Malory through T. H. White's influential version of the work, *The Once and Future King*. It was undoubtedly Malory's clipped and readable prose, and the comprehensiveness of his narrative, that made his version the most read and re-adapted version of the story in the post-medieval period.

When Caxton came to print the work, he chose to remove any references to Malory being a prisoner. We know this because in 1976 the British Library bought the manuscript of the *Morte* from Winchester College. To celebrate the sale, the manuscript was put on display next to the only complete copy of Caxton's print edition, lent by the Pierpont Morgan Library in New York. This persuaded the scholar Lotte Hellinga to think about the relationship between the manuscript and the book. She discovered something intriguing.[54] On several pages of the manuscript there were tiny smudges and blots of a different kind of ink from that used by the scribe. This kind of ink was a 'quick-drying oil-based ink'.[55] In other words, this was printer's ink. Further investigation revealed that the print smudges were in a particular pattern, which matched typesets that had been used by Caxton. (You can see the ghostly smudges of the dark, sticky ink on some the manuscript's folios when you look at it online.)[56] This meant that the manuscript had been in Caxton's workshop. Scholars were therefore able to get a better sense of the editorial changes made by Caxton, which included not mentioning the fact that Malory had written the work in prison.

At the end of the essay in which he describes his extraordinary encounter with the Malory manuscript, Oakeshott compares his discovery to the biblical story of King Saul, who was sent to seek his father's lost asses:

> We are told that Saul the son of Kish went out to seek his father's asses and found a kingdom. The fate of the literary detective is comparable only in that, if he finds anything at all, he will find something different from that for which he is looking. It is seldom a kingdom. The asses almost always

prove obstinately elusive. Certainly I did not, on this occasion, find them. All I could tell Oldham was that there were no bindings on the manuscripts to interest him.[57]

The lesson of 1934 – that remarkable year in literary history – is clear: you must always keep searching, because you might find something magical, beneath a mouse-eaten cover, while looking for something quite different altogether.

Oakeshott's story is also thrilling because it shows that sometimes discoveries can be made even on well-trodden ground. The Winchester Manuscript had passed through the hands of several generations of experienced scholars before 1934, but it had been miscatalogued: it was never described as being a work by Thomas Malory.[58] Oakeshott reflected that the 'moral seems to be that there are chances for the humblest gleaner even when the harvest has been reaped by experienced hands'.[59]

Medieval manuscripts in major libraries are largely all catalogued and are slowly being digitised but, despite this, manuscript discoveries are still being made. In 2008 a new version of the *Encomium Emmae Reginae* (discussed in Chapter Three) was discovered in Devon Record Office. Produced around two years after the original text, it gives a different account of the last days of the pre-Conquest period in England. Discoveries like these remind us that there is still land beyond the sea. As a 1934 editorial in *The Times* noted, discussing the discovery of the Kempe manuscript, 'There is no knowing what treasures may yet be found in private libraries and muniment rooms which have existed for centuries undisturbed by the auctioneer or the bonfire.'[60]

Chapter Two

NEAR-DISASTERS

In truth infinite are the losses which have been inflicted upon the race of books by wars and tumults.

Richard de Bury[1]

Ted Hughes's 1997 poem 'Hear It Again' expands on Heinrich Heine's famous observation, '*Dort wo man Bücher / Verbrennt, verbrennt man auch am Ende Menschen*' ('Where they burn books, ultimately they burn people').[2] Hughes writes:

> Fourteen centuries have learned,
> From charred remains, that what took place
> When Alexandria's library burned
> Brain-damaged the human race.[3]

Hughes's point is, of course, that the destruction of books has bleak consequences, but his poem itself is also a monument to how we value books. This chapter is a story of terrible events and near-misses – a story of fires and fragments and forgetting. But it is also a story of survival, a story of the dedicated labours of book lovers and the efforts they went to, to preserve the material remains of the past.

What follows underlines how precious the manuscripts discussed in *Hidden Hands* are, because since the medieval period so many have perished. Each of the literary works discussed in this chapter is from the pre-Conquest period: this story of near-disasters shows that many of the earliest fragments of English history so nearly did not survive.

The Ashburnham House Fire

On his death in 1702, Sir John Cotton left his home and its famous manuscript collection, largely amassed by his grandfather, Robert Cotton, to the nation. Since Robert Cotton's time, the house had fallen into a state of disrepair, becoming damp and dilapidated. In 1706, the architect Sir Christopher Wren was consulted on what to do with the building. He recommended that the library be moved to the House of Lords, and noted that the collection 'may be purged of much uselesse trash, but this must be the drudgery of librarians'.[4] Mercifully, his advice on the library's contents was not taken and, after some parliamentary dithering, the collection was moved to rented premises – Essex House, off the Strand. Soon after, however, the government got into a dispute with the landlord over the rent. It was claimed that a lower rent should be paid because Essex House was surrounded by other buildings and 'therefore in Danger of Fire and in other respects very improper'.[5] In December 1729 the officers of the Board of Works wrote to the Treasury. They noted that they had 'heard of a House in Westminster by its situation much more safe from fire & more commodious in all other respects belonging to Lord Ashburnham who is willing to let it to his Majesty'.[6] This house – Ashburnham House – was in Little Dean's Yard, near to Westminster School – a fitting choice, as Robert Cotton had been a pupil there. The collection was moved again but, with a grim irony, this 'Ash-*burn*-'em House' was not as 'safe from fire' as had been hoped. Some two years later, on 23 October 1731, a fire broke out in a room on the floor below the library.

In this period the royal manuscript collection was stored alongside the Cotton Library.[7] The joint collection was cared for by one Richard Bentley. The previous librarian had been Bentley's father, also called Richard Bentley. In 1731 Bentley Senior was the Master of Trinity College, Cambridge. On the night of 23 October, however, he was in London for the night, visiting his son. As a contemporary letter reports:

> Dr Bentley being expected in Town that Night there was a goode fire made for his reception in a Stove chimney under the Library; The Dr himselfe is not sure whether he did not leave the Blower on the Stove when he went to Bed.[8]

At around 2 a.m. a 'great Smoak' was detected.[9] A fire had broken out in the apartments on the floor below the library. It began with a wooden mantelpiece and from there it spread along the wainscot. At first it was hoped that the blaze could be stopped at source, and initial efforts were focused on trying to put the fire out, rather than salvaging the manuscripts on the upper floor. This was an error. In fourteen bookshelves, or 'book presses', in the library above were two of the original manuscripts of Magna Carta, the largest collection of pre-Conquest manuscripts ever amassed by an antiquarian (including the Lindisfarne Gospels and the *Beowulf* manuscript), the manuscript containing the late medieval masterpiece *Sir Gawain and the Green Knight,* and the state papers of Henry VIII and Elizabeth I, amongst other priceless treasures.

It soon became clear that the fire could not be stopped, and the frantic effort to rescue the books began. The Library was long and narrow and was 'lined with free-standing book presses made probably of oak, fitted with lockable doors or covers'. (On top of each press stood a brass bust of an emperor; the presses were named after these busts.)[10] We can only imagine how tricky the work of salvaging the books was. The room would have been dark and, lighting candles to aid them, the librarians must have been afraid that these flames might have helped the fire to spread. On the night of 23 October, there was only a slim crescent moon to aid the rescuers.[11] The room probably contained 'a table or cabinet holding the alchemical instruments of the Elizabethan mathematician and astrologer John Dee'.[12] This may have made it difficult to manoeuvre in the semi-darkness. Added to this, the doors of the presses were locked, preventing the books from being quickly removed. I imagine the terrified librarians fumbling for the keys of each press, as the horrible fire crackled around them. At some point, schoolboys from Westminster arrived at the scene. One account reports that the 'scholars being alarmed came and assisted very much both in extinguishing the Fire and saving what they could of the books'.[13] We have to hope that the well-meaning efforts of the pupils were a help and not a hindrance in the darkness and confusion.

In November 2018 I went to visit what remains of Ashburnham House, which is now owned by Westminster School. The building has changed a lot since 1731 and it is difficult to work out where the fire began or how it travelled. A few things were clear to me, however. The room was long and cramped. It had two sets of windows at the south and north, and another two on the south-west wall, adjacent to the south-end ones. The house now looks out over Little Dean's Yard, which is a spacious flagstoned courtyard, entered from Dean's Yard through a medieval arch. I visited during the pupils' lunchtime and it was full of students, chatting in groups. In 1731 that yard was not there, however. Ashburnham House would have had a small yard in front of it and another small one behind, reached by an entrance (now closed off) through Westminster Abbey's cloisters. Despite the difficulty of reconstructing the house's original design in 1731, what is clear is that there would have been limited room for people to manoeuvre inside the building, and that there was likewise little room outside for the fire engines – such as they were – when they arrived.

The fire appears to have spread up the walls and ignited the backs of the bookshelves. Several whole presses were then removed, which must have been very difficult. But – according to the official Parliamentary Report – the fire engines were slow to arrive. At this point the bookcases 'were obliged to be broke open, and the Books, as many as could be, were thrown out of the Windows'. In these vital moments, the decisions of the librarians were crucial. At moments of crisis, personal biases play a role, and with hindsight perhaps we feel that different decisions could have been made. In the Vitellius and Galba presses 'priority was given to the volumes of sixteenth- and seventeenth-century papers', while the medieval volumes were left longer on the shelves.[14] The Parliamentary Report states that the first press that was salvaged was the Augustus press. The reasons for this are a little unclear. It was a smaller press which contained a collection of maps, papal bulls and charters. It may have contained drawers which made it easier to remove.

Equally, it had fewer items in it, which might mean that it was situated over a door, making it quick to grab and take out. Accidents of geography were key that night.

The next day, the Speaker of the House of Commons, the Chancellor and the Lord Chief Justice all visited the scene to ensure that 'what had escaped the Flames should not be destroyed or purloined'. They found that the surviving books 'had suffered exceedingly from the Engine-Water, as well as from the Fire'. There had been 958 volumes in the collection.[15] The Parliamentary Report into the fire reported that 114 volumes were 'lost, burnt or intirely spoiled' and a further ninety-eight were considered defective from damage.[16] Ashburnham House was 'a smouldering ruin' and all across Little Dean's Yard were scattered burnt fragments of former manuscripts.[17] In the aftermath of the fire some of the pupils from Westminster gathered up the fragments fluttering in the breeze. The British Library still houses boxes of them that have yet to be identified.

The damage to the manuscripts was grave and considerable. Cotton's 'pride and joy', the fifth-century Greek Book of Genesis, Otho B vi, was reduced to a 'pile of cinder-like fragments'. One of the two original copies of Magna Carta had, before the fire, preserved its original wax seal but, in the fire, it had melted into a lump. And over the following days, further damage was done to the manuscripts in the course of some well-meaning 'conservation' efforts. Three days after the fire, a committee met to discuss what was to be done about the damaged manuscripts. It was decided that, where possible, the manuscripts should be disbound (taken out of their bindings) and individual leaves hung up on lines to dry, like laundry. The committee decided that the manuscripts should be turned over to prevent the development of mould, and the paper manuscripts – which would have included many of the state papers – were washed in an alum solution.

Predictably, in the wake of the disaster, rumours about the night's events began to circulate. Sifting through them today feels as tricky as it would have been to sift the charred fragments of the library's manuscripts. According to the official Parliamentary Report on the fire, deputy librarian Richard Casley's first act was to remove the *Codex Alexandrinus* – a fifth-century Greek Bible, considered extremely important for biblical study. A different report, which may have originated with Bentley Senior himself, describes 'Dr Bentley's coming out in his nightgown and large wig, with the Alexandrian Old Testament Manuscript under his arm'.[18] Whether or not there is any truth in this – and it seems a little improbable that in the haste to save the library Dr Bentley would have had time to put on his wig – it does at least convey a sense of the librarians' hurried distress. Bentley had been at work for ten years on an edition of the New Testament, and his choice of what to salvage may have been coloured by his personal biases, or it may be that this story was one put about by Bentley himself in an attempt to assuage some of the guilt for the tragedy. The Edinburgh *Caledonian Mercury* reported that 'this Morning Part of the Lord Ashburnham's house near Westminster Abbey, was destroyed by Fire, as also Part of Dr Bentley's fine Library, and also some manuscripts of the Cotton Library, but the most valuable called the *Alexandrian Manuscripts* have received no Damage'. This story has the whiff of spin, focusing as it does on the saving of the *Codex Alexandrinus* and mentioning that Bentley's own library had come to harm.

It is clear that the fire was seen almost at once as a national tragedy. The newspaper reports of the time give us a sense of this. On 16 November 1731, the *Caledonian Mercury* published an account of the fire that concluded with the words, 'Such a Treasure of English History was here reposited, that no particular Nation nor Age could boast the like; and the Loss is irretrievable as few copies had been taken of the Manuscripts.' The fire also elicited poetic responses. The Reverend Thomas Fitzgerald (died c. 1752), who was an usher at Westminster School, wrote:

> All the past Annals of revolving Time,
> The Acts of 'every Age' and 'every Clime',
> The rich Productions of each studious Mind,
> The various Skill and Science of Mankind,
> Collected stand, the World's stupendous Boast!
> And all in one, one fatal Blaze, are lost.[19]

Fitzgerald's words, although moving, are not entirely accurate. The manuscripts were not 'all in one . . . fatal Blaze lost'. In fact, most were saved. The most recent census notes that thirteen manuscripts were destroyed completely, mainly from the press topped by the emperor Otho. Of course, many manuscripts were damaged beyond legibility, but there are crumbs of hope in this story. The disastrous events of 23 October 1731 led to calls for the creation of a national library which would safely house what remained of these priceless collections. It was partly because of the memory of that disastrous night that, in 1753, the British Museum was created by Act of Parliament, and the Royal and Cotton collections became two of the four founder-collections of the Museum's manuscript holdings. (In 1973, the British Library was created as a distinct entity from the Museum.)

Considering the impact of the fire today, there are other slivers of hope. The *Caledonian Mercury* lamented that 'Few copies had been taken of the manuscripts', but this is not entirely true, either. Cotton was part of a group of like-minded people who shared manuscripts between them, and some of them *did* make copies of the texts. And, even after the fire, people made transcriptions before the crumbling of fire-damaged folios made the works illegible. We are eternally grateful to these figures, these early lovers of books, without whose energies our sense of these manuscripts and the texts they contained would have been lost completely.

Asser's *Life of King Alfred*

In the library at Ashburnham House, on the first shelf, twelve manuscripts along, in the press under the bust of the Emperor Otho (BL Cotton MS Otho A xii) was a manuscript containing several texts from the early medieval period.[20] It contained, amongst other items, the only known copy of the *Battle of Maldon* – a poem about a battle between the English and the Vikings on 11 August 991. As well as this, it also contained the only known copy of a life of the pre-Conquest king Alfred the Great, written by the monk Asser. Alfred (849–899, reigned 871–899) is the only king in English history to have been afforded the epithet 'the Great' – a moniker given him by the Victorians.

Scraps of some of the texts from this manuscript survive in some sad, burnt fragments. The text of Asser's *Life*, however, was obliterated in the fire. Mercifully, though, the manuscript was one of a number of codices that were studied by a group of early antiquarian readers, passing through the hands of some of the most important scholars of the early modern period.[21] Several copies of it were made before the fire of 1731, including two printed editions in 1602 and 1722.[22] Were it not for these early scholars and their interest in the text, we would have a much poorer picture of the reign of King Alfred, and we also would have lost one of the great pieces of early Anglo-Latin prose.

Asser (died c. 909) was a Welshman from Saint David's, who later became Bishop of Sherborne. He was one of Alfred's closest companions. Alfred mentions 'Asser my bishop' in his preface to Gregory the Great's *Pastoral Care*. Asser was clearly a man of learning. He cites a number of sources in the text, but appears to have based his work on a famous *Life of Charlemagne* by the Frankish scholar Einhard (775–840). Asser's *Life* is important for a number of reasons, but one of the main ones is that it shows the human side of Alfred. We gain a sense of his interests, his childhood and his human weaknesses. The picture that emerges is of a man keen to promote religion and learning, with an interest in justice.[23]

Alfred obviously loved literature. We hear that through the 'shameful negligence of his parents and tutors he remained ignorant of letters until his twelfth year, or even longer. However, he was a careful listener, by day and night, to English poems, most frequently hearing them recited by others, and he readily retained them in his memory.' But Asser relates a story which suggests that some of Alfred's thirst for knowledge stemmed, in part, from sibling rivalry. He describes how Alfred's mother showed him and his brothers a book of English poetry. She promised to give the book to whichever of them was able to memorise it fastest. Asser says that, 'Spurred on by these words, or rather by divine inspiration, and attracted by the beauty of the initial letter of the book', Alfred immediately took the book away and learned it by heart.[24]

This love of literature persisted into adulthood. Asser tells us that the king's favourite activity was 'reading aloud from books in English and above all learning English poems by heart'. (As well as this, he found time for 'pursuing all manner of hunting; giving instruction to all his goldsmiths and craftsmen as well as to his falconers, hawk-trainers and dog-keepers; making to his own design wonderful and precious new treasures'.) Alfred promoted literature and learning by inviting important scholars (like Asser) to his court. Indeed, Asser describes Alfred's 'kindness and generosity' towards 'foreign visitors of all races', including 'Franks, Frisians, Gauls, Vikings, Welshmen, Irishmen and Bretons'.[25] Asser tells us that:

> just like the clever bee which at first light in summertime departs from its beloved honeycomb, finds its way with swift flight on its unpredictable journey through the air, lights upon the many and various flowers of grasses, plants and shrubs, discovers what pleases it most and then carries it back home, King Alfred directed the eyes of his mind far afield and sought without what he did not possess within, that is to say, within his own kingdom.[26]

In passages like this we see Asser's capacity for lively images and moving metaphors. He is, for a writer and scholar, a sympathetic figure. In Chapter 21 of the work, he admits that he has been distracted while writing:

> But (to speak in nautical terms) so that I should no longer veer off course – having entrusted the ship to the waves and sails, and having sailed quite far away from the land, I think I should return to that which particularly inspired me to this work: in other words, I consider the infancy and boyhood of my esteemed lord Alfred.[27]

Some fifty-two chapters later, Asser admits once more that the ship of his prose has meandered again. He promises to 'return to that point from which I digressed so that I shall not be compelled to sail past the haven of my desired rest as a result of my protracted voyage'. Asser's text is not only a key document for understanding the reign of the most famous of the pre-Conquest kings, but also a work which gives insights into the mind of both its subject and its author.

Asser's *Life* has been the source of some scholarly controversy. In 1995 Alfred P. Smyth argued that the now-lost manuscript was a forgery, and that the text did not date from the time of Alfred, but from around a century later.[28] He argued that it was by Byrhtferth of Ramsey and was written c. 1000. This debate encapsulates the importance of original manuscripts in historical study.[29] Some questions cannot be answered by copies or surrogates. And when a manuscript is lost completely, many important clues are lost with it.

Beowulf

Many manuscripts nearly succumbed to the same fate as Asser's *Life of Alfred*. One of these horrifying near-misses is the only surviving manuscript of *Beowulf*, which is singed at its edges, the fragile ends of its folios a chilling reminder of the fate it nearly suffered. *Beowulf* is, of course, the great gem of Old English literature. It was composed at some point between the middle of the seventh and the end of the tenth century. The manuscript itself dates from the late tenth or perhaps the very early eleventh century.

Set in a mythic past, in sixth-century Scandinavia, it tells the story of a hero, Beowulf, from the land of the Geats (in modern-day southern Sweden), who crosses the sea with a band of companions to the land of the Danes. The Danes, under King Hrothgar, are being harried by a hideous man-eating monster named Grendel. Beowulf fights and kills Grendel but is forced into a second encounter with the monster's mother, who comes to wreak revenge for her child's death. He travels to her watery home and kills her there before returning to Hrothgar's hall (which is called Heorot) as a triumphant hero. At this point, the poem swoops forwards. Beowulf has been ruling his native Geatland for fifty years, when his people – like the Danes fifty years before – begin to be terrorised by a monster. This time it is a dragon, and Beowulf decides to fight the beast. Both of them are killed. The poem concludes with Beowulf's funeral, when his body is burned on a pyre and his people lament, building a giant barrow to enclose his remains. The final lines of the poem describe how Beowulf was mourned:

> Swa begnornodon   Geata leode
> Hlafordes hryre   hheorðgeneatas
> Cwædon þæt he   wære wyruldcyninga
> Manna mildust   ond monðwærust
> Leodum liðost   ond lofgeornost.[30]

> *Thus the Geat people, his hearth-companions,*
> *Lamented their lord's fall.*
> *They said that of all the earthly kings,*
> *He was most merciful, most gentle,*
> *The kindest to his people, and most eager for fame.*

These last lines throb with resonance. Beowulf is a flawed hero: he was 'manna mildust' ('most merciful'), but he was also 'lofgeornost' ('most eager for fame'), and that lust for renown led him into an ill-fated fight with the dragon, leaving his people bereft, shorn of their 'hlaford' ('lord').

Beowulf is a window into an early medieval warrior society quite distinct from our own. As Seamus Heaney notes, the world of *Beowulf* – the Geats and the Danes – is 'a society that is at once honour-bound and blood-stained, presided over by the laws of blood-feud'. The poem describes a society whose inhabitants are 'in thrall to a code of loyalty and bravery, bound to seek glory in the eye of the warrior world'.[31] But, like all great works of literature, we can also find much in it that is familiar. The so-called 'Father's Lament' (lines 2444–62), for example, in which a father grieves for his son, has a timeless quality – speaking as it does to a universal human experience of grief for a loved one: 'Symble bið gymyndgad   morna gehwylce / eaforan ellorsið' ('each morning he awakes, to remember his child is gone').

Beowulf was once a fixture on many undergraduate English Literature courses, although it is becoming rarer today. For a long time it was only studied for its language, but after J. R. R. Tolkien published his 1936 essay 'The Monsters and the Critics', it came to be seen as a work of unity and artistry. For readers encountering it for the first time, it may seem narratively confusing, as the poet makes frequent digressions into an earlier history. As Heaney observes, 'Just when the narrative seems ready to take another step ahead, it sidesteps. For a moment it is as if we have channel-surfed into another poem.'[32] Its complex, interlocking narratives, which loop in and out of one another, are like the zoomorphic designs we find in pre-Conquest jewellery. Initially what we see is a maze of shapes, but these reveal a pattern when viewed as a whole.

These historical digressions have a bearing on the world of the poem's present.

To this day, *Beowulf* generates a huge amount of scholarly interest. This is partially because it is a collection of mysteries – the most basic details about its date, authorship and intended audience remain unclear. What is clear, however, is that it is a work of haunting beauty, which depicts a strange and mythic past with layered narrative and musical language.

Grímur Jónsson Thorkelin: 'Work Retrieved from the Ruins'

In July 1786 the Icelandic-Danish scholar Grímur Jónsson Thorkelin (1752–1829) visited Britain in search of materials relating to Danish history. He ended up staying in the UK for six years, getting several extensions to his research trip, including one in order that he could procure a British recipe for turning seaweed into potash.[33] Thorkelin travelled widely during his expedition, but when he wasn't travelling, he spent a good deal of time in the Manuscripts Reading Room of the British Museum. On 3 October 1786 – a few months into this stay – the Reading Room Register shows that he borrowed a certain 'Cotton MS Vitellius A xv'.[34] This was the *Beowulf* manuscript. At the time there was no edition of the poem, and its importance to English literature had yet to be recognised. Thorkelin had read a brief description of the manuscript (written in Latin by the antiquarian Humfrey Wanley), which claimed that, 'In this book, which is an excellent example of poetry in Anglo-Saxon, can be seen fine descriptions in which Beowulf, a certain Dane, originally from the royal line of the Scyldings, performs [in war] opposite the princes of Sweden'.[35] Based on this, he was keen to learn more about the Danish hero.

The manuscript wasn't the only codex he consulted that day. The Register shows that he also had several charters on his desk, and we can only wonder at how much attention he gave the manuscript; the Register indicates that he did not keep the manuscript on reserve for further study and gave it back the next day. Clearly, the work of studying the first great epic in English literature could wait. Over the course of the next few years, however, in between trips to Ireland and Scotland, Thorkelin became increasingly interested in the poem, and commissioned two transcriptions of the text. At this point in the late 1780s, only fifty years after the fire, the singed edges of the poem's folios were in better shape than they are now. Many words and letters now lost forever were still visible then. The transcriptions (done by a member of the British Museum's staff) preserved readings of the poem which are now impossible to make.

In May 1791 Thorkelin returned to Copenhagen to take up a role as Keeper of the National Archives. He took with him his two transcriptions of *Beowulf* and set about preparing the first ever printed edition of the poem. But in 1807 disaster struck, and the project was nearly destroyed. In late August of that year, British naval forces attacked Copenhagen, believing that the Danish would help Napoleon in his plan to blockade Britain. For five days the city was bombarded, and over a thousand buildings were destroyed. During this time, Thorkelin's home was devastated, his library was ruined, and with it his preparatory work for the *Beowulf* edition. Later, recollecting these events, he wrote:

> O! Those woeful days (the bitter memory of which brings back my old troubles and ineffable sorrows) that robbed me of my sumptuous home and all my scholarly tools,

which I had assiduously gathered for thirty years or more. My rendering of the Scylding epic, together with its entire scholarly apparatus, perished utterly.[36]

Despite these 'ineffable sorrows', Thorkelin somehow found the determination to take up the work again, stimulated by what he called a 'love of country' ('amor patriæ'). He says that thereafter he 'endured a very arduous labour'. It took him another eight years to produce the edition, entitled *De Danorum rebus gestis seculi II & IV. Poëma Danicum dialect Anglo-Saxonica* ('Of Events Concerning the Danes in the Third and Fourth Centuries. A Danish Poem in the Anglo-Saxon Dialect'), which appeared in 1815. There has been some debate as to how much of the work on the edition Thorkelin had actually completed when his house was shelled, but it's fair to say that for Thorkelin the destruction of one's home and city would have been a terrible blow, which would discourage even the most dedicated of scholars.

In the preface to his edition, Thorkelin wrote that, while he had 'endeavoured to render our poet and his periphrases word for word', he still begged the indulgence of his readers, 'for I have had to contend with the greatest confusion of letters and a motley variety of words whose meaning is ambiguous, vague and often wildly contradictory'. Today's scholars feel that Thorkelin's work was not always accurate, and at times plagued by confusion, ambiguity and vagueness. He held a number of theories about the poem which are now disregarded by scholars. He misdated the poem as a work of the third and fourth centuries, for a start. (As I noted, we now date the poem's composition to some time from the mid-seventh century, while the manuscript itself dates from c. 1000.) As well as this, Thorkelin was an unashamed nationalist and therefore convinced that the poem was a Scandinavian one translated into Old English. (Thorkelin was not alone in this: in the nineteenth century, as nationalism bubbled up in every quarter, *Beowulf* was also claimed by several German scholars.) He called it the 'incomparable work of the divine Danish bard' ('divini vatis Danici incomparabile opus'), adding with disdain, that – 'By Hercules!' – he was 'astounded' that 'a song that poured forth from the Danish bard' had been attributed to England.[37] Linguistic analysis indicates that the poem was indeed composed in Old English, not translated from Danish. But his idea that it was a translation has a kind of kernel of truth, in the sense that it was a cultural translation. The stories of the Geats and the Danes may have been passed down in some form through the generations. It's possible that versions of these stories were brought across the sea by the Angles, Saxons and Jutes who populated Britain after the departure of Roman forces in the fifth and sixth centuries. The poem was very likely to have been composed orally and passed down by 'scops' (pronounced *shops*, meaning 'poets'). The version of the text in the manuscript is a little like an insect trapped in a piece of amber: the text is simply one form of the poem from a particular moment in time – it probably had a different life before that.

Another of Thorkelin's theories pertained to the Christian aspects of the poem. He thought that Alfred the Great took the work 'into his protection' and that it was through his influence that the Christian aspects of the poem were introduced.[38] The truth is probably more complex: the poem is a mixture of a pre-Christian, mythic sixth-century past and the interventions of a more recent Christianised narrator. It is perhaps best to think of the poem as a fabric, with different coloured threads, representing Christian and pre-Christian elements. The word 'text' is, in fact, etymologically linked to 'textile'. The word comes from Latin *textus*, which means 'that which is woven, web, texture'. *Textus* itself is derived from *texere*, to weave. *Beowulf* is this textile – artfully woven and iridescently beautiful.

Despite Thorkelin's somewhat idiosyncratic opinions on the poem, even the most curmudgeonly of scholars now recognise that his work was vital in recording letters and words that otherwise would have been lost. It is an extraordinary irony that it was British forces who so nearly destroyed Thorkelin's work, for without his energies, the words at the fragile edges of the first great epic in English literature would have crumbled to nothing. Reflecting on Thorkelin's story, Robert E. Bjork wrote that 'it captures the poignancy of a life's work at least in part retrieved from the ruins of war'.[39] His phrase is an apposite one because Thorkelin's story is, in several senses, a story of a work retrieved from the ruins.

In his preface, Thorkelin quotes a section (3.30) of Horace's *Odes* in support of his allusion to the figure he calls the 'divina Danici vatis indoles' ('the divine genius of the Danish poet'). This poet, he says,

> Exegit monumentum ære perennius
> Regalique situ pyramidum altius
> Qvod non imber edax, non aquilo impotens
> Possit diruere, aut innumerabilis
> Annorum series, et fuga temporum.

> *Has erected a monument more durable than bronze,*
> *Loftier than the royal site of the pyramids,*
> *Which neither the destructive shower nor raging wind*
> *Can destroy, nor the countless*
> *Series of years, nor the flight of time.*

There's a chill in Thorkelin's choice of quotation here. There was in fact little that was durable about the only surviving manuscript of the genius poet (who probably wasn't actually Danish). But Thorkelin's work ensured a version of the text was able to evade 'the destructive shower' and 'the flight of time'.

Beowulf is especially precious because so little Old English poetry survives. The entire oeuvre stands at around 30,000 lines. *Beowulf* is just over 3,000 lines long – one-tenth of the surviving corpus. More extraordinary still, the great majority of this surviving corpus (around two-thirds of it) survives in just four books. The Old English period stretches from around c. 600 to c. 1200. That's equivalent to the space of time between the era of Chaucer and our own day. Imagine if only four books survived from that period in English literature – perhaps one work by Chaucer, one by Shakespeare, one by Dickens, and one of the *Harry Potter* series. What picture would that give of our literary culture?

'The Ruin' and the 'Exeter Book'

One of these four surviving books of Old English verse manuscripts is the 'Exeter Book' (Exeter Cathedral Library MS 3501), which contains some of the most moving and enigmatic literary texts of the medieval period in England. The Exeter Book was made in c. 960–980 – so not that long before the *Beowulf* manuscript; in fact, each of the four poetic codices were made within a fifty-year period of one another. An eleventh-century list of donations left by Bishop Leofric (died 1072), dated to 1069–72, mentions 'mycel Englisc boc be gehwilcu[m] þingu[m] on leoðwisum geworht' ('a large English book about many things written in verse').[40] In all likelihood, this refers to the Exeter Book.

The manuscript is indeed a mixture of 'gehwilcum þingum' ('many things'). The texts in the manuscript are diverse, and in their diversity they give us a powerful sense of the intellectual sophistication of pre-Conquest literary culture. There are almost a hundred riddles, several saints' lives, and a body of elegiac poetry. The Exeter Book is most famous for its elegies and its riddles, however. The riddles – sometimes sombre, but often playful – explore the fabric of the early medieval world through the prism of the everyday. They give voice to inanimate objects. Here disgruntled tools and ageing weapons jostle with eloquent animals and euphemistic vegetables. A number of them invite less than innocent readings, giving us a sense that early medieval monastic life was perhaps not as solemn as we might expect.

While *Beowulf* presents us with a vision of a heroic, warrior culture, steeped in glory, the elegies of the Exeter Book complicate that vision, giving voice to its darker consequences: death, loss and social exile. In one elegy, alone at sea, a sailor yearns for life onshore. The speaker of the poem may be a *peregrinus*, or wandering recluse, who put to sea and placed their trust in God's providence, with no sense of where they were going or if they would survive. Strikingly, many of the poems in the manuscript meditate on themes of loss and impermanence. One of the more enigmatic of these is one which has been editorially titled (since few Old English poems ever have original titles) 'The Ruin'. This haunting poem describes the forlorn ruins of a once glorious city. It is often associated with the ruins of Roman Bath:

Wrætlic is þes wealstan,   wyrde gebræcon;
burgstede burston,   brosnað enta geweorc.
Hrofas sind gehrorene,   hreorge torras,
hrungeat berofen,   hrim on lime,
scearde scurbeorge   scorene, gedrorene,
ældo undereotone.   Eorðgrap hafað
waldend wyrhtan   forweorone, geleorene,
heardgripe hrusan,   oþ hund cnea
werþeoda gewitan.   Oft þæs wag gebad
ræghar ond readfah   rice æfter oþrum,
ofstonden under stormum;   steap geap gedreas.[41]

Wondrous is this masonry, though wasted by fate,
The battlements broken: the work of giants perishes.
The roofs have fallen in; the towers have crumbled.
The barred gate is broken; there is frost on the plaster,
The walls are scored, hacked and withered,
Consumed by age. The earthgrip holds,
In a harsh embrace, the works of the builders.
Decayed and departed.
Over a hundred generations now have passed.
This wall – red-stained and lichen-coated –
has withstood many a storm, while kingdoms rose and fell.
But now the lofty arch has also fallen.

The poem makes use of some chilling imagery – the buildings, the works of humankind, are described as being held in the earth's grip, 'Eorðgrap', which the poet describes two lines later as a hard embrace or hard grasp, 'heardgripe'. Human life, and the monuments it produces, is transitory – 'rice æfter oþrum' (literally 'one kingdom after another') has fallen. With a strange symmetry, the text itself is a ruin: it is mutilated by a large diagonal burn across its folio. The next section of the poem is

almost unreadable, the fragmentary words and phrases a testament to impermanence:

> Wonað giet se . . . num geheapen,
> fellon
> grimme gegrunden
> scan   heo . . .
> g orþonc   ærsceaft
> g   lamrindum beag
> mod mo . . .   . . . yne swiftne gebrægd
> hwætred in hringas,   hygerof gebond
> weallwalan wirum   wundrum togædre.[42]

This is one of several places where the precious Exeter Book
has been damaged. The opening pages are missing from the
manuscript: the current first page has been used as a chopping
board and as a resting place for a cup.

Although the damage to the manuscript is disquieting, it
seems grimly appropriate. The texts in the manuscript appear
acutely aware of the fragility of their own existence. One of the
most iconic of the riddle texts is Riddle 47:

> Moððe word fræt.   Me þæt þuhte
> Wrætlicu wyrd,   þa ic þæt wundor gefrægn
> Þæt se wyrm forswealg   wera gied sumes
> Þeof in þystro,   þrymfæstne cwide
> ond þæs strangan staþol.   Stælgiest ne wæs
> wihte þy gleawra   þe he þam wordum swealg.[43]

> *A moth ate words. That seemed to me*
> *A weird happening when I heard of that wonder,*
> *how a thief in the shadows – a worm –*
> *swallowed the words of someone's song:*

both its glorious statement and its strong foundations.
Yet, the stealing guest was not a whit wiser for the words
   he swallowed.

The most common solution to this riddle is . . . the book-worm or 'book-moth'. (While Latin collections of riddles from this period often had solutions in the manuscripts, the Exeter Book riddles have none, so their answers are sometimes a matter of scholarly debate.) Today a 'bookworm' is a person who loves reading, but the riddle's composer had in mind the larvae of various different species of insect that are wont to devour books, and have done for centuries. Riddle 47 is a beautiful meditation on impermanence. It is a reminder that so many texts of this period have been destroyed by fire, flood, or invertebrate *stælgi-estas* – the 'moððe' or 'wyrm' is described as a 'stælgiest' (literally a 'stealing-guest', or 'pilferer'). The riddle describes the text that the worm eats as 'wera gied sumes' ('someone's song'), which is 'þrymfæstne' ('glorious'), but also ironically stands on 'strangan staþol' ('strong foundations'). More importantly, the riddle makes clear that the *wyrm* does not become *gleaw* (clear-sighted, wise, skilful, sagacious, prudent, good), despite the fact that it has consumed the *gied* (song, lay, riddle: i.e. the text it has eaten through). The image here is clever. Early medieval monastic readers were encouraged to practise *ruminatio*, from the Latin, meaning 'chewing the cud'. This reading practice meant reading with care, as if chewing over the words. The riddle is a reminder that such *gied* are impossibly precious. They need to be read with care to extract their meanings and carefully protected because they are susceptible to manifold destructive forces.

In November 2018, 287 years after the fire at Ashburnham House, I called up the remaining fragments of Cotton MS Otho A xii – which had once contained Asser's *Life of Alfred*. The manuscript had originally comprised several texts alongside each other. Nothing of Asser's biography is left, but a few fragments of the other texts which were once bound with it survive into our era. I had recently discovered, in the course of my research, that these fragments had actually been burned *twice*. In the nineteenth century the then Keeper of Manuscripts at the British Museum, Frederic Madden, set about trying to sort the fragments left over from the Cotton Fire. During this time, some fragments of Otho A xii had been identified and gathered together and were sent to the museum's bindery to be bound as one. On 10 July 1865, at 9 p.m., Madden was writing letters in his apartments when – as he noted afterwards in his diary:

> We were alarmed by a report brought up by the man-servant that Mr Panizzi's house was on fire! It was the work of a few moments to fly downstairs, put on my boots & overcoat, get out the Museum keys, and rush into the Court. The first thing I saw was a column of black smoke, followed by flames, rising apparently out of the corridor leading to Mr P.'s house, but on approaching closer, I perceived that the fire was not in the corridor, but in Tuckett's (the binder's) workshops! The sight was terrible, for I knew many MSS [manuscripts] of value had lately been sent down to him![44]

One of the 'MSS of value' was what remained of Cotton Otho A xii. To burn a manuscript once may be regarded as a misfortune, but to burn it twice looks like carelessness. Madden's account gives a powerful sense of the chaos that ensues in the event of a fire: 'There was a great deal of confusion! Policemen running to and fro and shouts for the "key" of the door of Mr P's garden and Tuckett's house and for the hose.' Madden refers to particular, local problems that night, to important people being on leave, and how, 'instead of the two <u>trained</u> policemen [appointed] in such cases, two ignorant fellows were sent who had never handled a hose in their lives'. I reflected that the pandemonium of that night was probably not dissimilar to the night of 23 October 1731. He concludes: 'Such a want of organisation I never beheld in my life.' Perhaps most chilling in Madden's account is the sense that, had the wind been in the east, the fire might easily have spread to the Manuscripts department:

> I feared greatly that the rooms of my Department (my study, my sorting rooms etc.) could have caught fire. Indeed, had there been an east wind, I do not think anything could have saved them and probably the whole of my Department from destruction! As it was the sashes of the windows were charred and blackened and the glasses cracked!

When I called up Otho A xii, what arrived from the stacks of the British Library was something that looked like an A4 ring binder. Inside it was a series of plastic wallet pages. Within these were the fragments, mounted onto yellowed Victorian paper pages. The vellum fragments are black-burnt in places and in others, the colour of milky coffee.The script is just about discernible, if not easily legible. Letters can be made out, but the heat of the fire has shrunk the vellum, and the script is only a few millimetres tall. In the surrounding area, on the paper mounts, are pencil notes by Edward Maunde Thompson (who joined the British Museum staff in 1861), which identify sections of text.[45] The edges of the vellum pieces are ragged. Most of the fragments are about 10 cm high and 6 cm wide, but some are no bigger than a thumb. They come in a variety of shapes – some roughly triangular, something like what I imagine a dinosaur tooth might look like, others a sort of D-shape. Turning the plastic wallet pages, I started to see faces in the shrivelled scraps, as if looking for medieval gargoyles. Occasionally, red initial letters appeared, surprisingly clear and crisp amidst the burntness. Although these letters have shrunk significantly from their original size, the red ink has survived well. I felt as though I were looking at an evidence bag in some sort of TV crime drama. It's hard to process the sadness you feel looking at the remnants of such destruction.

I had a similar sensation in October 2018, when the British Library mounted an exhibition of pre-Conquest manuscripts and artefacts. The star of the show, for me, was the Codex Amiatinus, which was made in the early eighth century, in the monastery of Wearmouth-Jarrow (where Bede was from, and where the Cuthbert Gospel was made). The manuscript is a single-volume Bible – a beast made from many beasts: its spine is half a metre tall, it weighs 34 kg and has 1,030 leaves, which means it was made from 515 animal skins. We can only wonder at the investment of time and resources necessary for the manuscript's production.

In 716, Ceolfrith, Abbot of Wearmouth-Jarrow, set off from Northumbria bound for Rome, taking the Codex Amiatinus with him. The anonymous *Life of Ceolfrith* describes how the monks sang and wept as his boat set sail on the River Wear. The book was intended as a gift for the shrine of St Peter in Rome, but it never made it. Ceolfrith died en route and the Bible ended up in the monastery of Monte Amiata in Tuscany (hence its name). Ceolfrith's abbey was a centre of learning, and its scriptorium produced works of great quality. The inky sweeps of the Bible's script are crisp and clear, and its illumination sophisticated. Until the nineteenth century it was thought that the manuscript could not have been made in England. The assumption was bolstered by some dedicatory verses which explained that the manuscript was a gift from 'Petrus Langobardorum' ('Peter of the Lombards') to 'Cenobium Saluatoris' ('the monastery of the Saviour'). But, as the Italian scholar de Rossi noted in 1888, these words are later additions. Some wily person had sought to claim the Bible for Italy. According to the *Life of Ceolfrith*, the words should have described how the book was a gift for the shrine of St Peter from 'Ceolfridus, Anglorum extimis de finibus abbas' ('Ceolfrith, abbot from the far-away lands of the Angles').

The *Life of Ceolfrith* also tells us that the abbot originally commissioned *three* of these giant single-volume Bibles (known as 'pandects'). One of these is lost and the other one partially survives in three sad fragments – a few leaves of it were discovered being used to wrap legal documents in the sixteenth century, others came to light in a shop in Newcastle in 1882, and a third fragment turned up among estate papers in Kingston Lacy in 1982. In the exhibition, one of these fragments was displayed alongside the monumental Bible, a chilling reminder of the fate it might have suffered. Looking at this sad fragment I thought about a line from the ruined 'Ruin' in the Exeter Book: 'brosnað enta geweorc' ('the work of giants perishes').

The work of giants has perished. But sometimes it has survived, often because of the dedicated labours of particular people. The Codex Amiatinus is a giant itself – a hefty marvel of a thing, and one that has been loved over the centuries. One person loved it so much they wanted to claim it as an Italian manuscript. That person was not so dissimilar from Grímur Thorkelin, who sought to claim *Beowulf* for Denmark but in the process saved parts of the first epic in the English language. And it was probably largely a love of books that brought the pupils from Westminster School running across Little Dean's Yard on the night of 23 October 1731. It was love of books that made the librarians break open the doors of the presses and throw the manuscripts from the windows. Whatever their motives, these people valued the books they encountered, and were it not for this, many manuscripts and the crumbling texts within them might never have survived.

Chapter Three

PATRONS

The praise of the queen is evident at the beginning, thrives in the middle, is present at the end, and embraces absolutely all of what follows.

Encomium Emmae Reginae[1]

Forty folios into the British Library's Royal MS 17 D VI, there is an image of a man in russet-coloured robes kneeling in front of a king.[2] The king is comically oversized by comparison with the kneeling figure, his stature a metaphor for his regal majesty. The kneeling man is presenting a book to the king, who stands resplendent in a lapis coat lined with ermine. Beneath the image, a stanza of verse addresses the

> Hye and noble myȝty prince excellent,
> My lord the prince [O] my lord gracious,
> I humble servaunt and obedient
> Unto your estate hye and glorious,
> Of whiche I am full tendre and full ielous,
> Me recomannde unto your worthynesse,
> With hert entier and spirite of mekenesse.[3]

The text here is Thomas Hoccleve's early fifteenth-century *Regiment of Princes*, which is addressed to Henry, Prince of Wales (later Henry V). Both the text and the image tell us something important about the system of patronage in the Middle Ages. Throughout the medieval period, and beyond, patronage remained key to the production of texts and manuscripts. Patronage was most often royal or ecclesiastical. (That is not to say that other kinds of patronage did not exist – they did. Aristocrats and, later in the period, the gentry and mercantile classes were all patrons of art and literature.) The manuscripts we will encounter here, however, are products of royal patronage. They reflect paradigm shifts, embodying the hopes and fears of their commissioners in a time of change.

The Elf-Gift: Queen Emma of Normandy (c. 985–1052)

Opening British Library Add. MS 33241, the first medieval folio you come to is a blank page with a brief descriptive ownership inscription on it: 'Gesta Cnutonis [...] Lib[er] S[an]c[t] i Aug[ustini] Cant' ('The Deeds of Cnut, [this] book [is from] Saint Augustine's, Canterbury').[4] The inscription was right in one sense only – the book did come from St Augustine's, but on the subject of the text, the inscription is revealingly inaccurate, if not sexist. The following folios are not strictly the deeds of Cnut (died 1035) but of his wife, Queen Emma. Cnut is a key player in the narrative, but the work – the *Encomium Emmae Reginae* ('In Praise of Queen Emma') – was commissioned by Emma herself, and is one of the most important sources for our understanding of the Danish invasion of England in the early eleventh century and the fractious environment of the royal court in the generation before the Norman Conquest.

Most people have never heard of Queen Emma, but she was a crucial, if not pivotal figure in early medieval English history. She was crowned Queen of England twice, was the mother of two English kings, and the great-aunt of William the Conqueror. It was her relationship to William that partially legitimised the invasion in the Conqueror's eyes. She was a key political player; some might say she was the axis on which English politics turned around the year 1000. Unlike so many medieval queens who remain shadowy figures, the *Encomium Emmae Reginae* – a poem written for her by a monk from Saint-Omer in northern France – gives us unprecedented insight into her life and world. Written in c. 1041, the *Encomium* is a piece of brilliant political propaganda, which illustrates the delicate balance of power in the English court in this period, where factionalism was rife, and monarchs held power on a knife-edge. It is a highly political work, commissioned by a shrewd operator.[5]

BL Add. MS 33241 was copied shortly after the text was composed in the mid-eleventh century. It was not the original copy made for the queen, but appears to be a close cousin of that manuscript, which is now lost. After turning the page from its dubious opening inscription, the reader is greeted with an image.

Here we see Emma, in a crown, wearing a gown made from a splendid patterned fabric. Her figure dominates the image. She is framed by a Romanesque arch, elegantly draped with curtains; she appears to be sitting not so much on a throne as an architectural edifice. The work's tonsured author kneels in front of her, reverently presenting the book to her. Behind him, two figures peer through the side of the arch. They have little

Family Tree Showing Emma of Normandy's
Marriages, Issue and Stepchildren

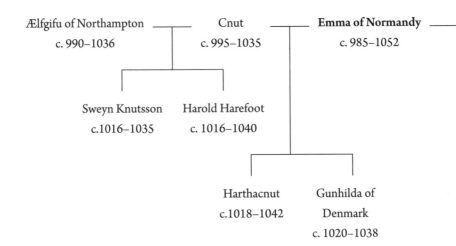

Ælfgifu of Northampton	Cnut	Emma of Normandy
c. 990–1036	c. 995–1035	c. 985–1052

Sweyn Knutsson	Harold Harefoot
c.1016–1035	c. 1016–1040

Harthacnut	Gunhilda of
c.1018–1042	Denmark
	c. 1020–1038

Emma of Normandy's Relationship to William the Conqueror

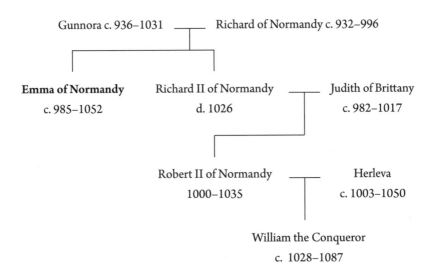

Gunnora c. 936–1031 — Richard of Normandy c. 932–996

Emma of Normandy	Richard II of Normandy	Judith of Brittany
c. 985–1052	d. 1026	c. 982–1017

Robert II of Normandy	Herleva
1000–1035	c. 1003–1050

William the Conqueror
c. 1028–1087

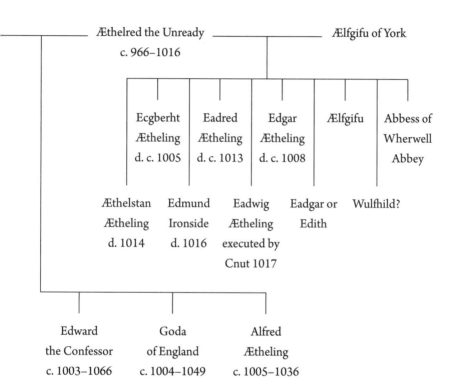

Æthelred the Unready
c. 966–1016
Ælfgifu of York

Ecgberht Ætheling d. c. 1005 | Eadred Ætheling d. c. 1013 | Edgar Ætheling d. c. 1008 | Ælfgifu | Abbess of Wherwell Abbey

Æthelstan Ætheling d. 1014 | Edmund Ironside d. 1016 | Eadwig Ætheling executed by Cnut 1017 | Eadgar or Edith | Wulfhild?

Edward the Confessor c. 1003–1066 | Goda of England c. 1004–1049 | Alfred Ætheling c. 1005–1036 fuzzy beards and are also wearing crowns. These figures are her sons, Harthacnut and Edward. The image encapsulates many of the fault-lines in Emma's world, fault-lines she had to navigate. Her life was one of intrigue, scandal and major reversals of fortune.[6] You would have no idea looking at this image that the two benign-looking figures in the background were competing claimants for the English throne, or that the kneeling figure in the foreground had produced an audacious piece of propaganda.

Emma was born in Normandy in the early 980s (her exact date of birth is not recorded). She was the daughter of the Duke of Normandy and was one of nine children, although we don't know which of these she was; her early life is obscure. She was probably in her early teens when she was sent across the English Channel to marry Æthelred the Unready in 1002.[7] (Æthelred's modern epithet comes from the Old English word *unræd*, which in fact means 'ill-advised'.) This was a period of high tension between England and its Scandinavian neighbours, when England was savaged by a series of Viking raids. The marriage was political – clearly part of a policy to strengthen links between England and Normandy as a buffer against Viking incursion. It was the first wedding of an English king to a foreign bride for over a century and a half.

Emma disembarked from Normandy at some point in the spring of 1002. On her arrival she was given a new name – Ælfgifu, which means 'elf-gift', after Æthelred's sainted grandmother, which was evidently an honour. That said, it was also the name of his previous wife. We can only wonder at what life was like for her, in this new court, with a new (or recycled) name and in a new language. Emma likely spoke both Norman and Danish, but not the form of English spoken at the time.

Within months of her arrival, an event occurred that illustrates the fragile political environment that Emma found herself in. The *Anglo-Saxon Chronicle* reports that:

> & on þam geare se cyng het ofslean ealle þa deniscan men þe on Angelcynne wæron, ðis wæs gedon on Britius mæssedæg, for ðam þam cynge wæs gecyd þæt hi woldon hine besyrewan æt his life, & siþþan ealle his witan & <habban> siþþan ðis rice.[8]

> *And in this year the king ordered to be slain all the Danish-men that were in England; this was done on St Brice's day [13 November], because it was made known to the king that they wished to deprive him and all of his council of their lives, and have thereafter his kingdom.*

This act of near-genocidal brutality illustrates Æthelred's weak and anxious hold on power. We know little about Emma's marriage to Æthelred. Writing a hundred years later, William of Malmesbury tells us that 'he was so offensive to his own wife that he would hardly deign to let her sleep with him'.[9] William's account is neither first-hand nor unbiased, but it's possible the marriage was not a happy one. Whether their marriage was harmonious or not, it is striking that after her arrival at court 'she was immediately accorded a prominent place in the witness-lists of the king's charters'.[10] (These charters – legal documents – give us an insight into the court's power structures.) Whether as a result of her own manoeuvring, or because of her status as the daughter of Richard I, Duke of Normandy, Emma appears to have exercised some power in her new court. Perhaps she had already learned how to be a political operator – a skill that would stand her in good stead throughout her life.

Emma's life in this period is largely obscure, but it was likely 'dominated by marriage and children'; she had three: Edward, Alfred, and a daughter, Godgifu.[11] But larger political concerns threatened in the summer of 1013, when King Swein of Denmark invaded England. Æthelred fled with Emma and her sons to Normandy. Swein died on 3 February 1014, and Emma and Æthelred returned to England, where they remained until his death on 23 April 1016. Edmund – Emma's stepson, Æthelred's son from his first marriage – was proclaimed king, but the country was soon attacked by Cnut – Swein's son. London was besieged twice in the course of 1016, and on 18 October Edmund was decisively defeated by Cnut at the Battle of Ashingdon. Thereafter, Cnut became the ruler of all England except Wessex (a kingdom in the south-west of England). On 30 November Edmund died. Mercifully for Emma, her son Edward had already fled England, because Cnut was ruthless with Æthelred's remaining heirs. Edmund's young sons were sent to the king of the Swedes to be executed, and Edmund's brother Eadwig was exiled and subsequently murdered on his return to England.

We are not sure where Emma was in this period; she may have been captured during the siege of London. At some point soon afterwards, in 1017, Cnut ordered Emma 'to be fetched' so that he might marry her. This looks like a brazenly political move 'to draw her away from the cause of her exiled sons in Normandy'.[12] He may have wanted to use her as a means to maintain continuity between Æthelred's administration and his own. We don't know where Emma was 'fetched' from; she may not have had a choice. The *Anglo-Saxon Chronicle*'s language here is bald: '& þa toforan kalendas Augusti het se cyng feccean him þæs oðres kynges lafe Æþelredes him to wife,

Ricardes dohtor' ('And before the first day of August, the king commanded that King Æthelred's other heirloom – Richard's daughter – be fetched such that he could make her his wife'). Emma is defined here in terms of her relationship to men, as 'Ricardes dohtor' and Æthelred's wife. The word *lafe* here can mean 'leavings, remains, legacy, heirloom'.[13] The language of the chronicler is clear: Emma was a chattel to be claimed. In an Old Norse poem by Hallvarðr Háreksblesi, composed during Cnut's reign, England is figured as feminine, and Cnut as the masculine conqueror, recalling 'earlier pre-Christian eulogies in which the conquest of a territory is expressed in sexual terms, as a forced "marriage"'.[14] Cnut may have seen his marriage to Emma as another form of conquest.

Emma was married to Cnut until his death on 12 November 1035. She had two children by him – Harthacnut and Gunhilda. When he died, she had been queen for thirty years at a court first presided over by Æthelred, and then Cnut. She might perhaps have felt secure in her status, but, in the closing weeks of 1035 Harold Harefoot (Cnut's son by his first wife) seized all her estates, and effectively disinherited Harthacnut. Emma tried to secure a position for Harthacnut (who was at the time in Denmark), but was not successful. Desperate to protect her own interests, as well as those of her children, she then tried to secure a position for Edward and Alfred (her sons by Æthelred the Unready), who were in exile in Normandy. In 1037 Harold Harefoot was formally chosen as king, and Emma went into exile. When Harefoot died in 1040, Emma returned to England, and it was then that she commissioned the *Encomium*. These are the bones of Emma's story, and seeing them helps us to grasp not only the story the *Encomium* wanted to tell, but also the stories it did *not* want to tell.

As this thumbnail sketch of Emma's biography makes clear, hers was a precarious political position. She was the mother of three separate claimants to the English throne, and the throne was claimed by several others – for each of her sons, there was a rival stepson. Her sons by her first and second marriage were in direct conflict with one another for the kingship of England. The *Encomium* therefore presents 'a particular picture of past glory and present peace as part of a deliberate attempt to intervene, on Emma's behalf, in the politics of the Anglo-Danish court'.[15]

The text opens with a prologue ('Incipit Prologus') in which the anonymous author addresses Queen Emma: 'o regina, que omnibus in hoc sexu positis prestas morum eligantia' ('O Queen, who excel all those of your sex in the admirable example of your life'). Strikingly, the prologue addresses the responsibilities of the historian, who 'should greatly beware, lest, going against truth by falsely introducing matter, he lose the very name which he is held to have from his office'.[16] Reading the rest of the text, these words are resonant. There are so many places where the author – the 'encomiast' – appears not to have adhered to his own words.

After the prologue, we find the 'Argument' – a short summary of the text's story. The story begins not, as we might imagine, with Emma, but with an account of Swein Forkbeard (the father of Cnut) invading England. The author seeks to refute any claim that this means the text is not entirely in praise of the queen, with a striking image:

> You are aware that wherever you draw a circle, first of all you certainly establish a point to be the beginning, and so the circle is made to return by continuously wheeling its

orb, and by this return the circumference of the circle is made to connect itself to its own beginning. By a similar connection, therefore, the praise of the queen is evident at the beginning, thrives in the middle, is present at the end, and embraces absolutely all of what the book amounts to.[17]

In other words, his text is a perfect O, looping back in reverent, circular praise of its queen, like the vocative 'O' in the 'O REGINA' of the prologue. In the Argument, the encomiast also signals his debt to the great Roman poet Virgil – a debt we see throughout the text: in places he even quotes Virgil directly.[18] (He also name-checks Horace, but the influence of a host of other writers is also discernible in the work.)[19] The *Encomium*, like Virgil's *Aeneid*, seeks to legitimise 'the claims of a contemporary ruler by recounting the foundation of her dynasty'.[20]

When the main text begins, the self-consciously literary style of the work is instantly apparent.[21] The author's description of the fleet of ships that set off to conquer England is pointedly Virgilian. He makes clear that this is no threatening war fleet intent on the murderous suppression of a neighbouring nation, but a beautiful and noble flotilla, describing the vessels as decorated with 'lions moulded in gold', golden birds and 'dragons of various kinds'. Elsewhere, there were 'glittering men of solid gold or silver nearly comparable to live ones, there bulls with necks raised high and legs outstretched were fashioned leaping and roaring like live ones'.[22] The encomiast tells us that the king was as beautiful as his vessels, and that beneath them, 'the blue water, smitten by many oars, might be seen foaming far and wide' – these ships so gorgeous that the sea itself foamed in excitement. (Shakespeare would use a similar image, centuries later, in his description of Cleopatra's barge as having silver oars 'Which to the tune of flutes kept stroke, and made / The water which they beat to follow faster, / As amorous of their strokes').[23] Such overwrought descriptions don't seem out of place from an author with an avowed love of Virgil, but there are other aspects of the *Encomium* that are not so much poetic licence as wilful perversion of fact.

The text describes the events of 1016–17, leading up to Emma and Cnut's marriage, as follows: 'the king lacked nothing except a most noble wife [*noblissima coniuge*]; such a one he ordered to be sought everywhere for him, in order to obtain her hand lawfully and to make her partner of his rule.'[24] Cnut sent his agents, it continues, to 'realms and cities', and the imperial bride was 'found within the bounds of Gaul'. Having identified the appropriate bride, 'royal gifts were sent, further-more precatory messages were sent'. In other words, Emma was wooed, because she was a woman 'of the greatest nobility and wealth [*stirpe et opibus ditissima*]'. There is no suggestion here that marrying Emma was a political move, because nowhere does it mention that she had been married to Æthelred.[25] It is a startling omission. And the *Encomium* goes further, attributing agency to Emma. It says she refused 'to ever become the bride' of Cnut 'unless he would affirm to her by oath, that he would never set up the son of any other wife'. The impression we get from the *Anglo-Saxon Chronicle* is that Emma – a woman defined in terms of her relationship to men – was an object to be left by one king and fetched by another. But the *Encomium* describes a woman in charge of her destiny. It paints a picture of a woman who well understood that her status was contin-gent, and that rival claimants to the throne were a threat to her and her sons. It is startling that the text mentions Cnut's 'other sons' (the encomiast says that Emma had received 'information that the king had sons by some other woman'), but it does not mention Emma's marriage to Æthelred.

It is clear that questions of succession were some of the stickiest for Emma. And the text finds deft ways to reframe the complicated threads of paternity that threatened her position. Describing the birth of Harthacnut – Emma and Cnut's son – the *Encomium* says that the two parents were happy in an 'unparalleled love for this child'. But it adds that they sent 'their other legitimate sons to Normandy to be brought up'. This is the first mention of Emma's other children. Predictably, her daughters are not mentioned, and revealingly, Edward (Emma's son with Æthelred) is described as one of 'their other legitimate sons' – in other words, the child of Cnut, not Æthelred. Seemingly under Emma's direction, the encomiast has re-described Emma's son from her first marriage as a son from her second.

There were other complicated threads of paternity to deal with. Emma was evidently concerned with furthering the interests of her children and not Cnut's children from *his* first marriage. To grasp her predicament, it is necessary to grasp the complexity of Emma's family tree (laid out above) and even then, the details can be a little dizzying. After Cnut's death, a faction of nobles installed Harold Harefoot (Cnut's son from his previous marriage) as the king. The *Encomium* describes him as 'one Harold, who is declared, owing to a false estimation of the matter, to be a son of a certain concubine of the above-mentioned King Cnut'. The author describes Ælfgifu of Northampton – Cnut's first wife – as a 'concubine', but more damningly describes Harold not as the son of this woman, but as the child of this still lowlier 'servant': 'the assertion of very many people has it that the same Harold was secretly taken from a servant who was in childbed, and put in the chamber of the concubine.' The words of the prologue, warning that 'the historian should greatly beware, lest, going against truth by falsely introducing matter, he lose the very name which he is held to have from his office', have a particular ring here.[26] The extraordinary claims about Harold are all the more surprising given that there are moments elsewhere in the text when the encomiast acknowledges the outlandishness of his story. In an episode in which he is discussing a magical banner of ravens carried into battle, for example, he writes: 'I believe that it may be incredible to the reader, yet since it is true, I will introduce the matter into my true history.'[27]

The concluding section of the work describes how Edward (Emma's son by Æthelred) asked Harthacnut (her son by Cnut) to 'come and hold the kingdom together with himself'. The encomiast assures us that 'the mother and both sons, having no disagreement between them, enjoy the ready amenities of the kingdom', offering thanks, in the final lines of the work, to 'Him, who makes dwellers in a house be of one mind, Jesus Christ, the Lord of all, who, abiding in the Trinity, holds a kingdom which flourishes unfading'.[28] Just as the work concludes with an image of the Trinity – the Father, Son and Holy Spirit – so too it enshrines a trinity of Emma, Harthacnut and Edward, united by shared parental love. The parallelism is plainly intentional, and it is indeed this very trinity that appears in the manuscript's opening image. The encomiast insists that his praise of Emma may be seen at the beginning, the middle and the end of his story, but his larger purpose – the projection of a harmonious family unit – is perhaps more visible.

The moment of glory that the *Encomium* describes was brief, however. Her son Harthacnut died in June 1042, and Emma was deprived of her treasures by Edward the Confessor and demoted from her former status. She lived the rest of her life in 'retirement' and died in 1052. She was buried at Winchester near the graves of Cnut and their son, Harthacnut.

Afterlives

In 2008 a different version of the *Encomium* came to light.[29] It was preserved in a manuscript copied later – in the fifteenth century – and presented a variant ending of the text written in the time of Edward the Confessor (the son of Æthelred and Emma). The text's new conclusion is a fascinatingly intelligent response to the original version. It reads:

> Now, O watchful reader, let your careful attention show itself and bring back to recollection what I said in my preface about the circle. I indeed recollect that I said that in making a circle there must be a returning to one and the same point so that the circle may attain the orbit of its round form. So likewise it was brought to pass in the arranging of the rule of the English kingdom. Æthelred, the foremost king – foremost because of all those of his time the most outstanding – commanded that monarchy.[30]

In a brilliant move, the reviser – or perhaps the original author, under new instruction – has taken a key image from the opening of the text and reframed it. Whereas in the original text Æthelred is unmentioned, here he is *returned to*, as though he had been there all along, as if to underline Edward's royal English lineage. (It might also suggest that a new ending was quickly slapped on when Edward became the sole ruler of the kingdom.) The discovery of this variant text is a reminder of how susceptible historical texts always are to change and alteration. The *Encomium*, in its different versions, reminds us that political agendas underpin the writing of history and the weaving of stories they tell.

The Broken Bones of a Story

In 2012, a conservation project began at Winchester Cathedral to examine the contents of six of the cathedral's mortuary chests.[31] The chests were supposed to contain the bones of fifteen people, including eight kings, two bishops and one queen, all from the late pre-Conquest and early Norman period. The chests are labelled, but during the Civil War, they were broken open and the bones scattered. A Royalist churchman, Bruno Ryves, describes how Parliamentarian forces, 'monsters of men', were seen to 'violate these Cabinets of the dead, and to scatter their bones all over the pavement of the Church'. Ryves was undoubtedly a biased informant, but the latest research supports some of his accusations. He describes the soldiers 'spurning and trampling on the bones of all' and subsequently using the bones as 'passive Instruments',

> of more than heathenish Sacrilege, and prophanenesse, those Windowes which they could not reach with their Swords, Muskets, or Rests [i.e. musket supports], they brake to pieces, by throwing at them, the bones of Kings, Queenes, Bishops, Confessors and Saints.[32]

After this, local people gathered up the bones and replaced them in the mortuary chests, but in the process the different skeletons got mixed up. In 2012, a team of biological anthropologists at the University of Bristol began work to sort the bones – reassembling dispersed skeletons and radiocarbon-dating them. They found that several had been broken in a way consistent with Ryves's account. In 2015 radiocarbon dating on selected bone fragments by the Radiocarbon Accelerator Unit at the University of Oxford revealed that the bones were indeed – as was suspected – from the late pre-Conquest and early Norman period. This accorded with the information on the outside of the chests. Using other techniques, the researchers were able to assess each skeleton's sex, age at death, and physical characteristics. They also used the 'marine reservoir' effect to determine the social status of the individuals. (In the medieval period, high-status individuals generally ate larger amounts of both freshwater and seawater fish, so their bones contain a different kind of radiocarbon.) Collating all of this information, the researchers were able to identify several specific individuals. They sifted through 1,300 bones and distinguished the skeletons of twenty-three individuals, rather than the expected fifteen. Amongst the bones, the researchers discovered the skeleton of a mature female, of a high social status. It seems very likely that these are the bones of Queen Emma.

Like her bones, Emma's story has been dismembered and scattered. Reconstructing the facts of her life is a complicated business. It's intriguing to speculate on whether she knew how stories, especially women's stories, become obscured over time. Perhaps she commissioned the *Encomium*, in part, to ensure that later ages would know something of her. This is the striking feature of the *Encomium* – it is so rare to find historical accounts from this period featuring women, let alone any commissioned by women. But what adds to the wonder of the *Encomium* is its acute awareness of how stories are contingent, easily altered and reframed. The encomiast acknowledges that parts of his story might seem unbelievable. And the discovery of the different, later version of the text shows how stories can themselves become broken, scattered and reconstituted.

Henry VIII (1491–1547)

Queen Emma is a figure almost completely unknown beyond academia. The contrast with our next patron could not be more marked. British Library Royal MS 2 A XVI is still in its original binding. This binding would once have been a luxurious, fluffy red velvet, but is now threadbare. Several elegant silver-gilt corner pieces and gilt edges remain, however, as does the suggestion of clasps: we have a sense of its former sumptuousness. Opening the initial folios, one of the first images to greet you shows an image of a plump and bearded king – one of the most famous of England's kings, King Henry VIII, sitting in his bedchamber. This king was the book's owner and commissioner. Henry looks a little sturdy here, but otherwise the image is an uncompromising display of royal power.[33] The room – airy and neo-Classical in design – is decorated with expensive fabrics and furniture. Henry is seen reading a manuscript in a red velvet binding with golden clasps – undoubtedly the very manuscript the image we are looking at appears within. Beside him on the floor are two similarly sumptuous volumes. Beneath the image, the opening text of the Psalms appears. It reads, 'Blessed is the man who has not walked in the counsel of the ungodly, nor stood in the way of sinners, nor sat in the chair of pestilence.' Henry's seated position may therefore be intended to suggest that he does *not* sit in that 'chair of pestilence'. The second verse of the Psalm exhorts readers to meditate on the word of the Lord day and night. Henry is shown in his bedchamber, but not asleep. It is daylight outside, but the scholar king has retreated to his chamber to study.

The text of the Psalms is written in an elegant script with perfectly straight ascenders, enclosed in a neo-Classical architectural surround, and decorated with an opulent initial depicting flowers and insects. Henry sits in a chair adorned with a lion's head. (The chair may have been observed from life. It is remarkably similar to a chair described in his personal inventory.)[34] This folio is striking for a number of reasons. It was common to find an image of the biblical David – the supposed author of the Psalms – at this point in a Psalter, but what is surprising is that here Henry is identified, iconographically, with David. Equally striking is the fact that beside the opening words of the Psalm, Henry has himself written 'nota quis sit beatus' ('note who is blessed'). This annotation, beneath an image of the king himself, is a potent display of Henry's belief in his own blessed status, which is appropriate for a man who broke with Rome and established himself as the head of the English Church.

BL Royal MS 2 A XVI was Henry's private prayer book. It was a personal commission and has a clear political agenda, embodying the desires and fears of its patron. Its images provide ample evidence of Henry's vanity, while its annotations provide an unparalleled insight into the mind of the tyrant-king whose personal, marital wrangles influenced the politics of Europe.[35] A remarkable commission, the manuscript brings us to the human heart of the one of most radical shifts in English cultural life in the pre-modern period.

The prayer book was written and illustrated by the French scribe and book-artist Jean Mallard in c. 1540. The manuscript is small and would have been easy for the king to hold in his hands, unlike some of the other works which Mallard produced for him which would have required a lectern to read.[36] It is written in an incredibly clear hand, which Henry may have favoured because of his failing eyesight. In 1535, when he was forty-four, Henry had written that he favoured a printing type that was 'easier to read'.[37] (This so-called 'humanist' script originated in Italy, and was modelled on the script developed in the reign of the ninth-century Emperor Charlemagne, which came to symbolise a revival of antiquity and ancient learning for Renaissance humanists.) Alongside its clarity, the manuscript has exquisite decorative details. The opening initial of Psalm 79, for example, shows a ladybird clambering over a plump cucumber.[38] Indeed, some of the most magical parts of the manuscript are its decorative details – tiny features so easily missed. In the opening initial a small frog can be seen, crouched amid briar roses. Elsewhere Mallard's initials contain snails, plump blackberries, butterflies, beetles, plants, a mouse chewing on an ear of corn, a parakeet, sweet-peas, fruit covered in caterpillars, a grasshopper and, rather alarmingly, two gutted rabbits, hanging up.[39] But the manuscript is most extraordinary for its larger images and its annotations.

The prayer book 'is more heavily marked up than any other book owned by Henry'.[40] The annotations happened in stages – in pen, pencil and red crayon. Sometimes he drew symbols in the margin – like the distinctive 'tadpole' sign which is a hallmark of his work. In some places he underlined pieces of text, while in others he wrote short notes in the margin. It was not unusual to gloss books in this period, but it says something of Henry's lavishness that he should have used the margins of so sumptuous a book to write notes in.[41] The annotations do not appear throughout: 'As elsewhere, Henry showed himself to have a short attention span and did not annotate the complete book.'[42] After Psalm 111, the book's margins are unmarked – a testament to regal boredom. In spite of this, Henry evidently knew much of the text well, and engaged with it thoughtfully, if not comprehensively. Erasmus – a scholar with whom Henry corresponded – wrote that 'it is generally agreed that among all the books of Holy Scripture, none is so full of such recondite mysteries as the book of Psalms, and no other book is wrapped in such obscurity of words and meaning'.[43] This was plainly thought to be a text demanding careful study.

The historical background to the prayer book's production is crucial, as the events of the previous decade – and, to some extent, the decade before that – directly informed the Psalter's decoration and annotations, and so I think are worth summarising here. Henry was born in 1491 and came to the throne in 1509. He married his brother Arthur's widow, Katherine of Aragon, on 11 June that year. The wedding was followed by a spectacular joint coronation thirteen days later. Their marriage was to last nineteen years, but it failed to produce the son and heir Henry so passionately desired. Katherine miscarried her first child, and the second, Prince Henry (born on New Year's Day 1511), survived for only a few days. Katherine was to have six pregnancies in ten years, but only one resulted in a surviving child: Princess Mary (later Mary I), who was born in 1516. In 1519 Katherine was pregnant again, but again miscarried. It must have hurt her deeply that in that year Henry's mistress Elizabeth Blount gave birth to a healthy son, whom Henry acknowledged (and created Duke of Richmond in 1525). In 1519 both Henry and Katherine were thirty-four. Henry's grandfathers had died at twenty-six and forty-one. He probably no longer saw himself as in the prime of his youth, and Katherine would have been thought of as entering the twilight of her fertile years.

In 1524 Henry abandoned intercourse with his wife, increasingly concerned that his lack of a male heir was proof of God's displeasure with him. Having married his brother's widow, he had become ever more anxious with a particular verse from Leviticus 20: 21, which states that if a man had sexual relations with his brother's wife, he would be childless. At some point in early 1526, Henry began to pursue Anne Boleyn, and in August 1527 he petitioned the Pope to have his marriage annulled and for the two of them to have permission to marry. They likely expected this would happen in a matter of months; in fact it would take another five and a half years.

After much legal wrangling, the pair married in January 1533. On 23 May, Thomas Cranmer, Henry's newly appointed Archbishop of Canterbury, declared that Henry's marriage to Katherine had been invalid. This legitimised his marriage to Anne, rendered Princess Mary illegitimate, and Katherine was demoted to Dowager Princess of Wales. Rome responded forcefully, ordering Henry to take Katherine back. The king formally denied papal jurisdiction in England and passed legislation that broke with Rome. He thereby became 'the only Supreme Head on earth of the Church of England', conferring on himself a particular status – now not only king of the nation, but head of its new religion.[44] This was a theocratic model of kingship.

The change in the new religion was widespread and sweeping, and it mirrored reformist movements in northern Europe. Between 1535 and 1540, under Thomas Cromwell, a policy known as the 'Dissolution of the Monasteries' was carried out. Monasteries and pilgrim shrines were attacked, and vast swathes of Church land and property passed into the hands of the Crown and ultimately into those of the nobility and gentry. A host of different practices were banned, including the worship of icons, the use of candles, the veneration of saints and the performance of pilgrimage. But this great change did not achieve one of its original aims. Although Henry reshaped the English religious landscape and declared himself head of a new English Church in order to marry Anne in the hope of having a son, no son was forthcoming. Henry turned against his second wife. She was executed in 1536, and Henry was betrothed to Jane Seymour the next day. They were married ten days later, on 30 May 1536; she gave birth to a coveted male heir, Prince Edward (later Edward VI), on 12 October 1537, but died twelve days later of complications related to the birth, possibly from a retained placenta. Two years later, in January 1540, Henry married Anne of Cleves. And it was in this year that the Psalter was produced. The marriage was not to be the most momentous event of that year: it was annulled; not long after, his trusted advisor Thomas Cromwell was executed, and Henry was married again, to Catherine Howard. Exactly when Mallard's commission was delivered, and how long he had worked on it, is unclear, but the weight of the previous decade's events is discernible throughout the manuscript.

The prayer book reflects Henry's status as the 'Supreme Head' of the Church. In his dedicatory epistle at the start of the book, Mallard addresses Henry as 'Defender of the Faith, King of England and France' (this fawning dedication is somewhat surprising from a Frenchman). Henry's status as the Supreme Head of the Church can be seen throughout the book, most obviously in the way it identifies him with the biblical David. David's story was used to justify and define Henry's supremacy, but it also had other quite striking resonances. David was the King of Israel and Judah. He was a young shepherd famed for his skills as a musician. He fought the giant Goliath, and became a favourite of King Saul and Saul's son, Jonathan. But Saul turned on David, and both Saul and Jonathan were killed in battle, and so David became king. He conquered Jerusalem and brought the Ark of the Covenant to the city. He reorganised the priesthood and created a new spiritual order. These parts of the story evidently resonated with Henry, who had established a new Church and who saw himself as battling against great evil. But there are other parts of the story that must have sounded equally strong, if inadvertent echoes. Once David had become king, he was walking one day on the roof of his palace when he saw a beautiful woman, Bathsheba, bathing. Enquiring about her identity, he was told that she was married to Uriah the Hittite, whereupon 'David sent messengers and took her, and when she came to him, he lay with her; and when she had purified herself from her uncleanness, she returned to her house' (2 Samuel 11: 4). She became pregnant, and he hoped to pass off the child as Uriah's, but when the latter stayed on the battlefield, refusing to come home, David arranged for him to be killed there in battle. One wonders whether Henry identified with both parts of this story of a murderous adulterer. No doubt Henry was more focused on the image of David as an ideal king, a musician, the author of the Psalms and the prefiguring forefather of Christ.

Henry's fascination with David had begun even before the Act of Supremacy. In 1528 he acquired a ten-piece set of tapestries depicting a 'riche historye of king david'.[45] But it was after the passing of that Act that royal iconography became particularly Davidic. In the frontispiece of the Great Bible – the English translation of the Bible that all English parishes were required by law after 1538 to purchase – Henry appears enthroned at the top, alongside a quotation from the Psalms: 'Lucerna pedibus meis verbum tuum' ('Thy word is a lamp to my feet'), Psalms 118: 105. And it was not only royal iconography that associated Henry with David. A number of writers also made the comparison, in ways both subtle and blatant.[46]

After the striking early image of Henry in the Psalter, several further illustrations in the manuscript link Henry with David and, more subtly, with Christ himself as heir to the House of David. The second image of the manuscript appears alongside Psalm 26 and shows David pitted against Goliath.[47]

As in the opening image, the illustration appears in a gold frame, but is different in a tiny, gorgeous detail: Mallard has drawn two golden chain links below the frame as holding the text's border decoration below. The text border is a *trompe-l'œil* knotted blue ribbon to which bunches of cucumbers, pears and cherries are attached. From the ribbon a kind of golden ox-yoke, decorated with a horned man's head, appears, as the text's lower border. This is a virtuoso piece of painting – three-dimensional and textured, conveying the weighty heft of the chains, the succulence of the fruit, and the delicate flutter of the ribbon-ends. You could so easily miss these details and, indeed, I wonder if Henry did. His attention was most likely attracted to the image above. There, the two figures of David and Goliath are fighting against a backdrop of elegant striped tents, green fields and a distant city, which makes artful use of aerial perspective. David has the face of Henry, as well as the distinctive black velvet cap we saw in the opening image. Goliath – an awkwardly oversized figure in neo-Classical golden armour – towers over him. David is in the act of drawing back his slingshot, ready to devastate Goliath, whom Henry no doubt saw as a metaphor for Pope Paul III – the pope who had decreed the second and final excommunication of the king in 1538. The *titulus* – or small, explanatory gloss – written out by Mallard in the margin at the start of the Psalm reads: 'Christi plena in Deum fiducia' ('Christ's full trust in God'). Next to this, Henry has made one of his characteristic 'tadpole' annotations, apparently denoting a particular interest in the text. He seems to have felt his complete trust in God would be rewarded.

This is something that recurs in several places in the annotations, revealing that Henry thought himself to be protected by God. In the margin two psalms later, next to the words 'Exaltabo te, Domine, quoniam suscepisti me, nec delectasti inimicos meos super me' ('I will extol thee, O Lord, for thou hast upheld me: and hast not made my enemies to rejoice over me'), he has written 'de gratiarum actione' ('concerning thanksgiving'). He seems to have been thankful that God had not made his enemies rejoice over him. We sense he expected those very enemies to be punished in another annotation next to Psalm 10: 7, where he notes well ('nota bene') that God will rain snares, fire, brimstone and storms upon the wicked. And at the end of the Psalm he writes 'nota de iusto' ('note concerning the just'). Henry evidently thought he would not be punished by God. Psalm 17: 26–7, for example, describes how 'God will be holy with those who are holy, but with those who are perverse, He will be a hard judge'. Next to this, Henry wrote 'de confortio' (of comfort).[48]

Annotations such as these in the prayer book suggest that Henry hoped the Psalms of David could teach him important lessons about his new role as Supreme Head of the Church of England, as well as about how to be a king. He highlighted Mallard's explanatory *titulus* 'exortatio ad principes' ('exhortation to princes'), and elsewhere directly aligns himself with David, as in an annotation attached to Psalm 88: 20, where next

1: Marginal detail, Domesday Abbreviatio, c. 1241,
The National Archives, E 36/284.

2: Æthelwine the Black (Egelwynus ye Swarte) and his wife Wynflæd,
who gave land to the abbey of Saint Alban in 11th century:
BL Cotton MS Nero D VII, fol. 89v.

3: An elaborate catchword in Jocelin of Furness, 'Life of St Patrick',
Cambridge, Trinity MS B 15 25, fol. 47v.

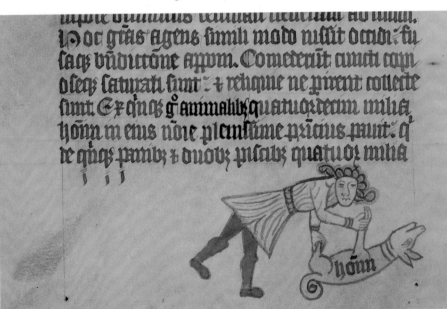

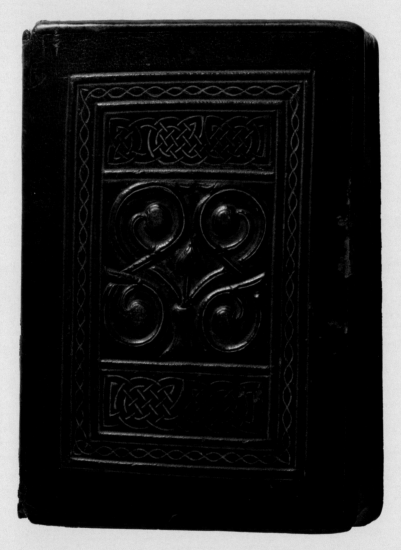

4: Front cover of the Cuthbert Gospel – the earliest intact
European book, BL Add. MS 89000.

5: The opening of *Beowulf* from BL Cotton MS Vitellius A xv (fol. 132r), showing the singed edges of the folios.

6: The author presents his work to its patron, Queen Emma, as her sons, Harthacnut (d. 1042) and Edward the Confessor (d. 1066), look on. From the *Encomium Emmae Reginae*, BL Add. MS 33241 fol. 1v.

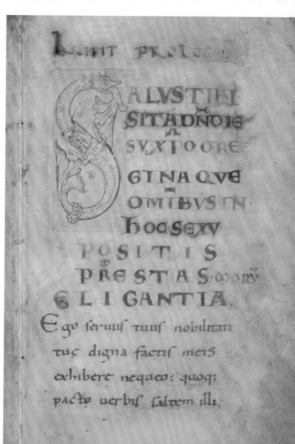

7: 'O regina': the opening of the *Encomium Emmae Reginae*, BL Add. MS 33241 fol. 2r.

BEATVS vir qui non abiit
in confilio impiorum, & in via
peccatorum non ftetit, & in cathedra pe=
ftilentiæ non fedit.

8: 'Note who is blessed', King Henry in his bedchamber reading, from the prayer-book of Henry VIII, BL Royal MS 2 A XVI, fol. 3r.

9: 'The fool hath said in his heart: There is no God', the opening of Psalm 13 in the prayer-book of Henry VIII depicting the king and his fool, Will Sommers. BL Royal MS 2 A XVI, fol. 63v.

10: David, figured as Henry, fights Goliath in the prayer-book of Henry VIII, BL Royal MS 2 A XVI, fol. 30r.

11: David, figured as Henry, is offered famine (birch scourge), flight (sword) or plague (skull) in the prayer-book of Henry VIII, BL Royal MS 2 A XVI, fol. 79r.

12: Three *putti* where once there would have been monks appear in the prayer-book of Henry VIII, Royal MS 2 A XVI, fol. 118r.

to the words 'I have laid help upon one that is mighty, and have exalted one chosen out of my people', he has written 'Promissa David facta' ('the promise made to David'), seemingly seeing David and himself as chosen ones.[49]

The manuscript's third major image appears at the beginning of Psalm 38.[50] It depicts a battle. The scene is crowded with knights on horseback, in early modern armour, armed with a forest of spears. In the foreground a man lies dead or dying, and another on foot stands to the right, while our eyes are drawn to a pair of figures in armour with white stockings who are engaged in combat. The relevance of the image isn't immediately apparent, but it seems most likely that the scene shows the death of Uriah, sent to his death by King David.

In the next major image, Henry's self-identification with the biblical David is more explicit. Here, above Psalm 52, which contains the line, 'the fool hath said in his heart, there is no God', we find an image of Henry with a harp – the traditional symbol of the biblical David.[51] Next to him is a man wearing a green hooded jacket and blue stockings. His hands are folded in front of him and his face is set in something of a scowl. He can be identified as Henry's jester Will Somers, with whom the king enjoyed a close relationship for over twenty years. Somers was born in Shropshire, and brought to court in 1525 by Richard Fermor, a senior merchant in Calais. He remained at court for the rest of his life, not retiring until the reign of Elizabeth I. In King Henry's later years, when he was suffering from a variety of medical conditions, it was said that only Somers could cheer him, and it is possible that this is why he was included in the Psalter's imagery. (Somers can be so confidently identified because he also appears in a painting in the Royal Collection at Hampton Court Palace.)[52]

The image accompanying Psalm 68, which begins 'Salvum me fac' ('Save me, O Lord'), illustrates an episode in the Bible when David is forced to choose between three terrible punishments (Figure 11).[53] The scene relates to 2 Samuel 24: 13–25, in which David was offered three alternative judgements for his sinful behaviour: either three years of famine, three months of flight from his enemies, or three days of plague. The image shows Henry VIII as a penitent King David, kneeling among the ruins. He is dressed in armour, but wearing the distinctive black hat with a white feather that he wears in several other images. Henry kneels in supplication, amid the ruins of a neo-Classical building. His crown appears on the floor beside him. His eyes are raised in the direction of an angel who appears in the sky in the upper-left corner of the picture, and who is holding three symbols to represent the three punishments: a birch scourge (three years of famine); a sword (three months of flight); and a skull (three days of plague). Overleaf, Henry has highlighted with the tadpole sign the verses which read, in translation:

> In the multitude of thy mercy hear me, in the truth of thy salvation.
>
> Draw me out of the mire, that I may not stick fast: deliver me from them that hate me, and out of the deep waters.
>
> Let not the tempest of water drown me, nor the deep swallow me up: and let not the pit shut her mouth upon me.
>
> Hear me, O Lord, for thy mercy is kind; look upon me according to the multitude of thy tender mercies.
>
> And turn not away thy face from thy servant: for I am in trouble, hear me speedily.

Attend to my soul, and deliver it: save me because of my
enemies.

The *titulus* – that explanatory rubric – reads: 'Christus in
angustia mortis inuocat Deum' ('In anguish at his death Christ
invokes God'). In so doing, David's torment prefigures
Christ's in the Garden of Gethsemane; and the image, *titulus*
and annotations link Henry with Christ as well.

One of the final images of the manuscript does not reflect
Henry's personal iconography, but does reflect a change
brought about by his religious policy. Next to Psalm 97, where
in a pre-Reformation manuscript you might usually find an
image of a group of monks in song, on this page we find instead
a group of plump-faced *putti*.[54] They appear in a historiated
(elaborately decorated) initial, wearing fetching robes in dark
purple, deep red and a burnt orange. They have ruddy cheeks,
chubby feet and boyish curls, and are singing from a manuscript
very like the one they appear within. Perhaps their youth was
intended to signal the promise of the new era – a new Church
of England, no longer populated by monks. And, it is not only
the manuscript's images that reflect the changes in religious
practice brought about during Henry's reign. Some of Henry's
annotations reflect it too, where he made notes next to verses
related to the use of religious icons and the role of confession
in religious practice.[55]

Thinking back on the events of 1540 – with the execution
of Thomas Cromwell and the annulled marriage to Anne of
Cleves – we can only speculate on a 'nota' mark Henry added
to Psalm 11: 3. The Psalm describes how the lips and tongues
of flatterers and braggarts will be cut off. Had Henry come to
see one of his most trusted advisors as a flatterer or a braggart?

His court was certainly a place where people jostled for advancement, a cut-throat arena of political manoeuvring, where a wrong move could prove fatal. We get a sense of this by looking at the cast of characters in play called *Magnyfycence* written by Henry's childhood tutor, John Skelton, which depicts a ruler surrounded by fawning courtiers. These allegorical characters have such names as 'Counterfet countenance' ('Counterfeit Countenance'), 'Crafty Conueyance' ('Crafty Guidance'), 'Courtly abusyon' ('Courtly Abuse'), and 'Clokyd colusyon' ('Cloaked Collusion').

Alongside these glosses, which point out issues of faith and practice, and hint at the environment of the court, there are also annotations that reflect more human concerns. The first half of verse 25 of Psalm 36, for example, reads: 'I have been young and now I am old.' Henry, who was between forty-nine and fifty-six years old when he made this note, seems to have felt that his time on earth was drawing to a close. He comments that this is 'a painful saying' ('dolens dictum'). And, near to Psalm 26: 4, he described as an 'apt petitio' ('appropriate appeal') its desire to 'dwell in the house of the Lord all the days of my life'. He added further *nota* signs next to Psalm 89: 9–10: 'Our years shall be considered as a spider: the days of our years in them are threescore and ten years' (the traditionally allotted span of human life being seventy). He may have been wondering if he would live that long. Elsewhere we see his concern for how his days may be numbered in the way he has drawn a line in the margin and added the tadpole sign next to Psalm 38: 'Notum fac mihi, Domine, finem meum, et numerum dierum meorum quis est, ut sciam quid desit mihi' ('O Lord, make me know my end. And what is the number of my days: that I may know what is wanting to me').[56]

One of the last, and perhaps most poignant, of the annotations in the manuscript appears next to Psalm 108.[57] The Psalm describes the punishment of the sinner: 'May his posterity be cut off; in one generation may his name be blotted out.' The events of the previous decade had been shaped by Henry's concern for 'his posterity' and an anxiety that 'his name may be blotted out'. The king highlighted the entire Psalm in ink in the margin. But at some point, he underlined a specific verse, relating to sinners, in pencil, and added the tadpole sign in the margin:

Fiant contra Dominum semper, et dispereat de terra memoria eorum: pro eo quod non est recordatus facere misericordiam.

May they be before the Lord continually, and let the memory of them perish from the earth: because he remembered not to shew mercy.

Henry seems to have wanted to utterly extinguish the memory of his enemies ('perish from the earth'), but the exhortation not to show mercy, doubly annotated by him, is doubly chilling. To the modern historian, however, the idea of how memory might perish from the earth is a constantly pertinent one, especially when we consider the two very different patrons we've met here, and how the story of one has lived on in the cultural memory, while the other has all but perished.

Henry VIII died some seven years after the Psalter was made, on 28 January 1547. After lying in state, his body was moved, on 16 February, to the vault of St George's Chapel, Windsor, where he was buried next to the grave of Jane Seymour. In September that year, formal instruction was given for an inventory to be made of his moveable property. It took eighteen months to complete. In its printed edition, that inventory stretches to just under 18,000 items. Item 3527 describes a 'Booke of Psalmes covered with crimson vellat and garneshed with golde': in all likelihood, this is Henry's prayer book.[58] The inventory is strangely compelling. The extensive list of Henry's books, tapestries, armour and furniture give a sense of regal opulence, but there are also parts of it that remind us of his human frailty. I paused over the two silver ear-picks, feeling a thrill of disgust at the thought of the royal earwax. To see a life laid out like this, in an itemised list, makes Henry simultaneously close and distant – a spoilt tyrant and a weak man. Enough of Henry's possessions survive today to make his presence still accessible to us, just under five hundred years later. I wonder if, in Henry's day, anything survived of Emma, who had died just under five hundred years earlier. None of her possessions survive today. Even her skeleton was dismembered, and has only recently been reassembled. It is impossible to know if she had any conception of how her story would live on, but she made a bold attempt to have her very selective version of events recorded. Like Henry, she commissioned a work that reflected her personal fears and biases, and enshrined a particular narrative of her life. Few women in history have had this power to record their stories.

Chapter Four

ARTISTS

It is typical of medieval achievement that we should find the work of one great artist so closely bound up with that of another, that the names of both should be unknown, and their personalities distinguished only because the hand of a master is almost always individual.

Walter Oakeshott[1]

In some ways, it is anachronistic to call this chapter 'Artists'. The word 'artist' did not appear in the English language until after the medieval period. Its arrival as a word, and concept, was concurrent with the emergence of early modern thinking which elevated painters from the status of craftsmen. In the medieval period, manuscript artists were often called 'limners'. (The word is an altered form of 'luminer', meaning 'illuminator', from the Latin *lumen*, meaning 'light'. Medieval artists were – in a literal sense – bringers of light.) Much like the scribes of the previous chapter, in the early medieval period, limners were often attached to monastic institutions, but as the medieval era progressed, they increasingly became secular professionals. (The Stationers' Company of London – a guild of scribes and limners – was formed in 1403.)[2] The examples I discuss here, however, are a mixture of monastic and lay artists.

This chapter is about the artists who wouldn't have called themselves artists, the people whose names and stories are now forgotten but whose strange and beautiful vision still captivates us today. The three manuscripts I explore here were produced by a *group* of artists. This is a key difference between our under-standing of the 'artist' and medieval practice. We tend to think of great artists as individual creative geniuses, who work alone and, in their lifetimes or after, become famous. This picture rarely applies to medieval manuscript artists, even those of the very highest status. The creation and decoration of manuscripts was a collaborative enterprise and the names of the people who made them rarely survive in the historical record.

In January 2019, a study was published in *Science Advances*.[3] It outlined the findings of a microscopic analysis of dental cal-culus found on the skeleton of a middle-aged woman buried in a church-monastery complex at Dalheim in Germany. Dental calculus, or tartar, is a hardened build-up of dental plaque. The teeth of the woman (radiocarbon-dated to 997–1162 CE) contained 'lazurite and phlogopite crystals, in the form of powder consistent in size and composition with lapis lazuli-derived ultramarine pigment'. In the Middle Ages, ultramarine was high-value pigment, which came from Afghanistan or Iran. It was used in the painting of manuscripts and frequently used for painting the robes of the Virgin Mary – its high price making its use a kind of reverence in colour form. The little particles in this woman's dental calculus suggested that she was a manuscript artist. She probably got the particles in her mouth when she sucked her paintbrush to bring it to a point, for more precise line filling.

We know almost nothing about who this woman was: we have neither a name, nor any dates of birth, but we do have these little particles – tiny pieces of evidence to show that, contrary to popular belief, women did work as manuscript artists in the medieval period and with the most precious materials in the trade. This pattern – no name, no dates of birth – is common for medieval manuscript artists, male or female.

The Winchester Bible

At some point around the middle of the twelfth century, a scribe set about work on a commission that was both hefty and spectacular.[4] This scribe was probably the most senior scribe in the scriptorium of St Swithun's Priory in Winchester – only someone with many years of experience as a copyist could be trusted with the task he was about to undertake.[5] He was, in all likelihood, a Benedictine monk, which meant copying manuscripts was an important part of his daily routine; time for such work was set aside during the hours of the morning.[6]

In front of him was a great bifolium of animal skin, probably sheep hide, which had already been carefully pricked and ruled, probably by a more junior member of the scriptorium. The parchment was of high quality – such high quality that it must have been made in specialist shop, rather than in the Priory itself.[7] This bifolium was to be one of many – in the end he would cover some 234 huge pieces (58 cm by 80 cm) made from whole hides, totalling 936 pages of text. The work of copying the text probably took him around 'four years or so' to complete: these hides would eventually make up a magnificent two-volume bible known today as the Winchester Bible.[8] The scholar Christopher de Hamel has called it 'a candidate for the greatest piece of art produced in England'.[9] It belongs to a group of large bibles made for religious houses in England (and on the Continent) in the twelfth century, but of this group, it is the largest English example and is possibly 'the finest'.[10] Its size and scale was a physical manifestation of the power the biblical text had for the community that made the manuscript.

Today the Bible can still be seen in Winchester Cathedral. (Winchester Cathedral was the church of St Swithun's Benedictine Priory in the twelfth century.)[11] Winchester had a long tradition of producing lavish illuminated manuscripts – bibles, liturgical books and charters.[12] This Bible was likely completed by 1161 and may have been commissioned by Bishop Henry of Blois (c. 1096–1171). Henry was Bishop of Winchester from 1129 until his death and was one of five sons of Stephen II, Count of Blois, by Adela of Normandy (daughter of William the Conqueror) and the younger brother of King Stephen. He had earlier commissioned another Bible (Oxford, Bodleian Library MS Auct. E inf. 2) for Winchester and was responsible for a number of changes in the Cathedral, including remodelling the east end of the choir to give pilgrims better access to the relics of St Swithun.[13]

The Winchester Bible is now displayed in a room in the Cathedral's south transept. A mural (from a later period) on the south wall shows a scribe at work, suggesting that this became the Priory's scriptorium. The area is traditionally known as the Calefactory – a heated place – heated perhaps to prevent the scribes and artists from getting cold hands. (Cold hands were something of an occupational hazard for scribes.)[14] I sometimes wonder whether the Bible's artists were afflicted by cold as they laboured to decorate its folios.

The Bible, which is now bound as four volumes after conservation work, was not intended for individual study but for ceremonial use by the monks of the Priory. After the text was copied, it was carefully corrected, and at some point accents were added to aid in reading the text aloud. When the text was completed, the work of decoration began. The Winchester Bible is an endlessly absorbing artefact because it provides us with an unrivalled opportunity to see medieval illumination *in progress*. The work of decorating it took some fifteen years but was never completed.[15] The plan seems to have been to have some ninety-three large historiated initials – initials decorated with human figures or particular scenes. Only forty-two completed initials survive.

We might imagine that when manuscripts were decorated, an artist would draw, gild and paint an image, and then move on to the next one. But the Winchester Bible shows us that sometimes these stages in artistic production were separated by many years and could be the work of several artists. Because it is unfinished, we still have a series of written instructions which tell us about how the manuscript was made: there are sections of text for the rubricator (who added text headings in different coloured ink), colour instructions for the decorated initials, and notes on the folio sequence in each quire. Sometimes the instructions are simple, as on a folio near an unfinished initial for the Second Book of Chronicles, where a note instructs that Solomon should be depicted in the temple (in keeping with the biblical story).[16] But in other instances we see the artists being given free rein. A note next to a space by the preface to the opening of the Apocryphal Book of Maccabees reads 'ad placitum' ('as you like').[17] The manuscript allows us to lift the bonnet and see the workings of the artistic engine.

Every stage in this process is represented – from the simple lead underdrawings to the rich, shimmering colours of the completed initials. The creation of a painted initial happened in stages. Firstly, a drawing would be made using a stick of lead alloy called a 'plummet' (sometimes these were held in holders – the forerunner of the pencil). After this, the lead drawing would be filled in using ink, to prevent particles of lead showing through the subsequent painting. The next stage was the gilding. To apply gold, a layer of gesso first had to be added as a ground. Gesso was a thick white substance usually made from chalk or plaster mixed with an adhesive. It created a raised surface onto which gold leaf could be applied (sometimes it was coloured red so that a warm red glow showed through the gold, although this only appears twice in the Winchester Bible).[18] After application, the gold leaf was then burnished. Gilding was a messy activity, and sometimes the gilded areas had to be trimmed with a knife. It was for this reason that it was done before the paint was applied. In Figure 13 we can see an initial that has been gilded but not painted. These initials, although perhaps not as beautiful as the completed ones, show the meticulous care that was taken in the decoration of the manuscript, connecting us to the labours of the artists. It is as if we have happened on a moment in time when, after drawing, pressing and burnishing, the artist sat back to consider what will come next.

After the gold leaf had been burnished, the coloured paints were applied. The paints were made from a mixture of animal, vegetable and mineral pigments mixed with egg yolk or gum arabic.[19] The rarest of the pigments – rarer and more costly even than the gold – was the ultramarine (the very particle found in the teeth of the manuscript artist from Dalheim).[20] In Figure 14 we can see an initial that has been partially painted, but not completed.

The Winchester Bible reveals the many stages involved in manuscript decoration, but it also reveals a sequence of different artistic hands that toiled over its folios. Like all the manuscripts discussed in this chapter, the Bible was decorated by a group of artists, but untangling the relationship between them and their work is a tricky business. These artists' work is entwined like the interlacing patterns we find in the manuscript's folios. Often initials were drawn by one artist and painted by another. In some places, it seems the artists worked alongside one another, but in others it looks as though earlier work was taken up and modified by later hands. The manuscript also holds in its pages evidence of changes in artistic styles over the period in which it was produced, as new artistic fashions arrived as a result of exchange and collaboration between English and European artists.

Around the year 1160, two artists appear to have begun the ambitious programme of decorating the Bible. All the artists who worked on the Bible are anonymous, but in the 1940s Walter Oakeshott (whom we met in Chapter One as the discoverer of the only manuscript of Thomas Malory's *Morte Darthur*) identified six different figures involved in the manuscript's artistic production. He gave them names – names which have largely been accepted by later scholars. These artists were probably lay professionals, brought into the Priory to work on the initials. It is the difference in their styles that hints at them being professionals – it implies they encountered diverse influences on their travels, as they moved from job to job.

The first of them is known as the Master of the Apocrypha Drawings. He may have come from the abbey of St Albans because a manuscript made there bears a striking resemblance to his style. It is possible that he was first trained in western France or Normandy. The second artist was known as the Master of the Leaping Figures. It has been suggested that he was the manuscript's 'primary designer'.[21] His work is characterised by its 'energetic mannered poses and gestures'.[22] He was probably English and was perhaps even trained in Winchester itself.[23] His style resembles the Winchester Psalter, which may have been commissioned by Henry of Blois. His figures are painted in a characteristic 'Byzantine dampfold style', which means they look as though they have just emerged from water and their clothes are sticking to them. This distinctive style came to England in 1130s, probably first at Bury St Edmund's. As the artist's name suggests, he created dramatic poses and leaping movements. Much of his work was painted over by later artists, in the period 1170–90, but his dramatic, fluid underdrawings remain. Those initials which he created that were not subsequently overpainted demonstrate how he got his name.

The initial for the Book of Exodus (Figure 15) is a tangle of figures, foliage and interlace. The episode depicted is one in which Moses kills an Egyptian overlord who has been tormenting a Hebrew slave (Exodus 2: 11–12). In the upper part of the image, the Egyptian slave-master can be seen grasping the arm of the Hebrew slave and poking a finger in his eye. His knee is bent, his body intruding into the space occupied by the slave, who seems about to topple over. Below we see Moses delivering the fatal blow to the abuser and the little pile of sand under which he will hide the Egyptian's body. These are images of fluid, colourful movement, with interlacing patterns which are different from the decorative patterns we find in the work of the other artists.

The Master of the Leaping Figures may have gone on working on the Bible for a long time, during which time his style may have changed and been influenced by new artistic fashions. But, at some point, a new set of artists took up the project. While the first two appear to have had connections with England, working there and perhaps partially training there, the next four appear to have been 'European travellers'.[24] Oakeshott named them the Master of the Morgan Leaf, the Master of the Genesis Initial, the Amalekite Master, and the Master of Gothic Majesty. (The work of the latter two is less impressive than the first and they may have been assistants.) These four artists use more of a Byzantine style (i.e. a style related to the artwork of Byzantium – the continuation of the Roman Empire in its eastern provinces through the Late Antique and medieval period). This style may be derived from Italian models. Many of the later images in the Bible are painted onto a gessoed gold ground, and shimmer like the mosaics of Cefalù Cathedral and the Capella Palatina in Palermo, Sicily.[25] Sicily was a notable centre of Byzantine art in the period. Henry II's daughter, Joan, married King William of Sicily in 1177, when she was twelve years old. Three years before the marriage his envoys visited her in Winchester, and it was from Winchester that she subsequently embarked on the journey to meet her husband in August 1176 (she arrived in February the following year). Perhaps she had English artists in her retinue who brought a Sicilian style back to England's rainy shores in their luggage. Her marriage was part of a larger pattern of Anglo-Sicilian relations in this period: the Archbishop of Palermo was an Englishman, and several members of Henry I's and Henry II's court visited Sicily in the twelfth century.[26]

The Master of the Morgan Leaf appears to have worked on manuscripts for the monasteries of St Albans and Westminster.[27]

He takes his name from a single leaf of the Bible, now held by the Pierpont Morgan Library in New York (New York, Morgan Library MS M. 619). The leaf, which contains scenes from the life of David, was painted separately but never sewn into the manuscript.[28] Although painted by the Master of the Morgan Leaf, it is based on drawings by the Master of the Apocrypha Drawings. Figures by the Master of the Morgan Leaf are solemn creatures, with sombre expressions. They lack the writhing movement that characterises work by the Master of the Leaping Figures. In Figure 16, we see a scene in which David covers his face in grief on learning of the death of his son Absalom. The artist used 'a softer, yet still intense, colour palette', investing his work with an emotion not seen in the more stylised poses of some of the other artists.[29]

Intriguingly, the work of the Master of the Morgan Leaf (as well as the other later artists who worked on the Bible) shows an affinity with some surviving wall paintings in Winchester Cathedral's Holy Sepulchre Chapel, suggesting that he was trained to work on frescoes as well as manuscript images.[30] This might seem strange to us – that artists of this period worked across such diverse media – but the Winchester Bible is endlessly informative about how medieval artists operated. Even more excitingly, there is evidence that one or more of the later group of artists – perhaps the Master of the Morgan Leaf – also worked on a series of wall paintings in the Chapter House of the Royal Monastery of Santa María de Sigena in northern Spain.[31] There are details in the Sigena paintings that only find parallels in English art, making it likely that they were created by English artists. The case is further strengthened by a number of striking stylistic similarities between the Bible and the frescoes.[32] There is a popular misconception that medieval people rarely travelled, but the Winchester Bible and the Sigena frescoes put paid to this idea. Travel was, of course, arduous and time-consuming – it was not to be undertaken lightly – so it is thrilling to imagine the artist (probably accompanied by assistants) making the journey from England to Aragon. Why he went remains unclear – it may have been a diplomatic mission or the result of international royal connections. It has been suggested that he may have visited Sicily on the same trip, although opinion is divided on whether the frescoes pre- or post-date the Bible, and not all scholars accept this theory.[33]

The other important artist of the later group is the so-called 'Master of the Genesis Initial', because of an extraordinary initial he painted for the opening of Genesis. Looking at this initial, the difference in this artist's palette by comparison with – say – the Amalekite Master (Figure 17) is immediately apparent. Here (Figure 18) the only warm colour is a deep coral red, and there is no purple or bright orange in the image. The greens and blues which form the roundel borders predominate, alongside the gilding. This artist's figures are sturdier than some of the others, and the faces of his figures have fearsome frowns. Like many of the Bible's artists, he had a talent for conveying narrative, even within the confines of an initial. In his image of Noah's Ark, we can see both the dove and the raven – both birds sent out by Noah after the flood. Genesis 8: 6–9 tells us that after forty days Noah sent forth a raven which 'did not return' and afterwards sent forth a dove, 'But she, not finding where her foot might rest, returned to him into the ark: for the waters were upon the whole earth: and he put forth his hand, and caught her, and brought her into the ark.'

Christian commentaries traditionally figured the dove and the raven in opposition to one another. The dove symbolised virtue, and the raven vice – some commentators held that the raven did not return because it was feasting on the corpses of the sinful who had been drowned in the Flood.[34] The Master of the Genesis Initial shows the corpses of the damned floating in the waters of the flood, while above, Noah – aboard the Ark – is seen reaching out an arm to gather the dove to him while to the left, the raven bends its head to peck at something grisly. The medallion captures within its round orbit the drama of the Flood, which was thought to wash away the sins of mankind. In the roundel above, we see an image of sin being created in the person of Eve.

For whatever reason, the decoration of the Winchester Bible was never finished – perhaps because of the death of its likely commissioner, Henry of Blois, in 1171. It has remained in Winchester Cathedral ever since, apart from a brief period after the Civil War when it was given to Winchester College by Oliver Cromwell. After the restoration of the monarchy, the Bible was returned to the Cathedral in 1669.[35]

The Bible has not always been well treated in its long history. Nine initials have been cut out of the manuscript since its creation. These removals happened at different points. A date of '1626' appears next to one hole – a depressing note, as though the vandal wanted to record the date of their crime for posterity. Other thefts were more recent. A report on the Bible written in Winchester in 1907 describes an incident when the verger was offered a bribe to look away while a 'souvenir' was taken from it.[36] And more chillingly, a letter dated 16 August 1927 thanks the Canon Librarian for an hour's 'consultation' of the Bible, which concludes with a dastardly 'P.S.': 'That initial "S" now ranks as the cornerstone of my possessions. But mum mum as to this!'[37] In 1948 one of the nine missing initials was identified, bought with the assistance of the National Art Collections Fund, and thereafter resewn into the manuscript.

Tragically, the frescoes in Sigena Monastery were largely destroyed by a fire in 1936 during the Spanish Civil War. (Thankfully they were photographed before their destruction.) The Winchester Bible has fared better by comparison, giving us a unique insight into the artistic *making* of a medieval manuscript. Its folios reveal the collaboration of many hands whose work with brush and gilding knife tell us about the international journeys they took, as well as something of their individual characters in the decisions they made as they realised the drama of the biblical story in such enduring shapes and colours.

The Luttrell Psalter

In the early decades of the fourteenth century Sir Geoffrey Luttrell (1276–1345) – a wealthy Lincolnshire landowner – commissioned a spectacular Psalter (BL Add. MS 42130) with around 400 decorative borders.[38] The manuscript was a weighty thing, and Sir Geoffrey may have intended it to be used for ceremonial purposes both in his lifetime and after his death.[39] A Psalter, as we've seen, is a copy of the biblical Book of Psalms and it contained much of the material used in the Divine Office, or religious services, in the Middle Ages. From our modern perspective we might imagine that such a manuscript would be decorated in a manner befitting the solemnity and power of the text it contained. Parts of the manuscript do meet such expectations – they contain images of the life of Christ, a sequence of saints, and other aspects of the biblical story. And parts of the manuscript owe a debt to the book's commissioner. In it we see idealised images of the feudal hierarchy – peasants labouring in the fields, Sir Geoffrey at his feast table surrounded by family and servants, repairs being carried out to the parish church. It is, seemingly, a vision of parochial English life, in which localised communities cluster around their lord. But the Luttrell Psalter, as it is now known, also contains imagery which we don't expect. In fact, it doesn't simply defy our expectations, it sets fire to them. Alongside its religious scenes and images of rural life, the Psalter artists depicted a different reality: a comedic and surreal world. The manuscript's margins portray people from the social margins – beggars, entertainers and pedlars.[40] This strange borderland is also home to bizarre creatures, with faces where their buttocks should be, or human torsos with animal legs. This is a world where knights tilt against snail-dragons, monkeys can be seen driving carts drawn by teams of horses, or riding goats, out hawking with owls. We are presented with a world turned upside down, a place of anarchy and rupture.

The surreal monsters and comedic scenes which adorn the Psalter's folios are not uncharacteristic of manuscripts produced in this period – the so-called 'Gothic' period in manuscript art (roughly 1200–1350). It is not impossible to find images fantastic, profane or scatological in the borders of sacred manuscripts, produced for important patrons.[41] So the Luttrell Psalter is not an outlier, but the scale and scope of its imagery sets it apart. It often seems as though the marginal imagery will overwhelm the text it surrounds, spilling riotously into the text's space, but we should approach with caution. There are some images in the manuscript that look strange to us, but would have made perfect sense to a medieval audience. One such image is that of a bishop in purple robes, who is pinching the nose of a bear-like creature, with a second face in its belly, using a pair of tongs.[42]

A medieval viewer would most likely recognise this as St Dunstan, who was said to have tweaked the nose of the devil with a pair of blacksmith's tongs.[43] An image like this reminds us that we should always be wary of how we – as moderns – interpret the manuscript's images, which bamboozle and delight in equal measure, but rarely offer neat explanations of their meaning. As in the case of the Winchester Bible, it is also important to remember that this manuscript was made by several figures, and the collaborative nature of the enterprise perhaps explains some of its uniqueness. We can almost imagine the group of artists working together, delighting in outdoing one another with their strange and comic imagery. Sometimes the manuscript's images feel like a long sequence of in-jokes: what the scholar Paul Binski has solemnly called 'small-group humour'.[44]

The Psalter was produced in one or two workshops of artists, but the exact nature of the workshop that produced most of it is unclear. It was likely a secular workshop based in a major urban centre. Geoffrey Luttrell lived in the village of Irnham in Lincolnshire, so a number of nearby towns have been proposed as a possible place of production – Peterborough was a day's walk from Irnham, but there is not much evidence for Peterborough being a centre of book production. Stamford – then a growing university town, which was half a day's walk from Irnham – is another contender, but Lincoln looks most likely: there is good evidence of it being a place where booksellers and illuminators worked.[45] The artists were probably laymen supervised by a churchman – probably, in this case, a Dominican; Geoffrey Luttrell had a Dominican chaplain in his household. It might seem strange to us that a churchman would sanction the creation of such strange images, but a medieval audience appears not to have felt that such images detracted from the solemnity and importance of the text they surrounded. In fact, our modern distinctions between 'sacred' and 'profane' would probably have made little sense to a medieval person. The scholar Michael Camille cites a Book of Hours – a prayer book – held in Trinity College, Cambridge, which contains an image of a man defecating and then presenting his faeces to a lady. This image appears beneath the text of Psalm 7. As Camille notes,

> Because we have so cleanly separated faeces from everything else in our lives, its medieval status, interwoven with the sacred text, makes us uneasy. Instead of turds being just what they are – matter – they become mysterious signs that we are unable to read, savour and enjoy with the gusto of our ancestors.[46]

The creation of the Luttrell Psalter happened in stages. First, the Latin text was written out by a single scribe. The perfect, architectural lines of his letters were likely formed with a single, thick quill, which made precise, angled sweeps. He also added gossamer-thin flourishes to some of the letters with a different (tiny) nib, or perhaps the angled point of his thick nib's edge. The result is a work that conveys weighty importance with touches of delicate beauty – appropriate for the place of the Psalms in medieval culture. The work would have taken the scribe 'many months, even years' to complete.[47] After this, the images and decoration were added by five or six artists.[48] There were four distinct phases in this decoration project, which was done booklet by booklet. Examining the different stages starts to give us a sense of the personalities involved in the manuscript's creation, but as in the case of the Winchester Bible, the work of the different artists is enmeshed and entwined.

The manuscript's decoration was created by artists who largely worked in teams. The first booklet, or 'quire', of the manuscript was actually decorated later than the rest, so the sequence of events begins with Booklet 2. Booklets 2–9 of the manuscript are a mixture of the sombre and the comic, and were the product of at least two artists working together. They contain bar borders and line-fillers populated by human figures, animals both real and magical, and hybrid monsters (sometimes called 'grotesques'). The monstrous creatures appear to have been designed by an artist identified as 'Hand C', but at the bottom of the pages in these booklets, narrative religious scenes appear, including moments from the New Testament and Apocryphal material. Here we see a narrative arc from the Annunciation (the moment the Angel Gabriel visits the Virgin) to the Last Judgement. There are also scenes from the Apocryphal Death of the Virgin. These images were painted by an artist, termed 'Hand D', who 'specialised in the specifically religious subjects'.[49]

The next phase, quires 10–12, have no figural elements. There, spaces were left for scenes to be painted, but they were left unfilled, for reasons that are unclear. But at the start of the thirteenth quire we get to the book's – justly – most famous section. What follows are six full quires painted by a single hand. The scenes are a marked departure from the earlier, more overtly religious ones. The work was all carried out by someone the scholar Michael Camille called the 'Luttrell Master', otherwise known as 'Hand A', whom he described as a 'highly individualistic illuminator'.[50] This artist used a softer, more naturalistic palette, by comparison with the religious scenes, which have bright blues and vermilion shades. The hybrid monsters that populate the borders of the manuscript here 'achieve astonishing new dimensions of ingenuity, imagination and scale'.[51] They are 'greasy, slimy, hairy, subcutaneous, phosphorescent, rubbery, metallic, velvety, and vegetal – they exhibit every possible malformation, often on one page'.[52] This artist tended to design the pages himself, leaving the floral borders to be completed by 'Hand B' and doing the figural work himself after the borders were finished.[53]

These quires, more than any others, show the identity of the manuscript's commissioner. They contain frequent images of its patron, as well as a sequence of images of farming and feasting. What is magical here are the places where the Luttrell Master has painted minute details, observed with forensic care. In a scene depicting a watermill, we can see the eel traps tied in the current.[54] Overleaf from the watermill, a stately carriage is pulled by five horses across the *bas-de-page* (the image at the bottom of the folio).[55] The details of the horses' tack here – the halters, bridles, bits, cruppers and girths – are meticulous, and they differ from the simpler equipment that is used on the horses pulling a cart loaded with bushels of wheat from the harvest on another folio.[56] These images are alive with narrative and movement. On the *bas-de-page* of a page a little earlier on, a man is sowing seeds in a field, scattering them from a basket hitched to his body.[57] It would appear to be a cold March day: he is wearing both a hood and a hat. In front of him, his dog chases away a crow, but behind him, out of sight, another crow feasts on a sack of seed.

Turning the pages, we sometimes feel we have stumbled across a private moment. At the foot of one folio we find an image of three friends playing a game in which one of them has to lift a pole over a molehill while the other two stand at each end of the pole.[58] These observations of agricultural life are stylised – presenting an image of a seemingly cheerful bucolic existence – but the small details lend touches of realism. In a scene of harvest on a double-page spread, we see women with sickles bent forward to cut wheat stalks.[59] Behind them, a man looks (perhaps lasciviously) towards their upturned bottoms. Another woman stands up to stretch, her back sore from bending. Across the page, one of the men piling the bushels of wheat together has taken off his gloves and tucked them into his belt. Perhaps he is warm from his work.

Of course, we should be wary about reading the Psalter images too literally. However, its carefully rendered details do offer an insight into the trappings of medieval rural life, a life contingent on that of the patron, not least by being paid for by him, and for depicting him frequently in its pages. Towards the end of the 'Luttrell Master's' stint, we find one of the manuscript's most famous images.[60] It shows a knight on horseback. He wears heraldic colours, as does his horse. Beneath him stand two women, who are passing him his shield and helmet. The knight is, of course, Sir Geoffrey Luttrell himself, and the women have been identified by their heraldic surcoats as Agnes Sutton (died 1340) and Beatrice Le Scrope – respectively his wife and daughter-in-law.

This is the so-called 'Dedication miniature' (the image in which a manuscript's patron is depicted). Dedication miniatures most often depict a patron kneeling in reverent prayer alongside the image of the Virgin or a patron saint, but here we see Luttrell, resplendent in armour on horseback. At the time of the manuscript's production, he was 'well past his prime and this specially commissioned image shows him in the glory days of his youth'.[61] The image appears next to the text of Psalm 109, 'I make thine enemies thy footstool' (the first Psalm of Sunday Vespers), but this image, which is 'closer in feeling to a knightly tomb', depicts martial strength rather than reverent prayer.[62] It is an unambiguous display of wealth and power which was probably produced on specific instructions from Sir Geoffrey.

Some five folios on, we find a double-page spread at the bottom of the pages showing Luttrell and his family at a feast.[63] On the left-hand page, we can see the food being prepared. Here the Master of the Kitchen wields a large knife which he uses to dismember a suckling pig and a fowl. At the same table another servant can be seen filling salt cellars. (Salt was a prized commodity in the period and this scene is an indication of Luttrell's wealth and status.) Two other servants are seen carrying platters into the hall (seemingly across the page gutter). There, on the opposite folio, Sir Geoffrey appears at the centre of his table. Behind him is a hanging decorated with his heraldic colours – silver martlets on a navy-blue ground. His wife, Agnes, sits to his right, flanked by Dominican or Austin friars. To his left sits his daughter-in-law Beatrice, his son Andrew, and another man, likely one of his other sons, Guy or Robert.

This is the last major image in the manuscript. After this, the quality of the work decreases. For reasons that remain unclear, these initial phases of work were stopped prematurely, and the manuscript was completed in a different workshop or by different hands. One scholar has argued that the project languished for at least ten years before being finished.[64] It seems that a different artist took over the work, and completed the last eight quires and the calendar of saints' days (which now appears at the start of the manuscript, in its usual place). After the feasting scene, the work was done 'cheaply and in haste'; the initials and line-fillers are in the 'crudest of styles'.[65] Towards the end of the century, the manuscript was in the hands of new owners. These new owners added obituary notes – names of deceased family members and their dates of death – to the calendar at the beginning. In the hands of these new owners, corrections and additions were made in the style of the earlier artists.

It is hard to know how many of the Luttrell Psalter's images were designed by the artists themselves and how many were the result of some kind of intervention by Sir Geoffrey, or perhaps the Dominican friar in his household. We do not have any surviving notes, as we do for the Winchester Bible, which might have given us more of a sense of the artists at work and the decisions they made. It is also hard to know how – if at all – we should interpret the manuscript. To a modern audience, the juxtaposition of the real and the surreal in the manuscript is strange. In the Psalter's folios the facts of medieval life are delineated. We find birth, marriage and death, sowing seeds and harvest time, and the words of the Psalms, which point to the inexorable, repeating pattern of the liturgical year. In one folio, a swaddled baby appears as a line-filler, while in another, youthful waywardness is represented by a boy stealing cherries – his shoes discarded at the bottom of the tree.[66] Elsewhere, the inevitable conclusion of this cycle of life is represented by an open coffin in which we can see a shrouded corpse.[67]

Yet alongside these images representing the course of the human life, we find a topsy-turvy world, like the scene in which a monkey, wearing a cap, can be seen driving a cart pulled by three horses.[68] Its expression is angry and it wields a huge whip. And more surreal still are the hybrid creatures that populate the Psalter. In the image of the monkey driving the cart, the horses, the cart and the monkey are all recognisably creatures or objects from the real world – the strangeness lies in their conjunction. But the Psalter's hybrids are unmoored from reality. Some have features that are half recognisable – like a bird's beak and wings – but these features are wont to appear on a beast with blue fur and a snail's shell for a head.[69]

What should we make of the manuscript, its conjunctions and contradictions? What is the relationship – if any – between the world of the margins and the text of the Psalms? At times, the marginal images appear deaf to the words of the text. The end of Psalm 30 reads, 'O love the Lord, all ye his saints: for the Lord will require truth, and will repay them abundantly that act proudly. Do ye manfully, and let your heart be strengthened, all ye that hope in the Lord' (Psalm 30: 24–5). These words, in Latin, appear next to a marginal image of a man climbing an oak tree to gather acorns for his pigs.[70] One of the pigs can be seen looking expectantly into the branches of the tree; another feasts on acorns below. The Psalm text promises punishment for pride, and exhorts the faithful to trust in the Lord. Are the acorns a metaphor for the fruits promised those who trust in the Lord? The marginal image appears at the end of Psalm 30 and the beginning of Psalm 31, which reads 'Blessed is the man to whom the Lord hath not imputed sin, and in whose spirit there is no guile' (v. 2). Might the pigs represent sin (pigs being symbols of sinfulness in the story of the Prodigal Son)? Might the man in the tree be a lost soul serving his sins? If there is a relationship between the words and the images, it is not altogether clear.

There are other places, however, where the text and image appear to be in conversation with each other, unlike in the image of the pigs. The famous farming sequence appears at the foot of the pages containing Psalms 94 and 95. Psalm 94 opens with the words, 'Come let us praise the Lord with joy. Let us come before his presence with thanksgiving,' and continues, 'For he is the Lord our God: and we are the people of his pasture and the sheep of his hand.' These words of thanksgiving for God's bounty appear above images of the sowing of seeds and ploughing of the earth.[71] Over two leaves, where we find an image of the harvest, the text of Psalm 95 declares, 'Let the heavens rejoice, and let the earth be glad, let the sea be moved, and the fullness thereof. The fields and all things that are in them shall be joyful.'[72]

In other places, the marginal imagery responds in diverse ways to the text it surrounds – responds in ways that are *both* playful and sombre. On a folio containing part of the text of Psalm 87, in the left-hand margin, sits an image of a naked man seemingly being drawn into an open hell-mouth beneath him.[73] Underneath this lies an open coffin, containing a shrouded corpse. These marginal images react to the Psalm's verses, which read, 'For my soul is filled with evils: and my life hath drawn nigh to hell' (87: 5–6) and, 'I am counted among them that go down to the pit: I am become as a man without help...like the slain sleeping in the sepulchres.' The final words on the folio are: 'Thy wrath is strong over me: and all thy waves thou hast brought in upon me. Thou hast put away my acquaintance far from me.' Further marginal decoration hangs from the word 'notos' ('acquaintance'). Here, hanging by three threads from the first *o* of *notos*, is a glass vessel being used by two young men, apparently playing a drinking game. One of the men lies underneath the open-ended glass vessel, while the other man pours liquid into it. What seems to be happening is that a piece of fruit has been placed at the bottom of the vessel and the game is to drink some of the liquid without getting drenched. This little scene of youthful japery hangs from the text like a hammock, as if mocking the words to which it is attached. Yet on the same folio, in the left-hand margin, we see the image of the hell-mouth and the shrouded corpse in the coffin. Taken together, the scenes act as a *memento mori* – a reminder that life is brief, the joys of youth are short, and the spectre of death and judgement are ever present.

The margins of the Psalter are playful and strange, resisting any neat interpretations – or, rather, resisting modern modes of interpretation. In places they present conventional religious imagery, and dutiful images of the manuscript's patron. But elsewhere they show strange events and outlandish beasts. You could be forgiven for thinking that the artists produced some of their paintings on a wild whim, perhaps beginning the outline of a snail's shell and then deciding to add the feet and body of a long-billed bird. Despite such curious juxtapositions, and the sense that sometimes the text and images are in a conversation that we have to acknowledge, there are parts of the manuscript that are resistant to interpretation. Opening the Luttrell Psalter, we feel as though we have walked in on a group of friends, making jokes and conversational references we will, centuries hence, still struggle to understand.

The Sherborne Missal

The Luttrell Psalter seems, at times, an anarchic manuscript, inviting puzzled interpretation. The Sherborne Missal, by comparison, is a highly ordered and meticulously produced book. It does not have the feeling of mad spontaneity that characterises some of the images in the Luttrell Psalter. Its borders depict scenes which enrich and complement the text they surround. Its allusions are subtle, and the decoration, which is extensive, follows a precise programme. It is a monumental manuscript – monumental not only in its size but also in the amount of decoration it contains.[74] And yet, like the Luttrell Psalter, even the ordered programme is sometimes disrupted by images that pose more questions than they answer. At a later stage in the manuscript's production, in a central portion of the book, one of the manuscript artists added forty-eight images of birds to the folio margins. They appear oversized by comparison with the scale of the illustration around them, and each one appears with a label giving their names in Middle English. The significance of this manuscript aviary is a perplexing mystery. Were these images a specific commission from the manuscript's patron(s) or the personal whim of the artist who added them? Do they have a symbolic meaning or are they merely decorative?

The Sherborne Missal was made c. 1399–1407 for Robert Brunyng, abbot of the Benedictine abbey of Sherborne, in Dorset. (A missal is a book containing all the Masses to be celebrated in the liturgical year.)[75] It is both vast and beautiful, weighing over 3 stone (20 kg), measuring 53 cm by 38 cm, and running to 347 folios. It likely took years to produce.[76] Inside, alongside the crisp lines of its text, it is decorated with a riot of floral, scroll and leaf designs, twisting colours, decorative sprays, and roundels depicting worthy saints, royal benefactors and strange beasts. Each page – with its complex, interrelated programmes of image and decoration – demands to be examined and re-examined.

It is difficult to convey the scale and artistry of the Missal, whose pages are dizzying in their beauty and intricacy. One scholar has noted that a description of all the images and decoration in the manuscript could make it sound 'grossly overburdened', but it is in fact 'delicate in impression'.[77] The manuscript represents a late manifestation of what is termed 'Gothic' style. This style is characterised by its use of rich, warm colours, impressive architectural designs and delicate, painterly use of human figures.

The Missal appears to be the work of five artists and one scribe.[78] They have been termed Hands A, B, B[1] (who was an assistant to Hand B), C and D by the scholar Kathleen Scott.[79] Hands A and B appear to have worked together closely. Hand C's style is slightly different from the others, and Scott has suggested he may have been influenced by Dutch artists.[80] Highly unusually, one of these hands is actually named in the manuscript. Hand A's name was John Siferwas, and – also very unusually – he depicted himself in self-portraits in several places.[81] He often appears alongside images of the scribe John Whas, and also of two other figures, Brunyng – the abbot – and Richard Mitford, Bishop of Salisbury.[82] Although Siferwas's name does actually survive, and thus he is more visible than the other artists discussed in this chapter, his name is not widely known. The names Brunelleschi, Donatello and Fra Angelico – who all worked in Italy at the same time that Siferwas was at work in England – might ring a bell for people today, but the names of artists whose work remains tucked in the folios of medieval manuscripts have remained unknown beyond the academy.

Siferwas's self-portraits show a man with a tonsure and a slightly beaky nose, perhaps rather serious eyes. He painted his self-portrait in ten different places. The first appears on the folio which contains the Mass for the first Friday of Lent.[83] Looking at the whole page you could miss the little portrait, tucked into a roundel beneath an image of a swan (the emblem of the Prince of Wales). Siferwas is looking somewhat wistfully to his left, his expression unreadable. In his final self-portrait, he appears almost unfurling a scroll which reads, 'Soli deo honor et gloria secula seculorum amen' ('Only to the honour and glory of God, for ever and ever').[84] Siferwas (fl. [i.e. active] 1380–1421), was one of the most important manuscript artists of late medieval England. His work survives in three manuscripts – the Sherborne Missal and two others.[85] He can probably be identified as the 'John Cyfrewas' of the Dominican community in Guildford.[86] There has been some debate about his origins. Elements of his style suggest the influence of northern Germany.[87] Some scholars have suggested he was from the Rhineland or Bohemia.[88] He depicts himself in Dominican robes, while depicting the scribe, John Whas, as a Benedictine. Whas probably belonged to Sherborne Abbey, while Siferwas may simply have resided there while working on the manuscript. It's clear that the two must have planned the work in tandem. It is hard to know, of course, who planned which aspects of the manuscript. Were smaller decisions about what scenes to paint in which roundels left up to Siferwas, or were those decisions taken by Brunyng? What is clear, however, is that like the Winchester Bible and the Luttrell Psalter, the manuscript was a collaborative enterprise.

Perhaps the most famous image in the manuscript is the full-page crucifixion image, which was painted by Siferwas. It appears on the inner face of an independent bifolium (i.e. a separate sheet, with a blank recto, which wasn't part of a quire), separating it from the opening words of the Canon (a section of the Mass). When turning the pages of the Missal, the reader would come across an anomalous blank page, only discovering the crucifixion painting when they turned it over. When the Missal was used during the Mass, this would mean that the crucifixion image would not have been visible at the moment of the consecration, but would have been symbolically revealed during its celebration.[89]

Having been kept safely within the pages of the manuscript, the colours in this image are perfectly preserved. It has a rectangular shape and is enclosed in an architectural border which looks like carved stone. At the four corners are eight-pointed rosettes depicting the Four Evangelists. Four other roundels depict Old Testament scenes that prefigure the crucifixion. The crucifixion image itself is one of extraordinary detail and colour. There are twenty-five figures in the composition, which depicts Christ crucified, the two crucified thieves flanking him on either side at a distance, and surrounded by a crowd of people. In the background, a crowd in armour and elaborate, gold-decorated headdresses, some on horseback, press in towards the cross shafts, gawping at the torment. The Roman soldier Longinus extends his spear into Christ's emaciated side, which gushes with blood. Mary Magdalene, her blond hair plaited elegantly around her head, looks towards Christ's shins as if looking at his face would be too much to bear. The striking feature of the image is that the iridescent crush of people does not, in fact, draw the eye. Instead, the viewer's focus is pulled towards the figure of the Virgin in the foreground, in an ultra-marine coloured robe. She lies, looking not at Christ, but down and away. Mary Cleophas and Mary, mother of James, hold her up, in a little sisterhood of grief. On the whole, the image is busy, sumptuous and colourful, covered in gold and scarlet. But the image of Mary in the foreground, in a flowing blue gown, provides a little oasis of calm, and a focus of grief amidst the crush.

The crucifixion image gives us a sense of scope and ambition of the Missal. It was an artistic achievement almost unparalleled in the period in which it was produced. Like the Luttrell Psalter, some of the smallest details are the most exquisite. In a historiated initial in the 'Sanctorale' – the sequence of masses associated with particular saints – we see an image of the Evangelist Luke painting the Virgin.[90] (According to legend, St Luke created the first icons of the Virgin. The idea gained currency and spread with the cult of Luke, and he became the patron saint of painters.) Unlike conventional images of the scene, here Luke kneels in the space of the initial and extends his paint-brush to the Virgin, who appears next to him in an architectural frame in the page's border. She is the same size as him, and both she and the Infant Christ are looking at him. There is a certain tenderness in the way his paintbrush gently sweeps the line of her robe; he looks in reverence up towards her face as he does it, as if hoping to see how she will react to being painted. There is nothing, visually, to demarcate which figure is the painting and which the painter. Kathleen Scott attributes this image to the work of Hand B[1] – the third identified artist to work on the Missal.[91]

Perhaps the most beautiful and perplexing details in the Missal are the images of birds which grace the borders in a central section of the manuscript. Scholarly opinion is divided over which of the manuscript's artists painted them.[92] Their function is something of a mystery. As one scholar has noted, 'No comparable series appears in any known European manuscript of the period.'[93] Many of the birds are accompanied by labels, in Middle English, which identify them. This makes the manuscript the earliest and most comprehensive collection of Middle English bird names in existence. There are some places where the choice of birds bears a relation to the rest of the manuscript page. For example, alongside the Communicantes – the prayer in the Mass in which important early saints are recalled – we find the robin, labelled as a 'ruddoke robertus'.[94] (The suffix '-ock' is a diminutive, like 'hillock', so 'ruddock' just means 'little ruddy one'.) It has been suggested that this was an 'oblique compliment' to the manuscript's commissioner – Robert (i.e. Robin) Brunyng, the Abbot of Sherborne.[95] And on the folio containing the Epiphany Mass, we find an image of a goldfinch.[96] The goldfinch was a common iconographic trope in images of the Virgin and Child, especially in Italy. Its blood-red head was taken as a symbol of Christ's Passion. Similarly, the skylark – traditionally associated with the celestial realm – appears next to a tiny image of the Ascension.[97] For the most part, however, the birds do not seem to relate to the text around them or follow any particular programme.

It is also striking that all of the birds in this particular section are wild: there are no domesticated birds, like chickens, nor indeed any birds used for the aristocratic pastime of falconry. In several places in the manuscript where we find images of its commissioner, Robert Brunyng, we find him accompanied by elegant hunting dogs, so, by the same token, we might expect images of hawks and falcons, but instead we find more prosaic birds: a dusky-coloured juvenile gannet and plain-plumaged quail. The collection feels a little like a bird-watcher's compendium. Intriguingly, many of the birds are coastal species that live on wetland or seashore. One scholar has suggested that as the birds are mainly northern coastal species, they may have been painted by a 'northerner who carried his sketches with him'.[98] They are observed with great care. The woodpecker can be seen with a long tongue, stretching out to gather insects; the heron is gulping down a fish.[99]

Another striking feature of the birds in the collection is that many of them have local, Dorset names, like the 'bergandir' for the shelduck, and the 'waryghanger' – a variant of 'wariangle' – for the shrike or butcher bird. It is possible that the birds may have 'been labelled as an afterthought by a specifically local hand'.[100] That said, it is also possible that the birds were themselves painted in later. Their scale in the context of the decoration they surround is outsized and they appear unlike other decorative details in the manuscript. In the page for the Christmas Mass, the robes of the angels at the top of the page have been carefully plaited in and out of the border at the page head. Some of the birds, by contrast, sit on top of the rest of the decoration, rather than integrating into it. At times they are integrated into the details around them, but these appear to be overpainted afterthoughts.[101] The thought of the Missal's bird-artist (whose ever hand it was) is intriguing. The manuscript's ordered design has been disrupted by these marginal images: in amongst the opulence of the Missal's pages, there is something delightful about the presence of the hungry heron or the homely thrush – their appearance making us wonder about the hand that added them, and why.

We have no idea of the names of the artists who made the Winchester Bible. Similarly, while the name and image of Sir Geoffrey Luttrell have been preserved, the artists who created the bizarre and topsy-turvy world at the edges of his Psalter have left nothing of themselves but the sweeps of their paint-brushes. Although we can name John Siferwas, he was only one of a group of artists who toiled to realise the Sherborne Missal's majesty.

In the Bibliothèque nationale in France, there is an image in a fifteenth-century manuscript depicting Tamaris – a painter who lived in the fifth century BCE.[102] According to Giovanni Boccaccio – the author whose work it adorned – Tamaris was the daughter of Micon the Younger, who 'scorned womanly tasks and practised her father's craft'.[103] In the image (Figure 31), Tamaris is hard at work in what looks like a busy workshop. A man can be seen grinding pigments at a table next to her. It's so rare to find images of manuscript artists at work, and this one is obviously not a 'portrait' in the way we would con-ventionally think of one, but I like the image of the man in the corner, his head bent, his gaze fixed on the work in front of him. His presence is a reminder of all the hidden hands that worked to produce medieval manuscripts.

Chapter Five

SCRIBES

is am fuar toirsech, cen tene, cen tugaid
[*'I am cold and weary, without fire or shelter'*]

Anonymous scribe[1]

In his *Institutiones*, Cassiodorus (c. 485–c. 585) wrote that the work of scribes and illuminators is:

> Felix intentio, laudanda sedulitas, manu hominibus prae-dicare, digitis linguas aperire, salutem mortalibus tacitum dare, et contra diaboli subreptiones illicitas calamo atra-mentoque pugnare. Tot enim vulnera Satanas accipit, quot antiquarius Domini verba describit.[2]

> *A blessed purpose, a praiseworthy zeal, to preach to men with the hand, to set tongues free with one's fingers and in silence to give mankind salvation and to fight with pen and ink against the unlawful snares of the devil. For Satan receives as many wounds as the scribe writes words of the Lord.*[3]

He figures the work of the scribe and the illuminator as sacred work, but in a martial vein. Each of the scribe's words harms the flesh of the devil. Some 900 years later, Geoffrey Chaucer wrote a wry injunction to his scribe, Adam (sometimes identified as Adam Pinkhurst).[4] Chaucer – whose works include translations of Boethius's *Consolation of Philosophy* and his own *Troilus and Criseyde* – berates Adam, threatening the curse of scabs ('scalle') on his head, should he not copy the work more correctly ('more trewe'). He complains that he is often forced to 'rubbe and scrape' the parchment folio in order 'to correcte' Adam's work:

> Adam scryveyn, if euer it þee byfalle
> Boece or Troylus for to wryten nuwe,
> Under þy long lokkes þowe most haue þe scalle,
> But affter my makyng þowe wryte more trewe;
> So ofte adaye I mot þy werk renuwe,
> It to correct and eke to rubbe and scrape,
> And al is thorughþy neglygence and rape.[5]

> *Adam scribe, if ever it falls to you*
> *Boethius or Troilus to write anew*
> *Under your long locks you must have the scale*
> *Unless you make my words more true;*
> *So many a day I must your work renew,*
> *Correct it and also rub and scrape*
> *And all that is from your negligence and haste.*

What we have here are two contrasting visions of the work of the scribe. Cassiodorus was a Roman Christian, who wrote his *Institutiones* from the monastery he founded at Vivarium, in the sixth century, while Chaucer was a fourteenth-century, London-based bureaucrat and poet. His texts were largely copied by professional scribes working in commercial workshops in and around Chancery (in London), while Cassiodorus's texts were likely copied by fellow monks who saw their work as in the service of God. The twin poles of Cassiodorus and Chaucer illustrate the way scribal work changed in the course of the medieval period, with the emergence of the professional scribe. As the period proceeded, scribal work was increasingly practised less in the monastery scriptorium and more in secular, commercial contexts. Wherever they worked, when we – as readers, centuries later – encounter the works of these scribes, we have an intimate connection with the figures who shaped the words on the folios we see. In this chapter we are going to encounter individual scribes, and try to reconstruct something of their lives, while in the next chapter we'll take a closer look at the way scribes moulded the texts they copied.

Bishop Eadfrith and the Lindisfarne Gospels

On the final page of the Lindisfarne Gospels (BL Cotton MS Nero D iv), at the end of the text, a note has been added.[6] It is in a later hand – small, spiky and cursive, by contrast with the stately letters of the main text. In eccentrically un-straight lines, the annotator has recorded that:

> + Eadfrið biscop lindisfearnensis æcclesiæ
> he ðis boc aurat æt fruma gode & sancte
> cuðberhte & allum ðæm halgum gimænelice ða ðe
> in eolonde sint.
>
> + *Eadfrith, bishop of the Lindisfarne church,*
> *originally wrote this book, for God and for St*

*Cuthbert and – jointly – for all the saints whose relics
are in the island.*

The note goes on to explain – in Old English – that the
manuscript was afterwards bound by 'Æthelwald, bishop of
the Lindisfarne-islanders', and then bejewelled by 'Billfrið, the
anchorite'. (The manuscript's jewelled binding was subsequently
lost in the post-Reformation period, before the manuscript
came into the hands of the collector Robert Cotton.) The note
was added by a monk named Aldred in c. 970 CE. Elsewhere in
the manuscript he added a continuous inter-lineal Old English
gloss to the Latin text of the Gospels – his work is the earliest
translation of the Bible into the English vernacular. For this, he
is beloved of linguistic historians, but his annotations are also
important because without them, we would have no idea who
made the Lindisfarne Gospels, which has been described as 'a
landmark of human creative achievement'.[7]

The Lindisfarne Gospels were probably made in a monastery on the island of Lindisfarne in Northumbria. Surprisingly, it
was the work of a single, brilliant scribe-artist. (This manuscript
might just as easily have been discussed in the previous chapter,
on 'Artists', because it contains beautiful artwork, but I have
decided to include it here because in the Lindisfarne Gospels
word becomes visual masterpiece, and letters artworks.) Many
medieval manuscripts were collaborative enterprises, but in this
case, the collaboration appears to have been confined to the
manuscript's now-lost jewelled binding. It was copied in the first
centuries of Christianity in Britain. (Christianity arrived in the
south of England in 597 but had been brought to the north by
Irish missionaries some time earlier.) If the note at the end of the
manuscript is to be believed,[8] it was made at some point between

the 'elevation' of St Cuthbert in 698 (when his veneration got under way),[9] and the death of its scribe, Eadfrith, in 721.[10]

The details of Eadfrith's life are hard to reach. We know nothing of him from before his becoming bishop in 698, but he was probably a monk from the Lindisfarne community. Once installed as bishop, though, it is clear that he promoted the cult of St Cuthbert – restoring Cuthbert's hermitage on Inner Farne Island and commissioning Bede and another, anonymous writer to write accounts of the saint's life.[11] The Gospels may have been made as part of this project of veneration. As well as promoting the monastery's own saint, Eadfrith also appears to have helped and encouraged the leaders of other nearby monasteries. According to a contemporary poem, he gave advice and instruction to an abbot named Eadmund at an unlocated monastery. In Eadmund's monastery there was a gifted scribe, named Ultán. It was said of him that:

> He could ornament books with fair marking, and by this art he accordingly made the shape of the letters beautiful one by one, so that no modern scribe could equal him [as if] the creator spirit had taken control of his fingers, and had fired his dedicated mind (to journey) to the stars.[12]

This contemporary description of scribal work is probably how Eadfrith perceived his role. He likely understood himself to be 'a channel between God and humanity', as he fired his dedicated mind and journeyed to the stars.[13] (It's also important here that Ultán is described as forming his letters 'one by one'. This painstaking method is characteristic of early medieval scribal work.)

We are not exactly sure when Eadfrith copied the book, and debate rages over whether it would have been possible for him to copy the manuscript while he was bishop. Alan Thacker contends that the manuscript took at least around two years of full-time work to complete, and therefore could not have been written after Eadfrith was bishop.[14] But some of the book's artwork is incomplete, suggesting that he may have died just before it was completed. If the book was a long-term, continuous project, perhaps it formed a kind of meditative retreat for the bishop as he sought to leave his administrative cares behind. If so, the manuscript was copied over a period of perhaps 710 to 722.[15] It has been suggested that he retreated to a hermitage on Cuddy's Isle, a tidal islet to the north of Holy Island, to work on it during Lent.[16] The idea is attractive. The Lindisfarne Gospels are a work of painstaking intricacy, which feels like devotion in book form. It seems fitting that Eadfrith might have withdrawn to a hermitage to carry out this spiritual labour over several years.

Opening the manuscript, the reader is first greeted by a so-called 'carpet page' – a densely complex array of patterns which cover the entire folio. The multifaceted decoration reveals new shapes at every glance. There are five of these carpet pages in the manuscript.[17] Four of them appear before the start of each gospel. Embedded in each of these four pages is an image of the cross – each one in a different form: Latin, Greek, Celtic ring-head, and the Coptic or Ethiopic 'tau cross'. In this way, the manuscript testifies to Lindisfarne's international connections, showing that its designer was familiar with the iconography of religious cultures far from England's shores.

The opening carpet page is followed by an 'incipit page' – from the Latin *incipit*, meaning 'here begins'. This page marks the start of a prologue introducing the Canon tables that follow. The incipit pages, of which there are a further four, are some of the most famous pages in the manuscript.[18] On these pages, letters become devotional icons – no longer simply alphabetical shapes but exquisite pictures. Here birds and beasts writhe in a complex interlacing pattern, set on a shimmering red-dotted ground. These tiny red dots, each so lovingly placed, with exquisite care, remind us of the words of Cassiodorus ('Satan receives as many wounds as the scribe writes words of the Lord'). It is as if every dot is a tiny wound in the back of the devil.

After the first incipit page, we come to the Canon tables.[19] These tables of information, common in Gospel books, were devised in the fourth century by Eusebius, Bishop of Caesarea, to help readers find parallel passages in the Gospels. Rendered simply as a list of references, the tables could be dull creatures, but in the hands of Eadfrith, the Lindisfarne Gospels' Canon tables are sixteen folios of intricate, iridescent architectural arches. The tables appear in pairs, with folios of similar decoration appearing on each double-page spread. Here we find – as in the opening incipit page – entwined birds, knotted beasts and braided designs 'cleverly moulded to fit an awkward space'.[20] As elsewhere, the use of alternating colours creates a shimmering, rippling depth. What is striking about the tables is that, by contrast with some of the models Eadfrith may have seen and used, the arches are not Classical forms, but distinctively 'Insular' – marvellous pieces of complex interlace pattern characteristic of early medieval English art.

Perhaps the most spectacular of the incipit pages is the 'Chi-rho' page that marks the start of the Gospel of Matthew.[21] 'Chi-Rho' (XP) is an ancient symbol for Christ – a monogram of the first two Greek letters of ΧΡΙΣΤΟΣ (*Christos*). It's quite hard to make out the XP shape, though, as the eye is drawn to a teeming mass of eddying beasts and knots. Their complexity is dazzling – Eadfrith plotted some of his designs mathematically.[22] But for all the complexity of the beast imagery, there is also sometimes something playful in the incipit pages. The decorated borders on the page for Luke are filled with cormorant-like birds, but terminate in what looks like a cat's head. Is the cat hunting the birds?

The decoration of the Gospels is not restricted to ornamental designs. The opening page of each of the Gospels – Matthew, Mark, Luke and John – is preceded by an image of each of the Evangelists, accompanied by their symbols: Matthew with the man, Mark with the lion, Luke with the bull, and John the eagle.[23] Matthew is attended by a mysterious haloed figure, holding a book, who peeps out from behind a curtain. They depict the Evangelists at work on their holy labour, writing out the words of the Gospels. We can only wonder at what Eadfrith felt as he drew these figures who, like him, bent their heads to realise divine words on the empty page.

The Text

The text of the Lindisfarne manuscript is a good copy of St Jerome's fourth-century translation of the Bible into the Latin Vulgate (this version of the text was the most widely used in the medieval West). It is written in a stately script called 'half-uncial', which has thick, round letters that terminate in neat little points. It would have been very time-consuming to write because it requires so many lifts of the quill (in contrast to the quick, cursive scripts we will meet at the end of this chapter). The name of the script derives from its half similarity to the Greek 'uncial' script that was used in manuscripts like

the Codex Sinaiticus (an important Bible manuscript dating to
c. 330–360). This script was criticised by Jerome 'for being so
luxurious and costly of materials and effort, its letters might be
an inch high (*uncialis*)'.[24] In its script alone, the manuscript of
the Lindisfarne Gospels demonstrates its luxuriousness.

Eadfrith's copy-text (or 'exemplar') was likely to have been
a good Italian one, akin to the copy-text of the St Cuthbert
Gospel (see Chapter One). It was probably derived from a
manuscript brought to the monastery of Wearmouth-Jarrow,
where Bede was from, which was most likely intended for
ceremonial use in church – carried in procession and used
for reading on special festivals. The beauty of the manuscript
was therefore designed to be 'in keeping with the status of a
book enshrining the Word of God'.[25]

How the Manuscript was Made

Although we know little of Eadfrith, his process in making the
manuscript can be partially recovered. He probably wrote the
text of the manuscript first, before coming to the illumination.
He appears to have kept the work of the illumination and
the text-writing quite separate. Three of the five carpet pages
(preceding Matthew, Luke and John) are not part of the original gatherings and were copied on different sheets before being
sewn into the existing gatherings.[26] For the main text he used a
black ink called iron gall ink, made from oak-galls and iron salts.
It was perhaps after writing the text that Eadfrith began to plot
the illumination. The manuscript contains many prick-marks
– small punctures in the parchment made to mark out the patterns on the carpet and incipit pages. These are ghostly traces
of the careful planning involved in the manuscript's creation.

Having marked out his designs with graphite and pricking, Eadfrith began to paint the illumination.

The illumination was created using animal, vegetable and mineral pigments – some of which were available locally and some imported. Eadfrith would have used a beaten egg-white preparation called 'glair' as an adhesive and mixed this with different pigments. For the black of the illuminations he used 'lamp black' made from soot (or – scientifically – carbon particles). The rich yellow colour was created using a pigment called 'orpiment'.[27] The greens were probably made either using 'verdigris, which is made by suspending copper over vinegar, or vergaut made by mixing blue and yellow pigments'.[28] The purple, crimson and blue colours were created using lichens and plant extracts such as woad and *folium* (turnsole), while the red and orange pigments were derived from toasted lead. The flashes of gold ink were made using gold leaf and powdered gold ink.[29]

Eadfrith probably applied the colours using reeds and quills. Holy Island is today renowned as a bird sanctuary visited by various species of goose, whose feathers would have made perfect quills. (One of St Cuthbert's miracles involved an uncooked goose, 'implying their presence locally'.)[30] The diverse pigments used in the creation of the Gospels reminds us of the investment of time and resources that would have been necessary to create the manuscript.

The beauty and intricacy of the Lindisfarne Gospels' text and decoration feel like an act of devotion in book form, created perhaps in silent retreat and contemplation. But the added note at the end of the manuscript gives us a sense of the community of devoted artisans who created the book and its binding. It also connects us, powerfully, to the scribe who laboured to create this masterpiece. So many scribes from the Middle Ages remain anonymous, but these names offer a tantalising glimpse of life in northern England in the earliest days of Christianity on the British Isles.

The Nuns of Nunnaminster

It would be easy to think that it was only men who worked as scribes in the medieval period. People often ask me if medieval manuscripts were 'all written by monks'. This popular assumption is wrong on two levels: firstly, many manuscripts were written by secular figures; and secondly, many were written by women (and this always seems to surprise people). In around 732 CE, St Boniface (c. 675–754) – a Christian missionary in Germany – received a letter from a young nun, named Leoba. In it, she requested that he pray for her parents, to whom he was related. And she included a poem in her letter, which she excused as 'exercising little talents and needing your assistance'.[31] This makes Leoba the first named English female poet. She added that she had learned to write poetry 'under the guidance of Eadburga', who was likely the Abbess of Thanet.[32] Leoba's letter is a clear indication that many early medieval English nuns were highly learned – not just literate, not just writing letters, but also composing poetry.[33] Later in her life, Leoba joined Boniface in his missionary work in Germany and became abbess of Tauberbischofsheim, but in the period of the letter she was part of the Benedictine double-monastery of Wimborne, in Dorset. Such an institution would probably have had a bustling scriptorium or perhaps even two – one for the male house and one for the female.[34] It's likely that Leoba copied manuscripts there. Her work may have been prized both inside and outside the institution. The abbess Eadburga, whom Leoba mentions in her letter, was a scribe so skilled that Boniface wrote to her in c. 735 to say:

> I beg you further to add what you have done already by making a copy written in gold of the Epistles of my master, St Peter the Apostle, to impress honour and reverence for the Sacred Scriptures visibly upon the carnally minded to whom I preach.[35]

This letter makes clear that the value of a manuscript was not only in the text it contained, but also in the visual beauty of its folios. (Later, Eadburga received a gift of a silver stylus from Boniface's successor, Lul, perhaps in recognition of her skill as a scribe.)[36] It is striking that Boniface does not want just any copy of the Petrine Epistles, but specifically requests Eadburga's penwomanship. A manuscript was not simply a repository of text but an embodiment, in visual and physical form, of the sacral power of Scripture. Such an artefact could not be created by anyone.

Tragically, Eadburga's manuscript does not survive. As ever in manuscript study, patchy survival is a problem, and hunting for the work of female scribes is challenging. There is a larger body of evidence for the work of medieval female scribes on the Continent, whereas most equivalent material in England often perished in Viking raids, the Norman Conquest, and the Dissolution of the Monasteries as part of the English Reformation.[37] Scribes, of either gender, did not often sign their work (although this became more common in the later medieval period), so their work goes unattributed. Female scribal hands are indistinguishable from male scribal hands. When examining a medieval manuscript from an uncertain place of production there is always the possibility that what is in front of you is the work of an unidentified female scribe.

Sometimes, however, manuscripts give us clues that they were made by a female copyist. British Library, Harley MS 2965 is known as 'the Book of Nunnaminster'.[38] Textually, it is made up of Gospel extracts, as well as a variety of prayers. It contains a prayer against poison,[39] and the oldest known copy of the 'Lorica of Laidcenn', an Irish 'breastplate prayer' for protection of the body,[40] which requests blessings on a long list of over a hundred body parts including 'skull', 'tongue', 'teeth', 'hams', 'spleen with winding intestines', 'joints, fat and two hands'.[41] The prayer's anxious catalogue of body parts is a very human reminder of the terror of disease that its readers must have felt. Perhaps the most intriguing aspect of the manuscript, however, is that it contains prayers in Latin with feminine word endings, which suggests the book was made by or for a woman. The manuscript's small size suggests that it was made for personal use – you could hold it easily in your hand. The text was written by a single scribe, in a clear round hand. It is delicately decorated with soft colour wash infills in some of the initials, and delicate dotting patterns around certain letters. Headings appear in red ink and some letters have animal heads, which writhe in an interlace pattern, characteristic of pre-Conquest English and Irish artwork.

It was probably created in the kingdom of Mercia (in the Midlands of England) in the late eighth or early ninth century, but by the tenth century it had made its way to the Benedictine Abbey of St Mary's, Nunnaminster, in Winchester. At this time someone added further prayers in Latin using nouns with feminine endings.[42] Tantalisingly, inscriptions were also added in Old English, describing the boundaries of a piece of land donated to Nunnaminster by Ealhswith (died 902), wife of Alfred the Great.[43] This could be a clue that the book had once belonged to Ealhswith, who was Nunnaminster's founder. The evidence is only suggestive, but Asser – Alfred's biographer (whom we met in Chapter Two) – describes Alfred's children Ælfthryth and Edward the Elder as studious and bookish, reading 'the Psalms, and books in English, [and] especially English poems'.[44] Asser describes Alfred himself being given a book of English poems by his mother. It would seem likely, therefore, that Ealhswith too shared Alfred's love of learning and promoted it to their children, as Alfred's mother had to him. A bequest of a personal prayer book to the convent she had founded would be in keeping with our picture of her.

The Book of Nunnaminster may suggest it had a partially female audience, provide suggestive clues to a female scribe, and hint at a female owner, but the evidence is frustratingly piecemeal. Very occasionally, however, a manuscript speaks to us in more unambiguous terms. MS Bodley 451, in Oxford's Bodleian Library, contains an anonymous moral treatise, a collection of sermons and a text on the monastic life called *Diadema monachorum* ('The Crown of Monks') by Smaragdus of Saint-Mihiel.[45] It was all written by a single scribe, in Nunnaminster (St Mary's Abbey, Winchester), which appears to have had a flourishing scriptorium in the early medieval period.[46] The scribe added a 'colophon' at the end of the text that reads, 'Salva et incolomis maneat per secula scriptrix' ('Save the scribe, may she remain unharmed forever'). The manuscript is written in a clear, neat hand with elegant 'rustic capitals' and rubrication, meaning that the text would have been easy to navigate. It was a carefully produced volume, with tiny thread page markers – which acted as bookmarks – the traces of which can still be seen. Unlike the Book of Nunnaminster, it seems to have been used for public instruction rather than private devotion.[47] One of the texts in the *Diadema monachorum* was one intended to supplement the 'Benedictine Rule' (the instructional manual Benedictine monks and nuns lived by). Smaragdus – the author of the *Diadema* – suggests that a chapter of the text should be read aloud at the evening meal. There are drips of wax and wax stains in the manuscript that suggest it was indeed used for this very purpose.[48]

It would seem that the scribe came back to her work, decades after it was finished, and added a note at the start of the manuscript concerning the genealogy of St Edburga – the granddaughter of Nunnaminster's founder, Queen Ealhswith, who may have owned the Book of Nunnaminster.[49] There is something compelling about her added note. It shows the book was retained by the abbey and likely read by generations of nuns. The manuscript appears to have been well cared for. When one of its leaves was lost or went missing, another scribe (probably another female scribe) replaced the leaf and copied the missing text in a hand approximately contemporary with the main hand. And the book went on being read and used for some time. Readers added forms of punctuation in the sermon collection to help them read aloud, and another scribe added a portion of a now-lost text describing a miracle associated with St Edburga.[50] Later notes and pen trials from the thirteenth century testify to several generations of (most likely female) readers.[51] In the tiniest of details – in traces of thread, drips of wax, and the three letters of the feminine word ending of 'scriptrix', we can begin to glimpse a lost world of female scribes and readers. Both manuscripts – the Book of Nunnaminster and the twelfth-century collection of sermons – testify to female patrons and owners, reminding us that women were involved in the production of texts in many different ways. These manuscripts offer a corrective to the popular perception that medieval manuscripts were 'all written by monks'. Our imagination of the past is delineated by patriarchalism infused with prejudice. If we were wrong in imagining that all scribes were men, what else might we be wrong about? The past is, as ever, richer and more intriguing than we imagine.

Each of the scribes described thus far was attached to a religious institution, but as the medieval period progressed, book production increasingly moved out of the monastery and into the lay world. The rise of universities in England from around the twelfth century created a demand for books outside of any specifically monastic context. (Students were being taught in Oxford in some form in 1096, and something approximating to a university developed after 1167, when Henry II banned English students from attending the University of Paris.) The growth in the number of lay scribes meant that, by the end of the twelfth century, 'monastic houses tended to acquire new books from professional scribes rather than relying on their monks to produce them'.[52] These changes are reflected in the appearance of the scribal hands. Eadfrith's letters are straight, careful, stately beasts, created with many painstaking pen-lifts. The Nunnaminster *scriptrix*'s letters are more interconnected, and look to have been made much quickly. But by the time we get to the scripts of the late medieval period, the scripts are 'cursive' (the letter forms are linked together, with single words being written in one fluid movement, rather than individual letters being formed as separate entities). These scripts are quicker, more functional and, especially in lower-status manuscripts, have none of the meticulousness of the scripts of the earlier period. It takes quite some time to learn how to read these hands. (There is a palaeography textbook that many students learn from called *English Cursive Book Hands*, which is known informally as 'English Cursèd Book Hands'.) Encountering the scribes of the late medieval period takes us away from the territory of the devotional or religious scribe, and we are now going to meet a group of scribes who worked for a single family in the fifteenth century. They often wrote in rapid, crabbed hands but, when deciphered, their words open up a world of family politics and social history.

The Paston Letters

What's under the microscope here is not a single manuscript, but a letter-collection containing the correspondence of several generations of the Paston family, who were from a village twenty miles north of Norwich. The surviving correspondence begins in 1422 and continues up to 1509, tracing the hopes, fortunes, loves and trials of William Paston and his descendants. Although the letters are the main seam of evidence about the family, other documents created for the Pastons also survive, such as inventories and legal documents, including petitions, indentures and wills. Through these letters and documents we gain an insight into the civil strife caused by the Wars of the Roses, but also more intimate aspects of the Pastons' lives. Sifting through the diverse documents, what becomes clear is that the family's lives were often entwined with those of their scribes. In the papers we see scribes becoming people, rather than names – their loves, losses and financial hardships traced in the documents they or their employers left behind. The family's relationship with its scribes can be mapped in some detail – and this is a story that evolved over decades, giving us a richer insight into the life of a scribe than any other single manuscript collection had ever done before.

The first member of the family to appear in the documentary record was Clement Paston (died 1419), who was a yeoman. His wife, Beatrice (died 1409), was said to be a 'bond woman' (or lowly servant). Their son William (1378–1444) was able to go to grammar school and train as a lawyer through the generosity of his uncle (Beatrice's brother). William's life was very different from his father's, and, in turn, his children grew up in a world dissimilar to theirs. William had a successful legal career and married, later in life, Agnes Barry (died 1479). She was from a well-known gentry family – the daughter of Sir Edmund Barry (died 1433); she brought William three manors and a degree of social standing he had not previously enjoyed. She and William had five children who survived into adulthood, the eldest of whom was John Paston (1421–1466), who married Margaret Mautby (c. 1422–1484). She was also from a prominent local family, and brought nine manors in Norfolk and Suffolk to her marriage. Crucially, however, she was – like her mother-in-law – well connected. She was related to Sir John Fastolf of Caister (1380–1459), a relationship that would come to shape the Pastons' fortunes. Margaret and John had seven surviving children: John II, and then (confusingly) John III, Margery, Edmund, Anne, Walter and William III.

Simplified Paston Family Tree

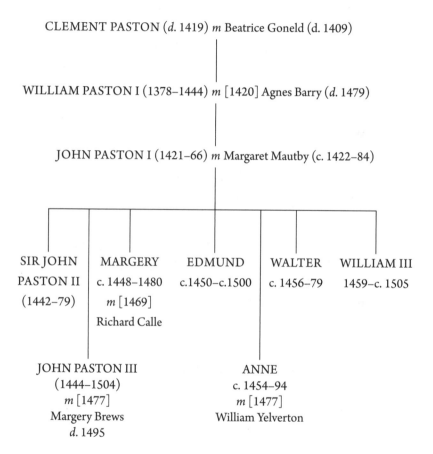

CLEMENT PASTON (*d.* 1419) *m* Beatrice Goneld (d. 1409)

WILLIAM PASTON I (1378–1444) *m* [1420] Agnes Barry (*d.* 1479)

JOHN PASTON I (1421–66) *m* Margaret Mautby (c. 1422–84)

| SIR JOHN PASTON II (1442–79) | MARGERY c. 1448–1480 *m* [1469] Richard Calle | EDMUND c.1450–c.1500 | WALTER c. 1456–79 | WILLIAM III 1459–c. 1505 |

JOHN PASTON III (1444–1504) *m* [1477] Margery Brews d. 1495

ANNE c. 1454–94 *m* [1477] William Yelverton

Through these canny marital alliances and professional suc-
cesses, the family's ascent through the social ranks might have
been assured, but in 1459 two events took place which shook
the family. In this year civil war broke out and Sir John Fastolf
died. John Paston claimed that Fastolf had made him his sole heir
in an orally dictated will. Fastolf owned the manor of Caister,
which was 'one of the most desirable contemporary houses in
the country'.[53] Unsurprisingly, the will was disputed by John
Paston's fellow executors. What ensued was the so-called 'war
of Fastolf's will', which cost the family dearly. John Paston I died
in 1466, with the will still in dispute. After some ten years of
conflict, the matter was referred to William Waynflete, Bishop
of Winchester, in 1470, who awarded Caister to the Dukes of
Norfolk. In a strange turn of events, however, at the unexpected
death of the fourth Duke of Norfolk, and through some political
manoeuvring, the family did eventually acquire the manor.

The letters offer a unique insight into the family's day-to-day
existence. Much of the correspondence is of an administrative
nature, but there are also moments of intrigue and fear alongside family squabbles and local gossip. At times we glimpse
a life where mundanity and danger sat side by side. In 1448
Margaret Paston wrote to her husband and asked him to buy
'1lb of almonds', '1lb of sugar', 'some cloth for gowns', as well
as 'two or three short poleaxes' and 'some crossbows'.[54] The
family's manor of Gresham was in danger of being attacked, and
Margaret wanted the resources to defend it;[55] yet this comes
alongside a request for material for the children's clothes.

What intrigues me most about the collection is that although
sometimes the letters were written by the Pastons themselves,
they often employed scribes. Perhaps the most famous letter
in the collection is a love letter from Margery Brews to John

Paston III (the son of John I and Margaret), which is thought to be the first Valentine's letter in the world.[56] It is written in the hand of Thomas Kela – a clerk to Margery's father, Sir Thomas Brews.[57] What was it like for Margery to dictate her declaration of love to an intermediary? This gives new meaning to our sense of scribal work – raising questions about the relationship between the scribes and their employers. In this sense, Margaret Paston is one of the most interesting figures in the collection. She was able to read, but appears to have been unable to write, meaning she had to dictate everything to an amanuensis. One hundred and four letters are authored by her, but all were written by scribes – twenty-nine different scribes, in fact.[58]

Other members of the Paston family used scribes for a variety of reasons, not simply because they weren't able to produce them themselves. Writing was – *is* – time-consuming, and the Pastons were busy people, usually requiring servants to write their letters. In one case, however, a letter survives in the hand of a professional scribe, William Ebesham. It is dated to April 1469 and is from William Paston II (the brother of John Paston I) and is addressed to his sister-in-law, Margaret.[59] Ebesham seems to have found employment with William in Norwich. We have to hope that William treated him fairly, because it would seem that other members of the family did not. A letter from Ebesham to John Paston II (the nephew of William II) survives. It describes all the work he has done and the outstanding payments owed to him. He opens by commending the ungrateful John, 'besechyng you moost tendirly to see me sumwhat rewardid for my labour in the grete booke which I wright vnto your seide gode masitirship' ('beseeching you most tenderly to see me somewhat rewarded for my labour in the Great Book which I wrote at your request, good master').[60]

The 'grete boke' he refers to here survives. It is now British Library Lansdowne MS 285 – a collection of English, French and Latin texts 'including descriptions of ceremonial occasions governing war and judicial combat', an English translation of a treatise on warfare by the fourth-century writer Vegetius, and a verse version of an Arabic text which purports to be a letter from Aristotle to his student Alexander the Great.[61] In short, it is a compendium ideally suited to a medieval would-be nobleman – a mix of the martial, educational and entertaining, in the languages of the court, the Church and the street.

In the letter, Ebesham describes how he has 'often tymes' written to Paston's employee John Pampyng requesting funds, and also put his case to an associate of the family, Sir Thomas Lovell, but to no avail. He describes how has been forced to seek 'seintwarye' ('sanctuary'), presumably from creditors, at 'grete coste' to him. Later in the letter he itemises the work he has carried out. It totals seven jobs; in each case he notes whether he had used 'parchemyn' (parchment) – an expensive material – or not. It's important to note that he would have been paid (in theory) for his work and not his time.[62] The letter is rather tragic, concluding with a request that John at least send him one of his 'olde gownes'.

The picture of William Ebesham begging for some clothing to keep him warm is a long way from our image of Eadfrith, bishop of Lindisfarne, retreating to Inner Farne Island to carry out his devotional labour, plaiting snakes and beasts together on the parchment folios of the Lindisfarne Gospels, making the pages shimmer with tiny red dots, like wounds on the back of the devil. What we can gather of Ebesham's story shows how precarious the life of the professional scribe in the later medieval period could be.

Ebesham is an unusual case in the Paston Letters. Apart from him, all the identified scribes used by the family were not professional. They were most often people in the family's service, in differing roles. The Pastons also wrote for themselves. One of the few surviving letters by Agnes Paston contains a note at the end which reads: 'Wretyn at Paston in hast þe Wednesday next after *Deus qui errantib*us, for defaute of a good secretarye & c' ('Written at Paston in haste, the Wednesday next after *Deus qui errantibus* for want of a good secretary etc.'). (The '*Deus qui errantibus*' here is the Collect, or prayer, for the third Sunday after Easter – it's a small reminder of the way medieval people measured out their lives by liturgical markers.) The letter is written in a clear, even hand. It would seem Agnes trusted none of her servants to improve on her writing. The letter can be dated to 20 April 1440 and is addressed to her husband. It is largely administrative, but with flashes of human detail. She reported that 'Yowre stewes [fish ponds] doe well' and asked that he bring her more gold thread for embroidery.[63] She also mentioned that on

> þe furste aqweyntaunce be-twhen John Paston and þe seyde gentilwoman, she made hym gentil chere in gyntyl wyse and seyde he was verrayly yowre son. And so I hope þer need no gret treté be-twyxe hym.

> *the first acquaintance between John Paston and the said gentlewoman, she made him gentle cheer in gentle wise [i.e. they got on well] and said he was truly your son. And so I hope there need [be] no great treaty [i.e. no difficult negotiations] between them.*

The 'gentilwoman' in question was Margaret Mautby, who became Margaret Paston not long afterwards. As I noted, all of Margaret's letters are in the hands of others, unlike Agnes.[64] For this reason, she is one of the most intriguing figures in the collection. I have often wondered what the experience of composing her letters was like. Recovering their original tone is difficult, and when we think about the fact that so many of them were dictated, that becomes especially hard. On 14 December 1441, Margaret wrote to John I, her husband of eight months. She opened by asking 'of yowre wylfare' ('your welfare'), before getting down to more pressing matters. She begs that he will buy her some cloth for a new gown, as he had promised because 'I haue no govne to weyre þis wyntyr but my blake *and* my grene . . . *and* þat ys so comerus þat I ham wery to wer yt' ('I have no gown to wear this winter but my black and green [one] and that is so cumbersome I am weary of wearing it'). She goes on to request a new girdle as well. The reason for her sartorial anxiety soon becomes clear: 'I ham waxse so fetys þat I may not be gyrte in no barre of no gyrdyl þat I haue but of on' ('I have grown so shapely that I can no longer get any of my girdles round me except one'). Margaret was pregnant, and in her next paragraph she reports that the local midwife has been ill, but has reassured her that she will be able to attend the birth even if she has to be pushed 'in a barwe' ('in a barrow'). In these lines we get a sense of Margaret's humour – describing herself as 'fetys' ('shapely', but also 'elegant'), and perhaps playing on her husband's anxiety by joking that the midwife might need to come in a wheelbarrow. But her words have a darker tinge: it is worth remembering that childbirth was very dangerous in this period and that as many as one in three women died.[65] A contemporary text called *Instructions to Parish Priests* by John Mirk or 'Myrc' (c. 1380–1420), an Augustinian canon, contains an unsettling reminder of the dangers women faced. Mirk encourages priests to impress upon the female members of their flock the hazards they were about to undertake: 'Wymmen that ben wyth chy[l]de / Theche hem to come & schryue hem clene, / For drede of perele that may be-falle' ('Women that are with child, teach them to come and clean themselves through confession, For they should be aware of the peril that may befall them'). Later there is a chilling instruction to midwives that if 'þe chylde bote half be bore' ('if child is but half born'), then the midwives should quickly 'crystene hyt and caste on water' ('christen it and cast on water').[66] Mirk suggests this because if the child is about to die, it must receive baptism of some kind to have a chance of salvation. Mirk goes on, saying that if the child cannot be born and the mother dies, the midwife is instructed to cut open the mother with a knife in order to give the infant baptism. Margaret Paston was facing a potentially fatal ordeal, for both herself and her child. Her letter concludes:

> I pre yow þat ye wyl were þe reyng with þe emage of Seynt Margrete þat I sent yow for a rememrav[n]se tyl ye come hom. Ye haue lefte me sweche a rememrav[n]se þat makyth me to thynke vppe-on yow bothe day *and* nyth wane I wold sclepe.

> *I pray that you will wear the ring with the image of St Margaret that I sent you for a remembrance till you come home. You have left me with such a remembrance that makes me think about you both day and night when I am trying to sleep.*

Margaret refers to the sleeplessness that often attends pregnancy, and we can only wonder whether there is affection and possibly sexual longing in the assertion that she 'thynke vppe-on yow bothe day & nyth'.[67] And the gift of the ring bearing the image of St Margaret was not simply intended as a reminder of her, but also had another purpose: Margaret was the patron saint of childbirth. Expectant mothers were known to wear amulet scrolls containing texts related to St Margaret around their stomachs during labour.[68] She was also asking her husband to invoke the intercessory power of the saint for her ordeal ahead. (It worked: John Paston II, the first of seven children, was born some time after.)

When we understand the context, Margaret's letter is full of layered meaning. Her words thrum with humour, affection, perhaps some veiled intimacy and also probably, beneath it all, fear. What was it like for her to tell an intermediary that she had grown so big in pregnancy, that she perhaps longed for the intercessory power of St Margaret, that the midwife was ill and might have to be pushed in a wheelbarrow to attend the birth? The scribe of this letter is 'unidentified' and it comes from a cluster of letters that were written around this time by different unidentified hands.[69] Who was this scribe, and what was their relationship with Margaret?

In other cases, the scribal hand can be identified, and we can grasp something more of the relationship between the scribe and the letter's author. Nearly thirty of the Pastons' letters are in the hand of James Gloys – the family chaplain. He appears in the records for the first time in 1448 and seems to have been in the family's service until 1473. He wrote seven letters – in total or in part – for John Paston I, and twenty – in total or in part – for Margaret. As she was unable to write, she was especially reliant on those who could do her business for her and Gloys appears to have been close to her. For complex reasons, he came

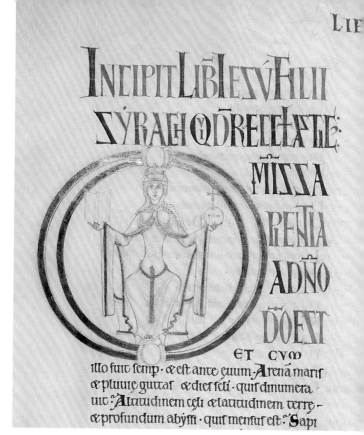

13: The initial for Ecclesiastes depicting Wisdom, Master of the Leaping Figures, drawn and gilded, Winchester Bible, fol. 278v.

14: Initial for Psalm 101 by the Master of the Morgan Leaf over a design by the Master of the Leaping Figures, drawn, gilded and partially painted, Winchester Bible, fol. 246.

15: The young Moses slays the Egyptian in retribution for the tormenting of the Hebrew, Master of the Leaping Figures, Winchester Bible, fol. 21v.

16: David covers his face in grief upon learning of the death of his son Absalom. The Morgan Leaf, from the Winchester Bible: Frontispiece for 1 Samuel.

17: Initial for 2 Samuel, by the Amalekite Master over a design by the Master of the Leaping Figures, Winchester Bible, fol. 99v.

18: Opening for the Book of Genesis: 'In Principio' showing Noah's Ark, Winchester Bible, fol. 5r.

ns misericordiam xpisto suo
id: 7 semini eius usqz in seculū.

19: A monkey, riding a goat, hawking with an owl, detail, Luttrell Psalter, BL Add. MS 42130, fol. 38r.

tis desertum. 7 commouebit
nus desertum cades.

20: St Dunstan pinching the devil's nose, Luttrell Psalter, BL Add. MS 42130, fol. 54v.

hiis qui seruant testamentum eius.
t memores sunt mandatorum
ipsius : ipsius : ad faciendum ea.

21: Eel traps tied in the current above a watermill, detail, Luttrell Psalter, BL Add. MS 42130, fol. 181r.

22: A carriage pulled by horses conveys a group of ladies and their pets (including a squirrel), *bas-de-page* double-page spread from the Luttrell Psalter, BL Add. MS 42130, fols. 181v–182r.

23: A man sowing seed on a cold spring day: his dog chases away a crow, while another feasts behind his back, detail, Luttrell Psalter, BL Add. MS 42130, fol. 170v.

24: 'Dns. Galfridus Louterell me fieri fecit' ('Sir Geoffrey caused me to be made'): Luttrell Psalter, BL Add. MS 42130, fol. 202v.

25: A baby appears in a line-filler, Luttrell Psalter, BL Add. MS 42130, fol. 23r.

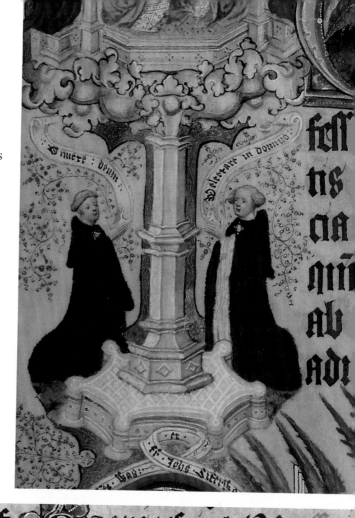

26: The scribe, John Whas (left), and the principal artist, John Siferwas (right), of the Sherborne Missal, BL Add. MS 74236, p. 276.

27: Self-portrait of John Siferwas, the principal artist of the Sherborne Missal, BL Add. MS 74236, p. 81.

28: The Crucifixion Scene, Sherborne Missal, BL Add. MS 74236, p. 380a.

to be resented by her sons. It is possible that after the death of her husband she came to rely on him more and more. On 8 July 1472, John Paston III wrote to his brother, John Paston II. The letter is in his own hand. It discusses a number of matters, which John III lays out as a list, beginning each point with 'item'. Item four reads:

> [T]he prowd, pevyshe *and* evyll dyposyd prest to vs all, *Syr* Jamys, seyth þat ye comandyd hym to delyuer þe book of vij Sagys to my brodyr Water, *and* he hathe it.[70]

> *The proud, peevish and evil-disposed priest to us all, Sir James, says that you commanded him to deliver the book of the Seven Sages to my brother Walter, but he has it.*

After writing the letter, he came back to it and added in a hasty hand, evidently as an afterthought: 'I prey brenne thys by[ll] for losyng' ('I pray you burn this letter in case you lose it').

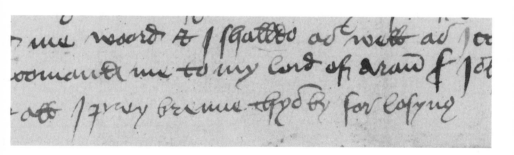

Later in the same year, John III's sense of disquiet about Gloys appears to have grown. On 16 October, he wrote again to his brother, again on several matters, but including the following paragraph:

> *Syr* Jamys is euyr choppyng at me when my modyr is present, ywith syche wordys as he thynkys wrathe <me> and

also <cause> my modyr to be dyspleaseid *wyth* me And when he hathe most vnsyttyng woordys to me, I smylle a lytyll *and* tell hym it is good heryng of thes old talys.[71]

Sir James is ever snapping at me when my mother is present, with such words as he thinks anger me and also cause my mother to be displeased with me. And when he has the most offensive words for me, I smile a little and tell him it is good to hear these old tales.

The family's relationship with Gloys suggests that those who were employed to write the Pastons' letters were often trusted intimates, perhaps too intimate for the liking of other family members. And Gloys was not the only employee whose familiarity with certain family members elicited concern.

Six of Margaret Paston's letters were written by Richard Calle, who was the bailiff of the Paston lands from around 1455.[72] He was evidently well trusted by the family, in part because he had been recommended to their service by the Duke of Norfolk. The sense of how important it was to be able to trust the people in their employ is conveyed in a little postscript added at the end of one of the letters Calle wrote for Margaret, addressed to her husband.[73] It reads: 'Yf it plese yow to send aney thing by the berer herof, he is trusty jnough' ('If it pleases you, send anything you wish with the bearer of this letter, he is trusty enough'). Calle was not the bearer of the letter as well as its scribe, but the note nonetheless illustrates a sense of anxiety about how written information could be used or misused.

Calle wrote letters for John Paston I, as well as for Margaret. On 28 July 1460 he took dictation from John, addressing a letter to Margaret.[74] It is business-like and full of administrative detail

and written in Calle's clear, cursive hand. It appears that after
he had finished writing it, he handed the letter to John to read,
and Paston amended the language in several places, crossing
out words and replacing them. In the top margin, Paston added
a more personal note: 'I requer yow be of god cumffort & be of
not heuynes if ye wil do owth for me' ('I ask you to be of good
comfort and be of not sadness if you will do anything for me').
John was able to give the letter a more personal and private
touch, in a way that Margaret could not. She had to entrust her
feelings to her scribes.

Calle's familiarity with the members of the family came to
be his undoing. On 3 April 1469, Margaret Paston dictated a
letter to James Gloys, her chaplain. The letter was addressed
to her son, John II, and is a mixture of administrative detail
and maternal advice. She sends updates on the manor of
Caister and encourages John II not to rush into marriage. Then
she adds:

> Also I wuld ye shuld purvey for your suster to be wyth my
> lady of Oxford or wyth my lady of Bedford or in summe
> othere wurchepfull place where as ye thynk best, and I
> wull help to here fyndyng, for we be eythere of vs wery
> of othere. I shall telle you more whan I speke wyth you. I
> pray you do your deveyre here-in as ye wull my comfort &
> welefare & your wurchep, for diuerse causes which ye shall
> vnderstand afterward, & c.[75]

> *Also I would like you to arrange for your sister to be with my*
> *lady of Oxford or with my lady of Bedford or in some other*
> *reputable place, as you think best, and I will help with her*
> *maintenance, for we are both of us weary of each other. I shall*
> *tell you more when I speak with you. I pray you do your duty*

herein, for my comfort and welfare, and your reputation, for many reasons which you shall understand afterwards etc.

Despite her somewhat guarded language, it was clear that Margaret was having a difficult time with her daughter and wanted her out of the house. (The daughter must be Margery, born in 1448, as later letters reveal.) As she hinted, it wasn't simply a question of a strained relationship, but 'diuerse causes which ye shall vnderstand afterward'. Gloys – the letter's scribe – would no doubt have been party to all the information here. It was probably this very familiarity that would enrage John II, in the letter quoted, three years later.

It is unclear whether Margery had indeed been found employment with 'my lady of Oxford or *wyth* my lady of Bedford', but a letter written a month later explains the cause of the difficulty between Margery and her mother. It is written in John Paston III's own hand and is addressed to his brother John Paston II.[76] The letter makes clear that Margery had fallen in love with Richard Calle, the family's trusted employee. The Pastons were a family newly socially elevated and evidently very keen to preserve their status. Calle was from a family of shopkeepers in Framlingham. The affair was a scandal and Calle was evidently unsure about how to broach the subject of a possible marriage. He had asked an intermediary to sound out John III. The conversation had not gone well. John III's words are cruel. He refers to his 'vngracyous sustyr' ('ungracious sister') and adds:

I answerd hym þat dan my fadyr whom God asoyle wer a-lyue *and* had consentyd ther-to *and* my modyr *and* ye bothe, he shold neuer haue my good wyll for to make my sustyr to selle kandyll *and* mustard in Framly[n]gham.

I answered him that if my father – whom God absolve – were alive and had consented to this, and also my mother and you both, he should never have my good will to make my sister sell candles and mustard in Framlingham.

Despite this strong opposition, the pair made solemn vows to each other in secret (effectively a wedding) late in the summer of 1469.[77] They may have tried to choose their moment strategically. The family were consumed with a threat to the disputed manor of Caister, which was stormed by the Duke of Norfolk in late August.[78] But when she heard of the secret marriage, Margaret was incensed. She had the pair kept apart and set about trying to have the union dissolved by the Bishop of Norwich. Her distress is clear in a letter dated to 10 or 11 September of 1469. It is addressed to John II and is written in the hand of Edmond Paston – the fourth of her children, who was nineteen at the time.[79] This private matter clearly had to be written by only the most trusted of scribes. The letter is much more open than the previous one which was written in Gloys's hand, and it makes for chilling reading. The depth of Margery's feeling was of little consequence to Margaret, whose primary concern was the family's reputation:

I pray ȝow *and* requere ȝow þat ȝe take yt not pensyly, fore I wot wele yt gothe ryth nere ȝowr hart, *and* so doth yt to myn *and* to othere but remembyre ȝow *and* so do I þat we have lost of here but a brethele.

I pray you do not take it too badly, because I know well that it goes right to your heart, as it does to mine and to others, but you should remember, as I do, that we have lost in her nothing but a worthless thing.

The word Margaret uses here, 'brethele', means 'a worthless person, a wretch; a pauper'.[80] (It is related to the word 'brothel'.) Later she writes that even if Calle died, Margery would never return to her affection.

The tone of the letter could not be more different from the tone we find in an extraordinary surviving letter written by Calle to Margery. He opens by addressing her as 'Myne owne lady and mastres and be-for God very trewe wyff' ('My own lady and mistress and before God very truly my wife'). His distress that 'we þat ought of very right [to] be moost to-gether ar moost asondre' ('we that have the most right to be together are the most apart') is palpable. Calle speaks of his faith and loyalty to Margery's mother and how upset he is to displease her, begging Margery to tell the truth about their union. He concludes with:

> Mastres, I am aferde to write to you for I vndrestond ye haue schewyd my letters þat I haue sent you be-fore thys tyme but prey you lete no creatur se this letter. As sone as ye haue redde it lete it be brent for I wold no man schulde se it in no wice. Ye had no wrytyng from me this ij yere, nor I wolle not sende you no mor therfor I remytte all this matre to your wysd<om>.

> *Mistress, I am afraid to write to you because I understand that you have shown the letters I have sent you before this time, but pray you, let nobody see this letter. As soon as you have read it, let it be burnt, for I do not wish any man to see it in any form. You have had no writing from me these last two years, nor will I send you any more, therefore I surrender this matter to your wisdom.*

The final line is perhaps most poignant: 'This letter was wreten wyth as greete peyne as euer wrote I thynge in my lyfe' ('this letter is the most painful thing I have ever written in my life').[81] The tone here is striking and has a particular significance because the voices of ordinary people like Calle rarely survive from the Middle Ages.

In the end, Margery and Calle's marriage went ahead and the pair were ostracised by the family. But as competent and trustworthy employees were hard to find, Calle did eventually find his way back into the family's service; there are letters in his hand from after the scandalous marriage.[82] However, it is unclear whether Margery, 'a daughter who had demeaned the family', was ever welcomed back.[83] She appears to have died after only ten years of marriage, perhaps in childbirth.

Calle wasn't the only figure whose familiarity with the family was viewed with suspicion. On 22 November 1473, some four years after the affair between Calle and Margery had shocked the family, John Paston II wrote to his brother John Paston III. He wrote in his own hand, perhaps feeling that these words could not be trusted to an intermediary:

> Item, as towchyng my sustre Anne I vndrestand she hathe ben passing seek, but I wend þat she had ben weddyd. As fore Yeluerton, he seyde but late þat he wold haue hyre iff she had hyre mony, and ellis nott; wherfor me thynkyth that they be nott very esewer. But amonge all other thyngys I praye yow be ware þat þe olde love off Pampyng renewe natt. He is nowe fro me I wott nat what he woll doo.[84]

Item, as to my sister Anne, I understand that she has been passing sick, but I hope she will be wedded. As for Yelverton he said lately that he would have her if she had her money and otherwise not, which makes me think it is not very sure. But among all other things I pray you be wary that the old love for Pampyng does not renew. He is not with me now and I do not know what he will do.

With an extraordinary symmetry, it seems that Margery's younger sister, Anne (1454–1494), had conceived of an affection for John Pampyng – another man in the family's employ. He wrote over twenty letters for the family and appears to have been in John I's service.[85] The letter makes clear that the marriages of the Pastons were seen predominantly as economic transactions. Three days later, on 25 November, he wrote again, again stressing his concerns: 'I pray yow take good hedde to my sost*er* Anne lesse the olde love atweyn hyr*e* and Pampyng renewe' ('I pray you take good heed of my sister Anne lest the old love between her and Pamyng renew').[86] Not long after these letters, Pampyng left the Pastons' service permanently, having been separated from Anne.

The interwoven stories of the Pastons and their scribes demonstrate the way scribal work could sometimes be intimate work, bringing the writer into the orbit of the author. Sometimes, of course, it was not. Poor William Ebesham, who begged for some clothing to keep him warm, clearly had little intimacy with his supposed patron, despite having copied a 'grete boke' for him. But for the others – for Calle, for Pampyng, for Gloys – the words they copied were emblematic of the familiarity they had with their employers, a familiarity that was sometimes viewed with suspicion. And for us today there is a certain intimacy we feel in reading those words. To be a scribe was to eavesdrop on an author's thoughts, and we – in turn – eavesdrop on the scribes when we read their work.

This feeling of intimacy is poignant when we encounter the work of people whose voices are not often heard from the Middle Ages. There is a thrill when we read the eloquent words of Richard Calle – the much-maligned shopkeeper's son – expressing his love for his would-be wife. There is a thrill when we see the words written by the Nunnaminster *scriptrix*, and see the notes she added later, as well as the wax stains and lection marks (annotations added to help the recitation or singing of a text) that testify to the generations of (female) readers who benefited from her words. And there is a thrill when we read the words written by Eadfrith, who perhaps hoped for a kind of intimacy with God as he formed the letters on the page, with what Cassiodorus called 'felix intentio' ('blessed purpose').

At the end of the Gospel of Matthew in the Lindisfarne Gospels, almost hidden in the page gutter, is a note: 'remember Eadfrið & Æthilwald & Billfrið & Aldred, a sinner; these four with God, were concerned with this book'.[87] Aldred – the enigmatic annotator of the Gospels – begs that he and the book's scribe and binders be remembered. And we hear him, a millennium later.

This obscure, tucked-away note is important because it allows us to attach names and partial stories to the hands before our eyes. We so nearly did not have the name of William Ebesham (he did not sign the 'grete boke' – BL Lansdowne MS 285 – he copied for John Paston III); we only know his name by marrying his hand with the letter in which he begs for money. And, of course, the name of the Nunnaminster *scriptrix* is lost.

Her story, like so many women's stories from the past, is now irrecoverable.

On the final folio of the Lindisfarne Gospels, near the page's right-hand edge, next to a Latin note declaring that this is the end of the Gospel of John, the following words appear:

> \+ Lit[er]a me pandat
> sermonis fida
> ministra
> Omnes alme
> meos fraters
> voce salvta [88]

> \+ *May the letter,*
> *faithful servant of speech,*
> *reveal me;*
> *salute all*
> *my brothers*
> *with thy kindly voice.*

Aldred invokes the power of the letter – the 'faithful servant of speech' – asking that the letters salute his fellow monks, with a kindly voice. And yet his letters did more than that. The letters written by Aldred, and by Bishop Eadfrith before him, and later the nuns of Nunnaminster and the Pastons' scribes, salute *us* with their distant voices.

Chapter Six

SCRIBES AND AUTHORS

Ælc gelæred bocere on godes gelaðunge ys gelic þam
hlaforde þe forlæt simble of his agenum goldhorde ealde
þing & niwe. [*Every scribe in the kingdom of God is like the
lord who continually brings out of his gold-hoard old things
and new*]

Ælfric [1]

Huntington Library MS HM 111 contains a copy of *La Male
Regle* by Thomas Hoccleve (1368–1426). Hoccleve was a clerk
of the Privy Seal (the office from which royal warrants were
issued), as well as a sometime poet. The poem is a witty account
of his dissolute youth in London, where – like many a young
office worker – he spends his evenings getting drunk, flirting,
gossiping and spending too much money.

> The outward signe of Bachus & his lure,
> Þat at his dore hangith day by day
> Excitith folk to taaste of his moisture
> So often þat man can nat wel seyn nay.
> For me, I seye I was enclyned ay
> With-outen daunger thidir for to hye me,

But if swich charge vp on my bake lay,
That I moot it forbere as for a tyme . . .

Of him þat hauntith tauerne custume,
At shorte wordes the profyt is this:
In double wyse his bagge it shal consume,
And make his tonge speke of folk amis;
For in the cuppe seelden fownden is,
Þat any wight his neigheburgh commendith.
Beholde & see what auantage is his,
Þat god his freend & eek him self offendith.[2]

The street sign and the lure of Bacchus
(Which hangs outside his door every day)
Entices people to take a sip of his liquid
So often that they can hardly say no.
As for me, I say that I was always inclined
To rush there without a second thought

Unless such a burden lay upon my back
That I must decline it for a while . . .

For he who haunts the tavern habitually,
To speak briefly, the 'profit' is this:
It will use up his money-bag twice over
And make his tongue speak wrongly about people;
For it's seldomly found at the bottom of a glass
That anyone compliments his neighbour.
Look and see what he gains, he who
Offends God, his friend and also himself.[3]

Reading these words in the Huntington manuscript has a particular thrill, because there they are written in Hoccleve's own hand, and we can imagine the poet forming these gently self-mocking words.[4]

We might imagine that this kind of manuscript was a common thing – that many medieval literary manuscripts survive that were written by authors themselves. In fact, author 'holographs' or 'autographs' (as they are termed) are surprisingly rare. The vast majority of medieval literary manuscripts contain the hands of scribes, not author-scribes.

When we open a modern, printed book we invariably see a title page, which gives us a whole set of clues about what to expect. We have a title, which is something many medieval texts did not have. (A large number of titles of medieval works are actually later, editorial inventions: the *Morte Darthur*, for example, which we looked at in Chapter One, is an awkward title given to that text by Caxton; the Old English poem 'The Ruin', discussed in Chapter Two, is a modern editorial invention.) We also have the name of the author, and often this name will mean something to us – we can perhaps google the author and find out what other works they wrote or have written, where they live or lived, and perhaps some personal details. But when a medieval reader came to a manuscript, their experience was probably very different from our own. They often had no title, no author (and if they did have an author's name, very little was likely known about this person), and they had nothing like a publisher or a place of publication to guide their reading of a text. Opening a medieval manuscript and encountering a medieval text might have been disorientating – like a kind of dream-vision – as if the reader had fallen asleep and woken in a strange land. (Indeed, the 'dream-vision' form, when a narrator falls asleep and wakes in an unknown place, was an extremely popular literary genre in the Middle Ages.) But this strange land – this textual world – was presided over by an obscure but powerful figure: the scribe.

Medieval texts were malleable things – malleable in a way that printed texts were not – and as such, they were often refashioned and reframed by the scribes and editors who worked on them. In each of the examples we'll encounter here, it will become clear that scribes often had an important role in shaping the meaning of a text – small details such as changes in wording or acts of extraction or anthologising (selecting texts and placing them alongside each other in a manuscript) could radically alter the way a work was understood. And sometimes texts only survived because of what feels like the whim of the scribe.

When I was an undergraduate, I began to realise that texts – and the manuscripts that contain them – are infinitely richer and more complicated than printed editions would lead you to believe. There is a huge disparity between the texts that appear in manuscript form and the sanitised, ordered blandness of the modern, edited text. The traditional understanding of the role of the modern editor held that they were vested with an important power, that they should act something like the author's holy representative on earth. Their job was to filter out the white noise created by scribes, and return texts to some kind of original form intended by the author. But recovering what this 'original form' may have been is often tricky. Many scholars are now shifting away from this earlier view, seeking to record faithfully the decisions of scribes, recognising that these decisions are often just as interesting as the decisions of authors, giving us fascinating insights into what a text meant in a particular time.[5]

We've seen that manuscripts are portals that connect us to lives in the past. But in this chapter, what becomes clear is that sometimes manuscripts get us close to the authors we seek – but never quite close enough. Those chosen here show us that sometimes they offer a more exciting encounter with the scribe than the author. In the previous chapter we met a series of scribes, and caught glimpses of their hopes and terrors – their devoted labours or joyless drudgery. Here we're going to explore scribes as active agents, making literary decisions and influencing how we come to see the authors whose work they copied.

The First Named English Poet?

At some point in around the 740s – perhaps as early as 737 – a scribe from the monastery of Wearmouth-Jarrow set about copying a version of Bede's *Historia ecclesiastica gentis Anglorum* (*Ecclesiastical History of the English People*). This text was written by the first great historian of Britain, who was himself from Wearmouth-Jarrow. It details the conversion of the inhabitants of early medieval England to Christianity and charts the establishment of the English Church. It was Bede's last major work. He completed it in 731 and would die only a few years later, on 25 May 735. The manuscript, known as the 'Moore Bede', is the earliest copy of the work. It was written by a single scribe using a type of script called 'Insular minuscule'. This script was cursive, and easier to write rapidly than some other kinds of more formal scripts, which require frequent pen lifts and generous spaces between the words (such as, for example, the formal script of the Cuthbert Gospel which we met in Chapter One.) Sometimes the spaces between the scribe's words are hard to make out and it can be tricky to read.

When the scribe got to the end of the text, he wrote out an 'explicit', in red ink, stating that this was the end of the work.[6] This left a space at the bottom of the folio. I sometimes like to imagine what this was like – when a scribe realised they had a whole, pristine piece of parchment to fill – or to take instruction on how to fill – at the end of text. Using the empty space, the scribe wrote out a little mini-chronicle describing the events of 731–734. The last entry records an eclipse of the moon on 30 January 734. This still left him with an entire blank space on the other side of the folio. He turned it over and, at the top of the next page, in smaller script, and with slightly paler ink, he wrote out what looks like another section of prose. Here he switched languages, taking up Old English – a vernacular language that was probably his mother-tongue. He wrote out three lines in Old English, cramming the text, with almost no word division, into a compact space at the top of the page. Despite looking like a concertinaed piece of prose, that text is now thought to be one of the earliest surviving poems in the English language.[7] English literature, it would seem, had cramped and inauspicious beginnings.

> Nuscylun hergeᵃn hefaen ricaes uard metudæs maecti end
>   his modgidanc uerc *uuldur* fadur
> sueheuundragihuaes ecidrin *yctin* or astelidæ heaerist scop
>   aelda barnū heben til hrofe
> *h*alegscepen· thaminᵈdun geardmoncynnæs uard ecidryctin
>   æfter tiadæ firum foldᵘ frea allmectig

Wrestling a poem out of this squished sequence of words is a little tricky, but the words can be reformatted to give us this:

> Nu scylun hergan   hefaenricaes uard
> metudæs maecti   end his modgidanc
> uercu uldurfadur   sue he uundra gihuaes
> eci dryctin   or astelidæ
> he aerist scop   aelda barnum
> heben til hrofe   haleg scepen.
> tha middungeard   moncynnæs uard
> eci dryctin   æfter tiadæ
> firum foldu   frea allmectig

> *Now [we] must honour the Guardian of Heaven,*
> *the might of the Creator, and his purpose,*
> *the work of the Father of Glory*
> *as he, the eternal Lord, established the beginning of wonders;*
> *he first created for the children of men*
> *heaven as a roof, the holy Creator*

Then the Guardian of mankind,
the eternal Lord, afterwards appointed the middle earth,
the lands for men, the Lord almighty.

As a devotional text, this little hymn is a masterpiece of formal economy and musical alliteration. Its opening invocation 'Nu' ('Now') grabs our attention and suggests that we are to participate in a communal act of praise. The poem's DNA is God – God appears, literally, in every line: 'hefaenricaes uard' ('the Guardian of Heaven') in line 1, 'metudæs' ('of the Creator') in line 2, 'uuldurfadur' ('Father of Glory') in line 3, 'dryctin' ('Lord') in line 4, 'scepen' ('Creator') in line 6, 'moncynnæs uard' ('Guardian of mankind') in line 7, 'dryctin' again in line 8 and 'frea allmectig' ('Lord almighty') in line 9. In line 5 – the central line of the *Hymn* – God appears more obliquely: *'he aerist scop   aelda barnum'* ('He first created, for the children of men'), but there's a clever little pun in this line. '*Scop*' can also mean 'poet', so the central line, the heart of the *Hymn*, draws our attention to acts of verse and uni-verse creation. (This short list shows the richness of Old English vocabulary relating to God – a plethora of words are used here which are often translated as the same word in Modern English.)

The scribe concluded the poem with the Latin words 'Primo cantauit Cædmon istud carmen' ('Cædmon first sang that song'). And after that, as if finding something useful to fill the space, he wrote out three Latin words, which perhaps he had difficulty with: 'arula', 'destina' and 'iugulum', with their Old English translations, 'hearth', 'feur-stud' and 'sticung', which translate as 'altar', 'buttress' and 'piercing/pig killing'. The Latin words do not crop up frequently in Bede's text (the first two only appear once each). After this, he added some information on Northumbrian history, including a list of the kings from 547 to 737 (and it is this information that helps to date the manuscript). The final section of the page was copied later by a scribe in Continental Europe.

The small, slightly squished top three lines of the page today have an important place in English literary history. Those lines, reformatted as a poem, often appear in anthologies as one of the earliest pieces of English poetry and have been treated with a degree of reverence that the scribe might have been puzzled by.[8] The reason the scribe's awkward gloss has become so revered in modern times is because of a story told by Bede in the *Ecclesiastical History*.

In Book IV, Chapter 24, of his work, Bede tells us the story of the poet Cædmon, who was active around 670, which makes him the earliest named English poet. He was not – as we might perhaps expect – a famous author who lived in a royal court. He was not of noble birth, nor did he leave an important oeuvre behind him. Cædmon was a cowherd who lived at the abbey of Whitby in the north of England.[9] He was an ordinary man living in an extraordinary time: Christianity had only reached parts of Britain under a century ago. Bede tells us that Cædmon was one of the greatest poets of his age, although you wouldn't have guessed this from his early life. According to Bede, he was so shy about singing or speaking in public that when people began singing at social gatherings he would leave 'as soon as he saw the harp approaching him'.[10] Bede describes how, one night, Cædmon saw the harp being passed in his direction, and he sloped away. He went to the cattle byre ('stabula'), as it was his turn to take care of the animals that night. I picture him alone there, the sounds of laughter and song from the abbey drifting across the night air, with sounds of the low rustles and murmurs made by the cattle, their feet stamping the straw, Cædmon enjoying their gentle warmth. My image of the scene is undoubtedly coloured by Christmas carols, but the comparison was probably one Bede intended us to make – for a divine event would occur in the stable that night. He wanted us to see this as in some way akin to the Nativity. Bede tells us that Cædmon stretched himself out in the byre and went to sleep. As he slept he had a dream in which someone came to him and instructed him to sing: *canta mihi aliquid* ('sing something to me'). Cædmon protested that he was not able to sing, which is why he had left the feast. The visitor in his dream replied, 'Nevertheless you must sing to me.' 'What should I sing?' Cædmon asked, to which the messenger replied, 'Sing of the beginning of creation.' After this, Cædmon 'straightway began to sing verses to the praise of God the Creator, which he had never heard before'. Bede then gives a description of the song Cædmon sang, in a Latin paraphrase, at the end of which he cautions that 'this is the sense but not the order of the words which he sang as he slept. For it is not possible to translate verse, however well composed, literally from one language to another without some loss of beauty and dignity.' Although Bede was describing a miraculous event – the divine gift of sacred song to an illiterate cowherd – he probably did not think it was worth recording the vulgar, vernacular text of that song.

Bede goes on to tell us that, the following morning, Cædmon went to the steward (his monastic superior) and reported his dream. The steward took him to the abbess, Hild, who instructed that he be examined by 'learned men'. (This is one of the many ways that Bede subtly sidelines the contributions of women in the early English Church – it is only the authority of learned *men* that can affirm the miracle that

has occurred, despite the fact that Hild is the abbess.)[11] Bede
stresses that Cædmon 'had never learned anything of versify-
ing', noting that 'he did not learn the art of poetry from men,
neither was he taught by man, but by God's grace he received
the free gift of song'.[12] The learned men confirmed that the song
which Cædmon had received was indeed a gift from God. It
becomes clear that Cædmon was illiterate, because to test him
further the learned men 'expounded to him a passage of sacred
history or doctrine' (the implication being that he could not
read it for himself), and the next day he returned, having rendered it 'in most excellent verse'. At this, the abbess instructed
him to take monastic orders. Bede says that 'he giving ear to
all that he could learn, and bearing it in mind, and as it were
ruminating, like a clean animal, turned it into most harmonious verse'. Here Bede is figuring Cædmon as an ideal monastic
learner. Medieval monastics were encouraged to practice *ruminatio* when reading a text – that is, they were required to read
deeply, to chew over the words of what they had read (as we
saw with the ironic book-moth riddle in Chapter Two). In this
way, Bede makes the illiterate cowherd a fitting model for his
monastic readers. And the reference to the 'clean animal' subtly
reminds us of the humble origins of the saintly Cædmon who
received a revelation in the *stabula*.[13]

Bede's point, in his story about Cædmon, is that poetry
is transformational, mystical and God-given. The implication
of the story is that this is the 'moment the native (Germanic)
traditions of oral song-making are allied with the subject of
Christianity and harnessed for the faith'.[14] This is a conversion story that maps neatly onto Bede's larger story about the
establishment of the English Church. But for literary historians
today, the story is also a perfect foundation myth for English

literature, as Cædmon is the first named English poet. Distilled down to its basic parts, you could perhaps render this event as 'Long ago, in a stable, a miraculous genesis occurred, and written English poetry was born'. Except that the story is more complex than that.

Apart from Bede's account, almost nothing else of Cædmon is recorded. None of the marvellous songs he composed are extant. And the hymn that Cædmon sang in the cattle byre that night might only have survived in Bede's described form, as an echo of a text – had it not been for the scribes, who began adding an Old English version of the poem into the spaces around Bede's Latin text, like the scribe of the 'Moore Bede' (see above), who added the vernacular text in amongst some annals and a gloss for a few random Latin words. Another very early copy of the text is found in the 'St Petersburg Bede' (National Library of Russia, lat.Q.v.I.18). This manuscript is roughly contemporary with the 'Moore Bede', and it was also produced at Wearmouth-Jarrow – Bede's own monastery. In this manuscript a scribe has added Cædmon's *Hymn* to the space at the bottom of the folio containing the text describing his divine dream.

After the eighth century, many more scribes added the *Hymn* to the spaces in and around the Latin text of Bede's *Ecclesiastical History*. It survives in twenty-three manuscripts (dating from the eighth to the fifteenth centuries), in four main recensions – essentially branches of a single textual family tree.[15] There has been some debate about the nature of the different versions of this little poem. Some scholars have suggested that the added Old English texts were simply translations of the Latin – back-formations without any sense of Cædmon's original poem. But the scribes who copied the *Hymn* may have had access to something like the original vernacular poem. Were you to translate Bede's version of the *Hymn* into Old English, the version you would arrive at would be different from both the early marginal versions added to copies of Bede's Latin *Ecclesiastical History*, and the later version produced under the reign of King Alfred.[16] This suggests that the versions we have of the *Hymn* pre-date Bede's text – that they existed in some form before Bede came to write his *Ecclesiastical History*.

Cædmon has probably become famous today, in part, because he is one of the few vernacular authors from the early medieval period who has anything that approaches a life story. Bede told the story of Cædmon as evidence of a miracle, but for modern scholars its significance lies in the way it provides an identifiable authorial biography for such an early figure. And the text – in its different versions – has taken on a life of its own, appearing in anthologies as a kind of foundational text of English literature. But it is a problematic work: textually a little confusing, of uncertain genesis. How much is Bede's story to be trusted? To what extent can we truly say that the *Hymn* was authored by Cædmon?

In spite of all these difficulties, Cædmon's *Hymn* is a beautiful metaphor for what is ephemeral, for the importance of manuscripts as tangible witnesses to a lost literary past, and a reminder of how fragile that past is. And it feels appropriate that the vernacular version of the *Hymn* should have been recorded as it was – unobtrusively tucked into the spaces around the Latin text, not unlike the shy Cædmon himself, hiding from the harp.

'Marie's my Name, and I'm from France'

BL Harley MS 978 is a 'miscellany' manuscript – a concoction of poems, fables, musical and medical texts. It dates to the thirteenth century, and in it you can find a dialogue on falconry, a glossary of herbs, a recipe for improving eyesight, a legend relating to the parents of Thomas Becket, a poem on the Battle of Lewes in 1264, a selection of Goliardic verse (satirical Latin poetry produced predominantly by clerics in the twelfth and thirteenth centuries), and a famous early English song, 'Sumer is icumen in, Lhude sing cuccu' ('Summer is coming in, loudly sing, Cuckoo').[17] The diversity of the manuscript's texts is mirrored by the diversity of its languages. Here there are texts in Latin, English and Anglo-Norman (the language of the educated elite in England after the Norman Conquest of 1066). This rag-bag of material is not unusual for medieval manuscripts, which are often more like a modern bookshelf than a modern book – they might hold several, unrelated works together in a single place.

Forty folios into the manuscript, an explanatory rubric at the top of the page reads, 'Ici cumence le Ysope' ('Here begins the Aesop').[18] The text is in Anglo-Norman, and would appear to be a translation of Aesop's *Fables*. There is no indication of the author or translator's name, but the final lines of the text read:

> Al finement de cest escrit
> Que en romanz ai treité e dit
> Me numerai pur remembrance
> Marie ai num, si sui de France

> *To end these tales I've here narrated*
> *And into Romance tongue translated,*
> *I'll give my name, for memory:*
> *I am from France, my name's Marie* [19]

These words tell us that the text is the work of the earliest named female writer of secular literature in the European tradition: Marie de France – a shadowy figure, so her words must sound ironic to us. Although Marie names herself 'pur remembrance', very little can be gleaned about her apart from the assertion that 'Marie ai num, si sui de France'. Her dates are tentatively given as fl. (i.e. active) 1160–1215, and she is generally accepted to be the author of three works: the *Lais*, the *Fables*, and the *Espurgatoire de Seint Patriz* (*St Patrick's Purgatory*). The *Espurgatoire* is the story of an Irish knight's visit to the fabled site of an entranceway to Purgatory, presided over by that saint. The *Fables* are based loosely on the work of Aesop, while the *Lais* are a collection of short lays (or tales) about love, loss and *aventure*. (This word *aventure*, which occurs repeatedly, launching the action of the tales, has a rich semantic range, meaning a 'happening', 'event', or 'piece of good fortune', but also a 'misadventure' and 'vagary'.)[20] The only contemporary reference to Marie comes from an English monk, Denis Piramus, who refers to a 'Dame Marie' and her popular 'lays in verse', beloved of both men and women, which, he noted, were 'not all true'.[21] Although she was 'de France', Marie probably lived in England and wrote in Anglo-Norman. Her poetry reveals her to be highly educated – it appears she was fluent in Latin, Anglo-Norman, English and Breton. In the prologue of the *Lais* she writes that she has composed the work 'En l'honur de vus, nobles reis, / Ki tant estes pruz e curteis' ('In your honour, noble king, who are so brave and courteous').[22] Scholars have long speculated on who this 'noble king' might be, and it is sometimes assumed to be Henry II of England (reigned 1154–1189), but Marie leaves us guessing.

In the *Fables*, which are often pithy and drily witty, with flashes of cynicism, we see Marie refashion a misogynistic form and make it her own. She made use of a long Latin fable tradition but altered the texture of her source material.[23] In the *Fables* she 'raises women from a position of moral inferiority to one of greater equality'.[24] But some of the scribes who copied her text had other ideas. Many introduced new lines to her verse, giving the texts a misogynistic ring. She has a fable called 'Del lu e de la troie' ('The Wolf and the Sow'). It describes how one day a wolf came across a sow who was pregnant with piglets and about to give birth. The wolf tells the sow he wants her to give birth quickly so it can have her piglets. The sow responds:

'Sire, cument me hastereie?
Tant cum si pres de mei vus veie,
Ne me puis pas deliverer;
Tel hunte ai de vus esgarder.
Ne savez mie que ceo munte?
Tutes femeles unt grant hunte,
Si mains madles les deit tucher
A tel busuin ne aprismer!'

'My lord, how can you hurry me?
When you, so close to me I see,
I cannot bear my young outright;
I'm so ashamed when in your sight.
Do you not sense the implication?
All women suffer degradation

If male hands should dare to touch
At such a time, or even approach!' [25]

The wolf therefore retreats and the sow escapes, her piglets unharmed. Coming across a fable called the 'The Wolf and the Sow', we might expect a cunning wolf and a seemingly stupid pig. But the heavy, lumbering, pregnant sow is more than a match for the wolf, who thinks he can outwit her. Her quick thinking allows her to escape and protect her piglets, as she claims that to be seen or touched would make her unable to give birth. In Harley MS 978 – considered to be the best text of the *Fables* – the story ends with:

> Ceste essample deivent oïr
> Tutes femmes e retenir:
> Que pur sulement mentir
> Ne laissent lur enfanz perir! [26]

> *All women ought to hear this tale*
> *And should remember it as well:*
> *Merely to avoid a lie,*
> *They should not let their children die!*

Marie's point seems to be that a woman should not be afraid to lie if to do so will protect her children. However, the scribe of a fourteenth-century manuscript of the *Fables* in Cambridge University Library changed the line 'Que pur sulement mentir' ('Merely to avoid a lie') to 'Por soulement lor cors garist' ('Merely to protect themselves'), refashioning this story of a protective mother into a tale that suggests that mothers might prioritise their own safety over that of their offspring. [27] (This is only one example of a pattern of misogynistic refashioning that we see throughout the variant manuscripts of Marie's *Fables*.) [28]

It's intriguing to speculate on whether Marie knew how her work could be susceptible to change and co-option. In the epilogue to the *Fables* she writes:

> Put cel estre que clerc plusur
> Prendreient sur eus mun labur.
> Ne voil que nul sur li le die!
> E il fet que fol ki sei ublie!

> *It may be that several clerks*
> *Will claim this work as their own labour.*
> *I'll not have any make this claim:*
> *A fool is one who is forgotten!*[29]

It is as if she knew that 'clerks' would seek to claim her work and reframe it. But these words have an ironic tinge. Apart from a few small snippets of information in some of her texts, almost everything about Marie's life has been 'ublie' ('forgotten') and her work was indeed reclaimed and reinterpreted by scribes.

Probably the best manuscript of Marie's work is BL Harley 978, which is often used as the basis for editions of the *Lais* and the *Fables*. It is the only manuscript to contain both texts in one manuscript. It is especially important as a witness to the *Lais* – it is the only manuscript to contain all twelve of her *Lais*, which appear in an order that seems close to the original authorial arrangement, and it also contains an important verse prologue to the text. But in spite of its importance, it is still several removes from Marie herself. It was probably put together between 1261 and 1265, around fifty years after we believe she died, and was written by multiple scribes, apparently in Oxford. (It may be the product of professional book producers in that relatively new university town.)[30] There is a note in the manuscript that hints at its commissioner: it reads, 'Ord.li. W. de. Wint', which may be an abbreviation of 'Ordo libri William de Wint' ('The list of the books of William of Wint').[31] This note about 'William of Wint' has been identified in various ways by scholars. Some suggest it indicates that the book belonged to W[illiam?] of Wycombe (fl. c. 1275), a music copyist and Benedictine monk who composed polyphonic alleluia settings and held the position of precentor – the most senior musical position – at Leominster Priory, one of the dependencies of Reading Abbey. (Elsewhere there are clues that the manuscript belonged to Reading Abbey, probably in the 1260s, as it contains notes recording the death of some of its abbots).[32] This William may have composed the song 'Sumer is icumen in', which appears in the manuscript.[33] Some scholars suggest, however, that 'W. de. Wint' could equally be William of Winchester, who – like Wycombe – resided at Leominster Priory.[34] This other William has been called 'something of a latter-day Abelard'.[35] Like his twelfth-century French counterpart Abelard, William was accused of having an improper relationship, his Héloïse a certain Agnes of Avenbury, an Augustinian nun of Limebrook (nine miles north-west of Leominster). In 1282, Thomas de Cantilupe, Bishop of Hereford, lodged a formal complaint against William for scandalous misbehaviour. He failed to appear in court, sent a proxy, and was duly excommunicated and dismissed from office. Whichever of these two 'W. de. Wint' candidates it was (or indeed another), it is a great irony that we know more about these putative owners or commissioners than we do about the author of the *Lais* and the *Fables*, which appear uniquely alongside (but not adjacent to) each other in this manuscript.

Bede's story of Cædmon has the contours of a biography – a pleasing creation story that details the transformation of the pious cowherd into the divine poet. Yet all but one of Cædmon's texts are lost, and the versions of the *Hymn* that do survive have a complicated history. Marie de France is a different case – with her we have a body of texts, in which she carefully embeds her name to signal her authorship, but we have nothing of her biography that isn't conjecture, and her texts have been subjected to alteration by scribes.

In the prologue of her *Lais*, Marie writes:

> Ki Deu ad duné escïence
> E de parler bon' eloquence
> Ne s'en deit taisir ne celer,
> Ainz se deit volunters mustrer.[36]

> *Whomsoever God has given knowledge*
> *And the gift of speaking eloquently*
> *Must not keep silent or conceal the gift*
> *But must willingly display it.*

There is something almost tragic in these words, because the shadowy Marie had spoken up, did not conceal her gift, but almost everything of her life has been lost. And, over time, she receded from view – the best manuscript of her two most famous works dates to around fifty years after she died, while other versions of her works have often been altered by scribes with their own agendas. Happily, unlike some of the authors we will encounter in the next chapter, Marie's work has never completely disappeared from view. Her work was known to later figures, including Chaucer, and subsequently studied by antiquarians and historians. The shadowy Marie's 'gift' has not been completely obscured.

Geoffrey Chaucer (c. 1343–1400)

BL Royal MS 18 D II contains an image of an assembled group of men on horseback, in brightly coloured clothing. You may recognise the image in figure 37 and associate it with the pilgrims from *The Canterbury Tales* – Geoffrey Chaucer's most famous work. The late fourteenth-century *Tales* is a collection of stories held together by a framing device: it describes a group of thirty-one pilgrims who meet while travelling to the shrine of Thomas Becket in Canterbury. While at an inn at the start of the journey, the innkeeper suggests that to pass the time on their journey, they should each tell two tales to the assembled company on the journey there and the journey home. If you own an edition of the *Tales*, it may well have this image of the pilgrims on its cover. You might imagine, therefore, that the image comes from a manuscript of the *Tales*, but it doesn't. The manuscript dates from around fifty years after Chaucer died, and the image illustrates a poem called *The Siege of Thebes* by the fifteenth-century poet John Lydgate, who was a devoted follower of Chaucer. Lydgate's text has a framing device, like Chaucer's. In it, he imagines himself meeting Chaucer's pilgrims on the road to Canterbury and telling his own tale (about the struggle between the two sons of Oedipus for control of the city of Thebes) to pass the time on the road.

This image of the Canterbury pilgrims reflects a larger pattern. Today we often view Chaucer through the prism of later ages. He is frequently hailed as the 'father of English literature', but his place at the supposed head of the English literary canon owes much to the generation of poets who came after him, who created what one scholar has termed a kind of 'cult', in part as a way to advertise their own worth.[37] In positioning themselves as heirs to Chaucer's legacy, they vested themselves with literary power. Successive editors, antiquarians and collectors did much to cement Chaucer's position as a dearly loved author. And, in a very literal sense, we see him through the prism of later ages because it seems none of his manuscripts dates from his lifetime.[38] The Chaucer we know is 'the product of his fifteenth-century readers and writers'.[39]

This sits in stark contrast to the surviving documentary records relating to Chaucer's life, most of which was spent in the service of the Crown, which is why we know how much was paid in ransom for his release (£16) when he was taken prisoner in France in 1360, as well as the fact that he was accused of 'raptus' (possibly rape) in 1380 and that he was robbed on a highway in Deptford a decade later. And yet, of the nearly five hundred 'life-records' that survive relating to Chaucer, 'not a single one gives him the title of poet or links him with any kind of poetic activity'.[40]

Understanding Chaucer as a poet is made all the more difficult by the fact that several of his works are unfinished, and the manuscripts of his work often present messy versions of incomplete or divergent texts.[41] Of the seventeen surviving manuscripts of *Troilus and Criseyde* – his great exploration of love and loss set during the Trojan War – only two of them name him as the author of the poem.[42] Indeed, the word 'anonymous', used to describe a literary text, only appears in the sixteenth century.[43] Our age cares much more about authorship than Chaucer's did.

The Canterbury Tales was written towards the end of Chaucer's career and is probably his defining achievement. The poem is, however, apparently unfinished.[44] The manuscripts of the *Tales* often differ both in the number of pilgrims' tales they contain and their ordering. Although the poem survives in ninety-two manuscripts, of varying levels of completeness (some no more than fragments, others complete codices), no manuscript is in Chaucer's own hand.[45] A Google search for 'Chaucer' and 'manuscript' is likely to bring up images of a manuscript like the Ellesmere Manuscript held in the Huntington Library in San Marino, California. This manuscript is handsomely produced – its script is neat and upright, with elegant flourishes; it is decorated with fine border illumination and it has twenty-two images of the pilgrims in its borders, including an iconic one of Chaucer himself. Seeing the image of Chaucer, it would be wonderful to imagine this was a portrait of him taken from life and that the author had overseen the production of the manuscript, but this is not the case.[46] And, this expensive star item does not give a true impression of the manuscripts of the *Tales* – manuscripts which are as diverse, messy, surprising and delightful as the text of the *Tales* itself.

In 1924, the American scholars John Manly and Edith Rickert embarked on a project to examine all the manuscripts of the *Tales* and produce an authoritative edition of the text. (Rickert had earlier translated the *Lais* of Marie de France).[47] Hitherto all editions had used particular manuscripts rather than examining them all. What they probably hoped to find was a definitive manuscript – perhaps not Chaucer's own version, but something closely related to it. They envisaged that the project would last 'several years'.[48] In the end, it lasted for sixteen. Their work required them to identify and photograph all the manuscripts, research their provenance, transcribe the texts, and compare each textual variant, word for word. The variants were compared on 60,000 collation cards.[49] This sounds like a truly daunting task, but dealing with large bodies of complex information is something they had experience with from their time working as code breakers for the American War Department during the First World War. The eventual eight-volume work exacted a heavy toll on them both. Edith Rickert died a few months before the first volume of the edition was published, and Manly six months afterwards. (Predictably, Rickert's work was undervalued, as it still is today. In the introduction to the edition, Manly praised Rickert for having a 'woman's capacity for enormous drudgery', and to this day, Manly has an entry in the *Dictionary of American National Biography*, but Rickert does not.)[50]

Manly and Rickert's task was made all the more complicated by the fact that after Chaucer died, he was put to many uses. The scribes who copied his work prodded and poked him, squishing him into moulds and fashioning him in their own image. A small, unglamorous manuscript held in the British Library exemplifies how this process was enacted. BL Harley MS 2382 is a small paper manuscript, copied by a single unnamed scribe. Paper was, of course, a much cheaper writing material than parchment. The scribe wrote in a cramped cursive script (meaning the writing is speedily 'joined up'), and the manuscript as a whole is a plain old thing. Its only decoration is the occasional use of red ink (for the underlining of rubrics, running titles, and highlighting of the first letters of poetic stanzas). The manuscript contains several texts, which are split up over the codex and crammed into the available space. One text breaks off midway and is followed by a new text, before the scribe returned to copying the earlier one. The overall impression is one of economy and slightly haphazard planning.[51] Manly and Rickert suggested that this was 'a book which a country parson might have written for himself'.[52] It has been called 'a labour of love, evolving as the scribe worked on it'.[53] Throughout the manuscript, the texts are glossed with heavily abbreviated Latin annotation. This annotation is in a cramped and scrawled cursive script, which is difficult to decipher, which probably means that the scribe was producing this gloss either for himself or a group of readers who were similarly Latinate.

Unlike a showy parchment manuscript like the Ellesmere Manuscript, which may have been made for an elite patron, this manuscript appears to have been made by a scribe probably working in a provincial location, who was making the manuscript for himself or for circulation amongst a group of friends or acquaintances. It is different from Ellesmere not only in its cost and appearance, but also in the version of the text it contains. It is emphatically not a complete copy of the *Tales*, but instead is a devotional compilation of religious and moralising material, containing a number of saints' lives, devotional texts and miracle stories. In this collection there are two texts, labelled 'ffabula monialis de *sancta* maria' ('The fable of the nun of St Mary') and 'Vita Sancte Cecilie virginis' ('The life of St Cecilia the Virgin'). These two texts are in fact, two tales from *The Canterbury Tales* – the Prioress's Tale and the Second Nun's Tale.[54] What is striking is that nowhere is Chaucer named as the author of these tales, and they have been stripped from their original context in the *Tales* as a whole.[55]

These tales are unlikely to be the ones that people study at school today, in part because they are some of the most overtly religious of them. The Second Nun's Tale tells the tale of St Cecilia – a virgin martyred for her faith in a boiling bath, which she survives miraculously unharmed before ascending to heaven. (The Second Nun is not one of the pilgrims described in the Prologue of the *Tales*.) The Prioress's Tale is an altogether more disturbing story, set in a city in Asia that contains both a community of Christians and a community of Jews. A young Christian boy in the city grows up to revere the Virgin Mary; he sings the 'Alma Redemptoris Mater' ('Nurturing Mother of the Redeemer') every day, although he does not understand the words. Some Jews are incited by the devil 'that hath in Jues herte his waspes nest' ('that hath in Jews' heart his wasp's nest') to murder the boy and dump his body on a dunghill.[56] Later, the boy's body is found, still miraculously singing the 'Alma Redemptoris'. The boy's Jewish murderers are drawn by wild horses and hanged; the boy later dies.

The way the scribe has reframed the tales in this manuscript is problematic for modern readers. The scribe clearly admired the stories for their devotional content, annotating parts of the story that could be used as prayers. Modern scholars have often pointed to the frame of *The Canterbury Tales*, pointing out that this grim story is not spoken by the narrator of the poem as a whole – the story is instead told by the Prioress, who we understand to be a provincial person with an air of intellectual and courtly pretension. It seems we are being invited to see this disturbing story as a feature of the Prioress's ridiculous, small-minded view of the world. But in the way the scribe of Harley MS 2382 has stripped the tale out of its original context, the sense that this story is *ironic* has been lost. It becomes just a straightforwardly anti-Semitic story. What is striking about this manuscript is that in it we find a scribe selecting a very particular kind of Chaucer for his collection. Today, the Chaucer that we value is the writer of secular verse, a writer who is bawdy, witty, self-referential. But the scribe of Harley MS 2382 did not care for the Chaucer we would recognise. Instead, he wanted a sober, devout moraliser whose texts contain medieval tropes of anti-Semitism that today we find troubling. (Indeed, he did not even care to name Chaucer as the author of the poems he transcribed.) The manuscript makes clear that scribes were not always just mere copyists – many made important literary decisions.[57] As the scholar Michael Johnston observes, scribes were 'interpreters of literary texts and co-participants, along with authors, in the creation of meaning'.[58]

Early printed editions of Chaucer's work continued this trend, refashioning the texts to suit the agendas of editors. In 1532, William Thynne, a courtier and antiquarian, published the first 'complete' edition of Chaucer's works. For his second edition, in 1542, he included amongst the texts he attributed to Chaucer a work entitled 'The Complaint of the Plowman', which was written at the end of the fourteenth century by a Lollard author. (Lollardy was a heretical movement associated with the religious reformer John Wycliffe, who sought ecclesiastical reform, changes in sacramental practices, and access to the Bible in the vernacular. The heresy is sometimes seen as a proto-Protestant movement.) This spuriously appended tale sought to reframe Chaucer as a reformist, which likely satisfied the appetites of readers in post-Reformation England.

These two examples of Chaucer's work – one print, one manuscript – illustrate the way he has been refashioned for different audiences across time. Sometimes, however, while reading Chaucer's work, I sense he might almost have enjoyed the way his texts were altered. And maybe he wasn't too worried about the way several of his texts were left unfinished or came to be lost. His work seems to invite us to not take the idea of the author too seriously, and he was probably aware that his texts would be subject to alteration. His famous injunction to a scribe, Adam, which I quoted at the start of the previous chapter, is worth revisiting here:

> Adam scryveyn, if euer it þee byfalle
> Boece or Troylus for to wryten nuwe,
> Under þy long lokkes þowe most haue þe scalle,
> But affter my makyng þowe wryte more trewe;
> So ofte adaye I mot þy werk renuwe,
> It to correct and eke to rubbe and scrape,
> And al is thorughþy neglygence and rape.[59]

> *Adam scribe, it ever it falls to you*
> Boethius *or* Troilus *to write anew*
> *Under your long locks you must have the scale*
> *Unless you make my words more true*
> *So many a day I must your work renew,*
> *Correct it and also rub and scrape*
> *And all that is from your negligence and haste.*

As ever, Chaucer's tone is playful. The poem is also important because it seems to show that Chaucer was aware that his text was out of his hands and in the hands of someone else. It should be noted, however, that this little poem only survives in one manuscript from the medieval period, written between twenty-five and fifty years after Chaucer died, by a scribe named John Shirley. Shirley wrote chatty rubrics (snippets of introduction) at the start of the poems he copied, to supply his readers with information on their authorship and the circumstances of their creation. This poem appears with a rubric that reads,

'Chuauciers words a Geffrey vn to Adame his owen scryveyne' ('Chaucer's words, he Geoffrey, unto Adam his own scribe').[60] These rubrics are often assumed to be trustworthy, but Shirley seems to have copied his manuscripts for commercial purposes, apparently creating a little circulating library of manuscripts. The rubrics might be supplying biographical colour with only a pinch of truth – the ascription of the poem to Chaucer might be a marketing strategy, adding to the prestige of Shirley's collection.[61] This much beloved self-characterisation by Chaucer may not, in fact, be genuine. If the work is Chaucer's, then we can say that he showed an awareness of how his works could be altered by scribes; and if it isn't, then the text is itself emblematic of the problems of attribution and reliability that we encounter reading his work.

In Chaucer's work more generally, there is a playfulness in the way he presents himself and, indeed, the idea of authorial fame. His extraordinary dream-vision *The House of Fame* exemplifies this playfulness. In it, the narrator falls asleep and wakes in a temple made of glass where he finds a brass tablet depicting the story of Dido and Aeneas. The narrator steps outside the temple in the hope of working out where he is, only to be gathered up in the claws of a giant eagle. This eagle, who has been sent by Jupiter, addresses the narrator as 'Geffrey' (line 729) and teases him, telling him he is heavy to carry ('thou art noyous for to carye', line 574), and then chiding him for his habits:

> For when thy labour doon al ys,
> And hast mad alle thy rekenynges,
> In stede of reste and newe thynges
> Thou goost hom to thy hous anoon,
> And, also domb as any stoon,

Thou sittest at another book
Tyl fully daswed ys thy look.
And livest thus as an heremite
Although thyn abstynence is lyte.[62]

For when all your work is done
And you've done all your calculations,
Instead of rest and new business
You immediately go home
And, as completely dumb as any stone,
You sit at another book
Till fully dazed is thy look,
And so live like a hermit,
Though you practise little abstinence.

The eagle accuses 'Geffrey' of liking nothing more than to return home after a long day of 'rekenynges' than to sit down 'domb as any stoon' with yet another book and read until he looks 'daswed' ('dazed'). (This description of making 'rekenynges' is often understood to refer to Chaucer's job as 'comptroller' in the port of London, in which role he was responsible for the import and export taxes on wool, skins and leather.) 'Geffrey' appears to prefer the company of books to people, living 'thus as an heremite', but in another jibe at his weight, the eagle remarks that his 'abstynence is lyte'. These moments show Chaucer in a playful, self-mocking mode, blurring the boundaries between the narrator and his authorial persona. And unlike the injunction to Adam, there is no doubt about attribution. This playfulness is apparent throughout the poem, which is a wider reflection on the nature of authorial fame. The eagle takes Geffrey to the house of the goddess Fame. When he arrives, he sees it is built on top of a huge mound of ice on which are engraved the names of famous people, slowly melting away and becoming 'unfamous'.[63] Literary fame appears to be a fleeting thing.

Time and again, Chaucer asks us to think about what an author is, and suggests – perhaps – that we should not take them too seriously. And the scribes who copied his work, as well as the work of Marie de France, did indeed seek to reframe and refashion the words they copied, treating these authors with varying degrees of reverence. This contrasts with the scribes who copied Cædmon's *Hymn*, who seem to have had a certain reverence for that ephemeral, vernacular text – a reverence not shared by Bede, who only thought it worth recording in paraphrase.

Today we deify great authors from the past and are fascinated by their biographies. This modern fascination has complex origins, but we can see the seeds of it in the period immediately after Chaucer's death, when a generation of poets began to talk about him in gilded terms. John Lydgate (c. 1370–1450) referred to Chaucer in his *Fall of Princes* as 'my maistir [master] Chaucer' who was now 'ded, allas, cheeff poete off Breteyne' ('dead, alas, chief poet of Britain'). Lydgate exhorts his readers to 'lat us yiue hym laude & glory / And putte his name with poetis in memory' ('let us give him praise and glory / And memorialise his name with other poets').[64] In so doing, poets like Lydgate were strategically situating themselves within an important literary tradition, figuring themselves as heirs to the now-dead master poet. This deification of Chaucer was reflected in the work of *some* scribes – like John Shirley, who copied the poem purportedly addressed to the scribe, Adam. But other scribes seem to have been indifferent to the cult of the author, like the one who stripped out the Prioress's

Tale and the Second Nun's Tale for his devotional anthology and failed to attribute the works to Chaucer.

Chaucer is buried in Westminster Abbey, in what is now called 'Poets' Corner'. It was not called that in around 1400, when he was buried there. His body was placed in the abbey not because of his status as a poet, but because he had been a Clerk of Works of the Palace of Westminster. In 1556, the antiquarian Nicholas Brigham paid for the erection of a splendid tomb into which his remains were transferred. In 1599 the poet Edmund Spenser was buried nearby, and the tradition of Poets' Corner was born. Chaucer's tomb is a monument as much to him as it is to the way later ages have come to valorise 'the author'.

Today, we have a very particular idea about what an author looks like: we like single, identifiable figures, preferably with lives that we can read into their works. But medieval texts disrupt many of these notions. Many medieval texts have no authors, while others have multiple authors. And even when authors are identified, they may have no biography. And, perhaps most disruptive of all, the manuscripts that preserve medieval texts are complex, messy things, shaped by the whims, political ideologies, devotional feelings or nakedly commercial interests of the scribes who preserved them.

Chapter Seven

HIDDEN AUTHORS

The struggle of man against power is the struggle of memory against forgetting.

Milan Kundera [1]

In around the year 705, Aldhelm, Abbot of Malmesbury, dedicated a treatise to Abbess Hildelith and her nuns at Barking Abbey. The prologue of the work describes the lively correspondence Aldhelm had with the Barking community. He describes the 'rich verbal eloquence and the innocent expression of sophistication' which he finds in their letters. He imagines the abbess and her nuns 'roaming widely through the flowering fields of scripture' and 'scrutinising with careful application the hidden mysteries of the ancient laws'.[2] But Aldhelm's words have a tragic note. Only one side of the correspondence survives: the work of the nuns is lost.

To sift the remains of the past is to be aware of how much has been lost. As we saw in Chapter One, were it not for the discovery of Margery Kempe's *Book* in 1934, we would have lost a unique text – a work of openness and honesty, which describes the experiences of a non-elite woman from fifteenth-century

Lynn in Norfolk. And as we've seen elsewhere, manuscripts are susceptible to many dangers: fire, flood and unthinking book-worms (which the Exeter Book vividly describes as *stælgastas* – 'stealing-guests'). But in some cases, material does not survive for ideological reasons. Most of history is, after all, a story written by the powerful. Certain voices have been excluded and erased from the literary canon and the historical record. This chapter is about some of those voices nearly silenced, and biographies nearly or completely lost.

Much of the discussion in previous chapters has focused on single manuscripts. Here, by contrast, the sources on the female authors in this chapter are spread across several codices. Recovering something of their lives is an exercise in uniting fragments (not unlike the burnt fragments of the Cotton Library that fluttered in the breeze on the day after the fire at Ashburnham House). We are reliant on scraps of information – brief references and partial and corrupted textual witnesses. This is a chapter devoted not so much to single, monolithic manuscripts, but to the gaps between them, and to the ghosts of those we have lost.

Searching for the Earliest English Women Writers

At some point between 776 and 786, an English nun in the Bavarian monastery of Heidenheim hid a secret code in the space between two texts. Here the lines over the words indicate abbreviations. Transcribed as it appears on the folio, this reads:

Secdgquãr. quĩn. nprĩ. sprĩx quãr. ntẽr.

cprĩ. nquãr. mtẽr. nsẽcun. hquĩn. gsẽcd

bquĩnrc. quãrr. dinando hsẽcdc. scrtẽr.

bsẽcd. bprĩm

With the expansion of the abbreviations, the text reads:

Secundumgquartum. quintum. nprimum.
sprimumx quartum. ntertium
cprimum. nquartum. mtertium. nsecundum.
hquintum. gsecundum
bquintumrc. quartumr. dinando hsecundumc.
scrtertium.
bsecundum. bprimumm

This code was not deciphered for some 1,200 years, until – in 1931 – the scholar Bernard Bischoff untangled it. He realised that the code-writer had replaced all the vowels with abbreviations for ordinal numbers – so for example, 'Secd' stood for 'secundum' ['second'], meaning the second vowel, *e*. The code can be cracked as follows, with the words in italic indicating vowels:

Secundum g *quartum. quintum.* n *primum.*
s *primum* x *quartum.* n *tertium*
c *primum.* n *quartum.* m *tertium.* n *secundum.*
h *quintum.* g *secundum*
b *quintum* rc. *quartum* r. dinando h *secundum* c.
scr *tertium.*
b *secundum.* b *primum* m

Which gives us: *Ego una saxonica nomine Hugeburc ordinando hec scribebam.* This translates as, 'I, a Saxon nun named

Hugeburc, composed this.'[3] This Hugeberc was the author of both texts – accounts of the lives of Saints Wynnebald and Willibald – but had left them anonymous, describing herself at the start of one as no more than an 'indigna Saxonica' ('unworthy Saxon woman'). She was a missionary who travelled from England to Germany to assist Bishop Boniface in his proselytising work in the region. The survival of her work is startling – an early copy of the text from c. 800 is held in Munich (Bayerische Staatsbibliothek, MS Clm 1086).[4] I like to think she stitched this code into the space between the texts because she had some inkling of the way authors' names were often lost in manuscript transmission. When manuscripts were copied, there was no guarantee that an author's name would survive copying and re-copying, especially if that name was a female name. As the scholar Diane Watt observes:

> Medieval texts most often circulated anonymously, or were ascribed or re-ascribed (regardless of who actually wrote them) to renowned figures from the past, who were almost invariably male. No matter how powerful they were in religious or political terms, medieval women were perceived by others – and perceived by themselves – as lacking the authority to be described as authors.[5]

The word 'author' is a cousin of the word 'authority', and in the Middle Ages, authors were called *auctores*. An *auctor* was thought to have *auctoritas* (authority): in 'a literary context, the term *auctor* denoted someone who was at once a writer and an authority, someone not merely to be read but also to be respected and believed'.[6] Watt's point is that women were often deemed not to have the *auctoritas* that would make their texts worthy of preservation. It was only because she embedded a clue to her identity in a cipher between two of her texts that Hugeberc's name survives. But 'nothing else is known of her except the sketchy information given in her writings'.[7]

Hugeberc's texts are something of an exception. A number of anonymous works survive from the medieval period which are clearly female-voiced, and it's possible that some of them were written by women whose names have been erased, whether by accident or design. The Exeter Book – a tenth-century manuscript collection of poems in Old English, which we met in Chapter Two – contains two female-voiced elegies (the feminine grammatical endings indicating that the speaker is female). These texts have no title in the manuscript, but came to be titled 'Wulf and Eadwacer' and 'The Wife's Lament' by editors.[8] They are complex works that invite multiple interpretations. The poems appear in the manuscript alongside a section of riddles – and this placement may be intentional: they are tiny, emotional riddles that describe the pain of loss. Both poems describe their narrators being separated from loved ones. Yet who these loved ones are, and why they are separated, has elicited much scholarly debate, in part because both poems use dense, polysemous language (in the opening line of 'Wulf and Eadwacer', for example, we find the Old English word *lac*, which can mean 'battle', 'sacrifice' or 'gift' – each translation lending a different meaning to the line). 'The Wife's Lament' appears to describe a woman who is separated from a lover, or husband, who had earlier set out over the 'tossing waves'. After his departure, she was made an outcast by her beloved's kin, forced to live under an oak tree in an *eorðscræfe* ('earth-cave') amid dark valleys tangled with briars, where she meditates on all she has lost.

In 'Wulf and Eadwacer' the speaker is separated from 'Wulf', whom she addresses as 'Wulf min [my] Wulf'. The identity of this Wulf remains unclear, though we are told that he goes on long journeys and that the rarity of his visits has made the speaker ill. The speaker is on an island, guarded by 'blood-thirsty men'. In the final lines of the poem she asks, 'Gehyrest þu, Eadwacer?' ('Do you hear me, Eadwacer?'). *Eadwacer* literally means 'property-watcher': it could be a name, or it could be a nickname. Is this the woman's husband, who is set up in opposition to the lover, Wulf? Or is it the same person as Wulf, who could be her husband? Or is Wulf her child? The poem ends, enigmatically, 'þæt mon eaþe tosliteð þætte næfre gesomnad wæs, / uncer giedd geador' ('that may be easily separated which was never bound, / the song of us both together'). Can we say these texts were authored by women? It's impossible to say so conclusively, and we have to be wary that the definition of 'author' in this context is a slippery one. These vernacular texts likely circulated orally for some time before they were copied down, perhaps centuries later, in a very different cultural context – likely by monastic scribes. And authorship in the pre-modern period was often collaborative, and texts were altered over time by scribes and revisers.

The Voices of Enclosed Women

The female-voiced elegies of the Exeter Book encapsulate many of the difficulties inherent in searching for women's writing and female authors in the pre-modern period. We can make educated guesses on the authorship of texts, but often lack definitive proof. And the nature of authorship itself, as we saw in the previous chapter, is complicated. These problems also beset a group of texts produced in the West Midlands region of England, in the thirteenth century.

'Mi druð, mi derling, mi drihtin, mi healend, mi huniter, mi haliwei, swetter is munegunge of þe þen mildeu o muðe' ('My dear, my darling, my lord, my saviour, my honey-drop, my balm, sweeter is the memory of you than honey in the mouth').[9] These are the opening lines of a meditation appearing uniquely in a British Library manuscript from the thirteenth century. The narrator is a woman: 'yif that I wile ani mon for feirnesse luve, luve I wile the, mi leve lif' ('if I will love any man for beauty, I will love you, my dear life').[10] The prayer is anonymous, but it's not unreasonable to assume it was written by a woman. It is a work of passionate love and longing, which describes Jesus as 'mi lives luve, min herte-swetnesse' ('my life's love, my heart's sweetness').[11] In the meditation the speaker compares Christ to different kinds of worldly men – men famed for their nobility, virtue, largesse, wit, power, honour or beauty. Each worldly virtue is itemised, and each time the speaker concludes that such men are no match for Christ, with the refrain, 'A, Jesu, swete Jesu, leove that te luve of the beo al mi likinge' ('Ah, Jesus, sweet Jesus, grant that love of you be all my pleasure').[12] These are words of romantic love: 'A, swete Jesu, thu oppnes me thin herte for to cnawe witerliche and in to reden trewe luve-lettres, for ther I mai openlich seo hu muchel thu me luvedes'.[13] ('Ah! sweet Jesus, you open your heart to me, so that I may know it inwardly, and read inside it true love-letters; for there I may see openly how much you loved me.')[14] The language throughout is quasi-sexual: 'hwen thu for me swa rewliche hengedes on rode, ne hafdes in al this world hwerwith that blisfule blodi bodi thu mihtes hule and huide' ('when you so pitifully hung for me on the cross, in all this world you had nothing with which to cover and hide that blessed bloody body').[15] The focus on the physical body of Christ is striking. Contemplating Christ on the cross, the speaker says, 'A, that luvelike bodi that henges swa rewli, swa bodi, and swa kalde' ('Ah! that lovely body, that hangs so pitifully, so bloody and so cold').[16] The text is written in a sing-song alliterative style. Some of the best alliteration comes in pairs and triplets, such as 'blisfule blodi bodi' and 'hule and huide'.

At the end of the text, the speaker says, 'Broht tu haves me fra the world to bur of thi burthe, steked me i chaumbre'[17] ('You have brought me from the world to the bower of your birth, locked me in a chamber').[18] And, a little later: 'mi bodi henge with thi bodi neiled o rode, sperred querfaste withinne fowr wahes, and henge I wile with the and neaver mare of mi rode cume til that I deie'[19] ('my body will hang with your body, nailed on the cross, fastened, transfixed within four walls. And I will hang with you and nevermore come from my cross until I die').[20] This reference to being locked in a chamber – figured as a cross – is one of several indications that the speaker of the text is an anchoress. An anchoress ('anchorite' is the male form) was a person who permanently enclosed herself in a cell to live a life of prayer and contemplation. The word comes from the Greek ἀναχωρεῖν (anachorein), meaning 'to retire or retreat'. In the Middle Ages in England, as elsewhere in Europe, the practice was relatively widespread – there were around a hundred recluses across the country in the twelfth century and by the thirteenth century this figure swelled to two hundred. Strikingly, women outnumbered men in this vocation. There were around three times as many female recluses in the thirteenth century and twice as many in the fourteenth and fifteenth centuries.[21] Anchoritism emerged in the late eleventh century in tandem with a monastic reform movement and a growth in spiritual enthusiasm which has been dubbed the 'Medieval Reformation'.

The narrator of the meditation, called Þe Wohunge of Our Lauerd (The Wooing of Our Lord), is evidently an anchoress, but it is also possible that it was authored by an anchoress. The text appears in a manuscript alongside several texts associated with a group of anchoresses who lived in the West Midlands region of England in the thirteenth century. These texts are all written in a distinctive style, sharing similarities of dialect, theme and imagery. The longest of them is a haunting work known as the Ancrene Wisse (Anchoress's Guide).[22] This anonymous work, likely written by a Dominican friar, is addressed to three sisters. The author tells them, 'You are much talked about, what well-bred women you are, sought after by many for your goodness and your generosity, and sisters from one father and one mother, [who] in the bloom of your youth renounced all the joys of the world and became anchoresses.'[23] (It is clear that they were genetic sisters, not spiritual ones.) Although the text is addressed to the three sisters, soon after it was composed, it was modified in a later manuscript so that it was addressed to 'the anchoresses of England, in such a large group twenty now or more'.

Between 1225 and 1250, the text was copied at least five times into manuscripts that were probably produced for anchoresses. Alongside the Ancrene Wisse, the scribes also added other texts suitable for the edification and instruction of an anchoritic audience. These texts – appearing in different combinations across a key group of manuscripts – included female saints' lives, a text on the values of virginity, and a series of meditations. One of these meditations is the *Þe Wohunge of Our Lauerd*. We know nothing of the group of anchoresses associated with these texts. We have no names or biographies or knowledge of when exactly they lived and died. Even the three sisters to whom the *Ancrene Wisse* is addressed are anonymous, despite the fact that the text was popular. (It survives in nine manuscripts.) But we can get a sense of their lives and the life of the possible author of *Þe Wohunge* from the extensive body of advisory literature produced for anchoresses throughout the medieval period in England.

Life as an anchoress began with a death. The liturgy of the enclosure ritual is theatrically macabre. In places it is indistinguishable from a funeral service; once enclosed, a recluse was dead to the world. When the moment for the enclosure arrived the *recludendus* (would-be recluse) would process with the celebrant, choir and others out of the church and into the graveyard, as the choir sang 'In paradisum deducant te angeli' ('May angels lead you to paradise') – usually sung when a body was conveyed to a grave. The procession would travel to the cell built onto the side of the church, usually – in England – on the north side, where the wind was most biting and the least sun shone. Some *ordines* ('liturgical directions') state that the *recludendus* should pause at the opening of the cell and the bishop should say, 'Si vult intrare, intret' ('If he/she wishes to go, then allow him/her to go in').[24] An antiphon drawn from the Book of Tobias was sung, concluding with 'Be of good courage, thy desire from God is at hand.' Upon entering, the *recludendus* would climb inside a grave dug inside their cell. Lying in this grave, they were sprinkled with earth – ashes to ashes; dust to dust – as the antiphon 'De terra plasmasti me' ('You have created me from earth') was sung, and the door of the cell was bolted. Once inside, they were be to enclosed for the rest of their lives. A thirteenth-century record for a church in Frodsham, in Cheshire, shows that an anchoress named Wymark was enclosed there for around fifty years.[25]

It was not only during the moment of enclosure that anchorites were invited to meditate on their death to the world. The *Ancrene Wisse* instructs that this grave should be daily enlarged, that recluses should use their bare hands to 'scrape up the earth every day from the grave in which they will rot'.[26] The text also prescribes the daily recitation of two psalms from the Office of the Dead, noting elsewhere that there is no difference between 'a smiret ancre' ('anointed anchoress') and an 'ancre biburiet' ('buried anchoress'), because 'hwet is ancre-hus bute hire burinesse?' ('what is an anchorhold but her grave?').[27] It was not uncommon for anchoresses to be buried in their cells after they died. At St Anne's in Lewes, an anchoress was buried in a grave positioned in the exact place where she would have knelt at a small window in order to see the high altar, meaning 'she would have had to kneel daily in her own grave'.[28]

A would-be anchoress would have had to apply to her local bishop in order to be enclosed. Her application had to demonstrate that she was of good character, suited to the contemplative life and also that she was of independent financial means or had a patron or patrons. Recent scholarly work on anchoritic patronage has shown that anchorites were supported by people from almost every level of society.[29] And this patronage could take various forms. Wills and household accounts reveal that often it was money that was bequeathed. In other cases, it was gifts of bread or books. In 1435, William Fylham, Canon of Exeter Cathedral, left 'three canonical loaves' per week, for a year, to an anchorite at the church of St Leonard.[30]

A decade earlier, Thomas Dunham, rector of Little Torrington, left twenty shillings and 'a book of Sunday sermons written in English' to an anchoress in Exeter named Alice.[31]

Anchoresses were required to remain in their cells (on average twelve feet square). The cells typically had three windows. One, known as the 'squint', opened onto the church's sanctuary, another onto the graveyard or street, and a third onto a servants' parlour. Recluses were tended to by a servant, or sometimes two, who brought them food and took away waste through the window. Some had access to walled gardens or adjoining rooms, but most remained inside a single room. When not in use, their windows were covered by a thick black curtain. They were encouraged to fast frequently and to maintain silence as much as possible, resorting to sign language if necessary. Even sleep was seen as an unnecessary luxury. The thirteenth-century *Walter's Rule* says that recluses should vary where they sleep in their cells – sometimes sleeping standing up, and sometimes on the floor. They are advised to sleep on nothing softer than a rush mat and use their arm in lieu of a pillow. This was a life of sensory deprivation, with limited light, fresh air, conversation, laughter or touch. The squint became a conduit of sensation. If their parlour window was covered by a curtain, the light from candles on the altar, glimpsed through the squint, might at times be the only source of illumination. And through it they might hear the sounds of the sung liturgy, smell incense and, importantly, receive the Eucharist. I imagine they got used to their own smell. *Walter's Rule* says that a recluse should shake out their clothes 'when required', but says nothing about washing.

Their contact with the outside world was limited. They might receive visitors at their windows, and it seems their counsel was often sought, but several texts exhibit concern for what such visits might entail. The thirteenth-century *Dublin Rule* recommends that before speaking to a visitor the recluse should cross themselves upon their mouth and not look too long on the face of their visitor lest they be tempted to some kind of sin by the encounter.[32] Walter Hilton's *Scale of Perfection*, which was addressed to an anchoress, advises her to receive visitors with grace and humility, offering them words of comfort. But should their talk turn to idle chatter, she should 'give little answer', and if the visitor is a man of the Church, she must only ask questions and never instruct him for 'it is not your place to teach a priest'.[33]

The *Ancrene Wisse* prescribes a life of privation predicated on the idea that the recluses were inherently sinful creatures. They were forbidden to touch anyone from the moment of their enclosure. It stipulates a virginity so totalising that even the intrusion of a person's hand into the anchoritic cell was a sinful penetration. The anchoresses' bodies became one with the cell, and being one with the cell, became organs of the church that could be controlled and contained. Their life was regulated by bizarre restrictions, which included crossing the legs, affecting a lisp, arching the eyebrows with moistened fingers, certain kinds of embroidery, owning gloves, wearing pleated garments and writing without the permission of the confessor. They also had to seek permission to wear a belt made of 'irn' (iron) or 'here' (hair) or 'ilespiles felles' (hedgehog skins). The text says that the anchoress should 'ne beate hire þer-wið, ne wið scurge ileadet, wið holin ne wið breres, ne biblodgi hire-seolf ne binetli hire, ne ne beate biuoren, ne na keoruunge ne keorue' ('not beat herself with them, or with a scourge weighted with lead, with holly or with brambles, or draw blood. She should not sting herself anywhere with nettles, or scourge the front of her body, mutilate herself with cuts').[34] These self-inflicted tortures are like treats to be rationed, and permissible only with authorisation. Bodily mortification was seen as a form of *imitatio Christi* – a way to experience Christ's suffering and thereby commune with him. Anchoresses were thought to be mystically married to Christ.

Knowing what we know about the realities of the enclosed way of life, reading *Þe Wohunge* and the other texts associated with it pulls us in different directions. The texts are beautiful – richly allegorical works, full of sonorous language and rhetorical flourish. They are 'written with unexpected skill and elegance' at a time when great works of literature were generally written in Anglo-Norman (the language of the educated elite in post-Conquest England) and not English – their style is redolent of the rhythms and patterns of Old English literature.[35] Reading them, we feel a thrill at their artistry, but the lives of their intended audience can crush the delight we take in the texts. The *Ancrene Wisse*, like *Þe Wohunge*, is a sensuous reading experience. It is written in rhythmic, alliterative language. Like *Þe Wohunge*, some of its best alliteration comes in pairs, such as – below – 'swete ant swote' or 'woh of word':

> Mine leoue sustren, alswa as ȝe witeð wel ower wittes utewið, alswa ouer alle þing lokið þet ȝe beon inwið softe ant milde ant eadmode, swete ant swote iheortet, ant þolemode aȝein woh of word.[36]
>
> *My dear sisters, just as you guard your senses well outwardly, see to it above all that you are kind inwardly, even-tempered*

and modest, gentle and good-hearted, and patient with offen-sive remarks that are made to you.

The text's imagery is rich, allegorical and unforgettable. Its rhythmic language delights the ear and contorts the tongue of those who read it aloud. In other words, it glories in its own aesthetic, revels in its own sound and sense. In one passage, the author – always alive to sonic play – riffs on the dual meaning of the Middle English word *ancre*, meaning 'anchoress', and also 'anchor':

> For-þi is ancre 'ancre' icleopet, ant under chirche iancret as ancre under schipes bord forte halden þet schip, þet uþen ant stormes hit ne ouerwarpen. Alswa al Hali Chirche (þet is schip icleopet) schal ancrin o þe ancre, þet heo hit swa halde þet te deofles puffes, þet beoð temptatiuns, ne hit ouerwarpen.

> *The anchoress is called an 'anchor', and anchored under the church like an anchor under the side of a ship to hold the ship, so that waves and storms do not capsize it. Just so, all Holy Church (which is described as a ship) should anchor on the anchoress, for her to hold it so that the devil's blasts, which are temptations, do not blow it over.*[37]

This is a rhetorical pirouette – playing on the different meanings of the 'ancre', but also of the 'chirch' as both the physical building of the parish church, but also the global Church. It moves from particular, local detail (an anchor, a church building) to the cosmic battle between good and evil. The language makes the tongue take several trips: the *cr-*, *cl-*, *ch-* and *sh-* sounds half-echo each other while the repetition of 'ouerwarpen' loops the sentences together.

The use of allegory here is typical of the text. The author is fond of animal and bird allegories in particular, describing the angry anchoress as a pelican that kills its own chicks (figured as good works) with the beak of sharp anger.[38] In Part 4, he warns against the lion of pride, serpent of envy, the bear of sloth, the rhinoceros of wrath, the sow of gluttony and the scorpion of lechery. Each beast has offspring which are varieties of the sins. The sow's piglets have names like 'To Frechliche' (Too Greedily) and 'To Ofte' (Too Often).[39] You can't forget the snouting, scuttling, slithering, slouching creatures of this sermon.

The *Wisse*'s tone is also unsettling to us. Read one way, it is veined with hatred of women, but it is also a work suffused with love: 'Godd hit wat as me were muche deale leouere þet Ich isehe ow alle þreo, mine leoue sustren, wummen me leouest, hongin on a gibet forte wiðbuhe sunne' ('God knows I would rather see all three of you, my dear sisters, women dearest to me, hanging from a gibbet in order to avoid sin').[40] These words are intimate, affectionate: 'mine leoue sustren, wummen me leouest', but the image of three sisters hanging from a gallows sticks in the mind.

To understand these texts takes a tremendous intellectual leap. It is difficult for twenty-first-century readers to inhabit the thought-world of the anchoress. But, for those women, enclosing themselves was an act of love. *Þe Wohunge* is plainly a work of love: 'A, Jesu, swete Jesu, leve that te luve of the beo al mi likinge' ('Ah, Jesus, sweet Jesus, grant that love of you be all my pleasure').[41] And the *Ancrene Wisse* is also filled with the imagery of love. There is a famous passage about a lady who lives in a castle beset by enemies. A powerful king comes to her aid, giving her protection and showering her with gifts. She treats him with contempt. He visits her, he is 'of alle men feherest to bihalden' ('the handsomest of all men in appearance'), speaks tenderly to her, offers to make her his queen.[42] She continues to treat him with contempt. He tells her that she is in mortal danger, that she will be captured and put to a shameful death. He vows that he will die to protect her. He does, in an act of great sacrifice. It could be the plot of a romantic novel, except that the king is a metaphor for Christ.

We cannot be sure if Þe Wohunge was written by an anchoress. The idea first emerged in the nineteenth century and was given currency in 1958, when the scholar Meredith Thompson agreed with an earlier scholar that the text had a 'preponderance of enthusiasm and fantasy over thought', which he felt indicated that its author was female.[43] Some more recent scholars have argued that the work wasn't written by an anchoress, claiming that anchoresses were required to practise a 'strenuous passivity' which would have precluded them from writing.[44] This is hard to assess. In their cells, anchoresses followed a regime of prayer. When they were not praying, guidance literature advises that they should occupy themselves with reading, writing or activities suitable to the enclosed life, like mending church vestments or making cloth. The fifteenth-century Speculum Inclusorum (Mirror for Recluses) instructs that the moment a recluse's 'taste for prayer or delight in meditation decreases' they should 'immediately' read or perform some kind of manual work.[45] If they were unable to read Latin, they are advised to read in English, French or their vernacular language. One manuscript of this work, specifically addressed to a female audience, advises recluses that they should engage in the 'writyng of holy and edificatif thynges of deuocyoun' ('writing of holy and edifying things of devotion').[46] The Speculum is from around two centuries after Þe Wohunge, but it does not seem unreasonable to imagine that writing works of devotion could have formed a part of the anchoress's regime of prayer and contemplative activity.

Reading the *Ancrene Wisse* and *Þe Wohunge* side by side is complex. The *Ancrene Wisse* is a didactic work, written by a male author, which prescribes a life of extreme privation for its female addressees. I am sure that the author thought he was writing something that would offer kindly instruction to the three sisters, ensuring their eternal salvation. *Þe Wohunge* is likely a female-authored work – a work of passionate love and longing, which suggests a wholehearted desire to be enclosed in the confines of a dark cell. Or – more troublingly – might *Þe Wohunge* be the work of a man, imposing a vision of the cell as the 'bower of Christ' on its addressee? I confess I want it to be the former, I want the work to be authored by an anchoress. So little survives of the women associated with these texts. Even the names of the original three sisters to whom the *Ancrene Wisse* is addressed are not recorded. All we have of these women are the texts composed to regulate their lives.

If the text was written by an anchoress, we are able to glean a few details about the kind of person she might have been. The addressees of the *Ancrene Wisse* appear to have been from a well-to-do gentry family. Some recluses may have been of humble origin and there are accounts of aristocratic women being enclosed, but many seem to have been from the burgess and gentry class. They had a male patron. The text says they have 'no worries about food or clothing, either for yourselves or for your maids'. They have 'from one friend all that she needs' who will hand out provisions to their maids 'at his hall'.[47] I've sometimes wondered if the three sisters' patron was their father, brother or another family member. I suspect they left their family – such as it was – behind. Perhaps they had no immediate family left. There are several accounts of women becoming enclosed in widowhood.[48] Grief could drive you to seek a living death.

The original three sisters may have been enclosed together – there are accounts of anchorites sharing cells, but I sense it is unlikely.[49] The text states that the permission of the confessor must be sought before an anchoress may receive visits from friends or relations. A later version of the text says, 'Tendre of cun ne limpeð nawt ancre beonne' ('An anchoress ought not to be too attached to her family').[50] With 'the door of their cell bolted and the window covered with a black curtain, they lived as if at the gates of heaven.'[51]

From my own twenty-first-century prespective I struggle to understand the possible author of Þe Wohunge. What might have made her want to rend her own skin with a lead whip? Why might she have desired to get inside her own coffin for decades? Sometimes I think that the three sisters for whom the Ancrene Wisse was written were trapped in an abusive relationship with Christ. But their choices look more reasoned when you consider that becoming an anchoress was a way of avoiding the dangers of childbirth and the misery of a forced marriage. And to be an anchoress was to gain a position of authority and social standing. Margery Kempe – most boisterous of the late medieval English mystics, whom we met in Chapter One – describes how she sought the counsel of the anchoress Julian of Norwich, spending 'many days' with her – which likely means she visited Julian at the window of her cell over several days. (What Julian felt about this is unrecorded.)[52] In an all-male church, Julian's position was unusual. It is no small irony that one of the few ways women could achieve autonomy and social standing in this period was by imprisoning themselves.

The *Revelations* of Julian of Norwich (c. 1342–c. 1416)

There is only one text from medieval England that we are sure was written by an anchoress: Julian of Norwich's *Revelations*. On 8 May 1373, Julian lay in bed, believing that she was shortly going to die.[53] She had been ill for six nights. On the fourth night her condition had worsened and she had received the last rites, but somehow had 'lingered on' for another three days. On the morning of the seventh day, when she was dead to sensation from the waist down, she felt a desire to sit up in bed so as 'to have the mare fredome of my herte to be atte Goddes wille' ('to give my heart more freedom to be at God's disposition').[54] Those who were gathered around her bed sent for the priest, who came with his assistant. When he arrived, she was no longer able to speak and her eyes were fixed in a stare. To offer her comfort, the curate held a crucifix out in front of her. At this point her sight failed her and the room grew dim. It seemed to her that night had fallen, but the cross in front of her appeared illuminated like a household light. Everything around it was hallucinogenic terror – the room was full of fiends. She felt the upper part of her body begin to die. Her hands fell down at her side, her head lolled to one side, her neck no longer able to support it. And then, suddenly, all pain left her. At this moment, Julian experienced a series of fifteen extraordinary visions of God. Thereafter she recovered from her illness and lived for around another forty years.

Soon after this terrifying deathbed experience, Julian composed a text which described these visions. It is the first work in English that we can be sure was authored by a woman. It is known as the 'Short Text' of her *Revelations of Divine Love*.[55]

Over the next twenty years, however, Julian meditated on the meaning of her experiences and produced a longer version of this account. In the longer version we have a sense that she has *read* 'her memories of these showings [as she termed them] over and over again, as if they formed a treasured book'.[56] The 'Long Text' represents Julian's transition from visionary to learned theologian.

At some point after the events of 1373, Julian decided to become enclosed as an anchoress at St Julian's Church in Norwich. Little can be gleaned of her life before this point. Some have suggested she may have been a nun beforehand, but in her description of her deathbed terrors, she describes how 'My modere that stode emangys othere and behelde me, lyftyd uppe hir hande before me face to lokke myn eyen, for sche wenyd I had bene dede or els I hadde dyede' ('My mother who was standing with the others watching me, lifted her hand up to my face to close my eyes for she thought I was already dead or else I had that moment died').[57] This account of her imagined final moments, surrounded by people, including her mother, suggests she was not – at that point – part of a monastic order. A compelling suggestion is that she composed the 'Short Text' as part of her application for enclosure.[58] Whether it was part of the application or not, her application was approved. Bequests made to her show that she was an anchoress for at least twenty years, if not more.[59] The exact date of her death is unknown.

Julian's text (in its two versions) is important not simply because it is the first in English definitively authored by a woman, but also because she was a writer of exceptional quality. Her prose is characterised by its elegant rhetorical structure, but in spite of this it never feels scholarly or obtuse: instead it is a work of clarity and empathy. Many of her metaphors are domestic and familiar despite the gap of centuries between her age and ours. Even when describing divine revelations, she uses an accessible register. In a vision of the blood running from Christ's crown of thorns, Julian writes that the droplets were as plentiful as 'the dropys of water that fallen of the evys after a great showre of reyne' ('the drops of water which fall from the eaves after a great shower of rain'), and adds 'for the roundhede, it were like to the scale of heryng in the spreadeing on the forehead' ('as for the roundness of the drops, they were like herring scales as they spread on the forehead').[60] Later, when she is describing how she saw the devil's face, she says the 'color was rede like the tilestone whan it is new brent, with blak spots therin like blak freknes, fouler than the tilestone' ('the colour was red like newly fired tiles, with black spots on it like black freckles, fouler than the tiles themselves').[61] In these comparisons we imagine something of Julian's experience, living in the busy trading and manufacturing city of Norwich. Herrings would have formed a staple of the diet of her hometown – probably landed at somewhere like Yarmouth and brought along the River Wensum to the city. Her cell was nestled in a 'highly industrial location near the busy quays of King Street Conesford'.[62]

These images are also homely – 'homely' in the British sense of the word, as something domestic and familiar. Indeed 'homely' is a word Julian uses often to describe what she sees as the intimate love of God for humankind:

In this same time oure Lord shewed to me a ghostly sight of his homely loveing. I saw that he is to us all thing that is good and comfortable to our helpe. He is our clotheing,

29: St. Luke, patron saint of painters, painting the Virgin Mary, detail, Sherborne Missal, BL Add. MS 74236, p. 573.

30: Heron, detail, Sherborne Missal, BL Add. MS 74236, p. 393.

31: Tamaris and assistant in *De Mulieribus Claris* (*On Famous Women*),
Bibliothèque nationale de France, MS Français 12420, fol. 86r.

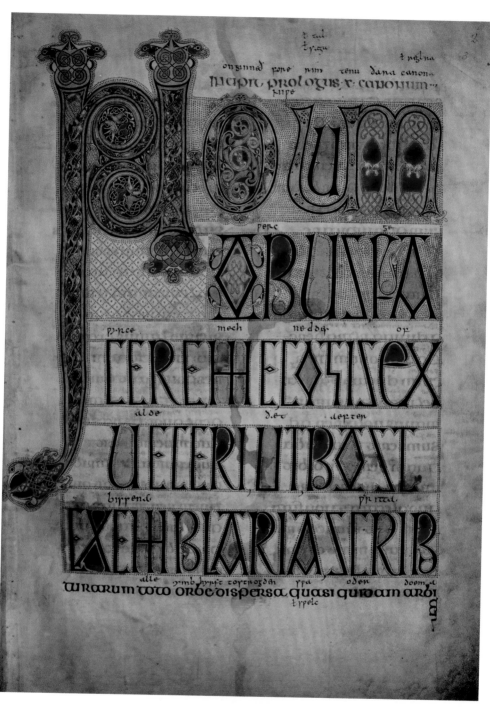

32: Incipit page, Lindisfarne Gospels,
Cotton MS Nero D IV, fol. 3r.

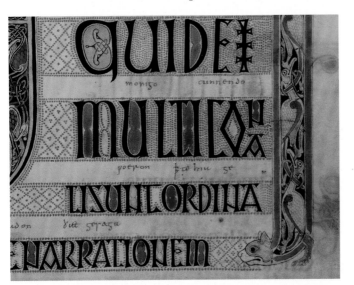

33: The tenth-century annotator, Aldred, leaves a note describing the book's creation, Lindisfarne Gospels, Cotton MS Nero D IV, fol. 259r.

34: Cat chasing birds, border detail, Lindisfarne Gospels, Cotton MS Nero D IV, fol. 139r.

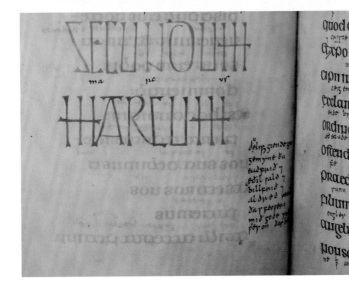

35: In a note almost hidden in the page gutter, Aldred, the tenth-century annotator of the Lindisfarne Gospels – BL Cotton MS Nero D IV – begs to be remembered alongside the book's makers (fol. 89v).

prouectioris aetatis consti-
tutus. nil carminum aliquando
didicerat. unde non numquam
in conuiuio cum esset lætitiæ
causa decretum. ut omnes
per ordinem cantare deberent.
ille ubi adpropinquare sibi
citharam cernebat. surgebat
a media cena. & egressus ad suam
domum repedabat. quod dum
tempore quodam faceret.
& relicta domu conuiuii
egressus esset ad stabula
iumentorum. quorum ei
custodia nocte illa erat
delegata. Ibiq; hora conpe-
tenti membra dedisset sopori.
adstitit ei quidam per somniu.
eumque salutans ac suo
appellans nomine. caedmon.
inquit. canta mihi aliquid.
at ille respondit. nescio
inquit cantare. nam & ideo
de conuiuio egressus huc
recessi. non poteram. quia cantare
rursum ille qui cum eo loque-
batur. at tamen ait

mihi cantare habes. quid
inquit debeo cantare.
& ille. canta inquit. principium
creaturarum. quo accepto
responso. statim ipse coepit
cantare in laudem dī conditoris
uersus. quos numquam audierat.
quorum iste est sensus.
nunc laudare debemus auctore
regni caelestis. potentiam crea-
toris. & consilium illius. facta
patris gloriae. quomodo ille
cum sit aeternus dŝ. omnium
miraculorum auctor extitit.
qui primo filiis hominum
caelum pro culmine tecti.
dehinc terram custos humani
generis omnipotens creauit.
Hic est sensus. non autem ordo
ipse uerborum. quae dormiens
ille canebat. neque enim
possunt carmina. quamuis
optime composita. ex alia
in aliam linguam. ad uerbum
sine detrimento sui decoris.
ac dignitatis transferri.
Exsurgens autem a somno

[Old English, lower margin, later hand — Cædmon's Hymn:]
Nu scilun herga hefenricæs uard metudæs mehti and his modgithanc uerc uuldurfadur sue he uundra gihuæs
eci drihten or astelidæ he ærist scop ælda barnum heben til hrofe haleg scepen
tha middingard moncynnæs uard eci drihten æfter tiadæ firum foldu frea allmehtig

36: Relegated to the bottom of the page, Cædmon's *Hymn*,
some of the earliest poetry in English, appears in Saint Petersburg,
National Library of Russia, lat. Q. v. I. 18, fol. 107r.

37: The Canterbury Pilgrims from *The Siege of Thebes*,
BL Royal MS 18 D II, fol. 148r.

38: The nun Hugeburc's secret code identifying her as an author,
Munich, Bayerische Staatsbibliothek, Clm 1086, fol. 71v.

[Manuscript text of *Þe Wohunge of Ure Lauerd*, BL Cotton MS Titus D xviii, fol. 127r, written in two columns of Middle English in a Gothic textura hand.]

39: The opening of *Þe Wohunge of Ure Lauerd*, which may have been authored by an anchoress, BL Cotton MS Titus D xviii, fol. 127r.

40: The enclosure of an anchoress, Cambridge, Corpus Christi College MS 79, fol. 96r.

41: The opening of the 'Short Text' of Julian of Norwich's
Revelations of Divine Love, BL Add. MS 37790, fol. 97r.

42: In a manuscript copied from a printed book, Anthony Woodville
is shown presenting the *Dictes and Sayings of the Philosophers* to Edward IV.
Lambeth Palace Library MS 265, fol. vi verso.

that for love wrappith us and wyndeth us, halsyth us, and
alle beclosyth us, hangeth about us for tender love, that
hee may never leave us. And so in this sight I saw that he
is al thing that is gode, as to myne understondyng.[63]

*At the same time our Lord showed to me a spiritual vision of
His homely loving. I saw that He is to us everything that is
good and comfortable to our help. He is our clothing, that for
love wraps us, winds us, embraces us and encloses us, hanging
about us for tender love, so that he can never leave us. And
so in this sight I saw that he is everything that is good, as I
understand it.*

Here the use of the word 'homely' indicates a gentle, familiar divine love. This passage precedes one of the most famous
of Julian's images:

Also in this he shewed a littil thing, the quantitye of an
hesil nutt, lying in the palme of my hand as me semede;
and it was as round as a balle. I lokid thereupon with
eye of my understondyng and thowte, 'What may this
be?' And it was generally answered thus, 'It is all that is
made.' I mervellid how it might lesten, for methowte it
might suddenly have fallen to nowte for littil. And I was
answered in my understondyng, 'It lesteth and ever shall,
for God loveth it; and so all thing hath the being be the
love of God.'[64]

*Also in this He showed a little thing the size of a hazelnut in
the palm of my hand, and it was as round as a ball. I looked
at it with my mind's eye and thought, 'What can this be?' And
the answer came to me, 'It is all that is made.' I wondered at
how it could last, for it was so small it might suddenly have*

disappeared. And the answer came to me, 'It lasts and ever shall because God loves it; and everything exists in the same way by God's love.'

Her hazelnut image is justly famous. It conveys simultaneously Julian's sense of God's omnipotence as well as his gracious love of mankind. The universe is as small as a hazelnut, a thing so small that 'it might suddenly have fallen to nowte': presenting the universe as so fragile a thing conveys Julian's feeling for the omnipotence of her God – that God might hold the universe in the palm of his hand. In her vision, Julian fears for this tiny nut of a thing, but is reassured that it 'lesteth and ever shall, for God loveth it'. The image – domestic and 'homely' – is instantly comprehensible. And the style of her description is effortless. Julian's writing often has this 'fluidity of talk' – sinuous but comprehensible.[65]

In this particular revelation, we see the different modes of Julian's visions – sometimes they are sensory or visual (as in the visualisation of the nut), and sometimes she receives revelations directly in her mind ('And I was answered in my understondyng'). At other times she receives insights that transcend the sensory or the verbal – in these moments, Julian will sometimes acknowledge the difficulty of conveying in language the nature of her visions.[66]

Elsewhere, Julian acknowledges her weaknesses, as she sees them. She calls herself a 'simple creature that cowde [knew] no letter'.[67] The exact meaning of this phrase is unclear. She may have meant that she could not read Latin, or she may have meant that she was illiterate and dictated her work to an amanuensis. But this seems unlikely. In the text she writes, 'I have techyng with me, as it were the begynnyng of an ABC', which suggests that she could at least read and had learned the alphabet.[68] And, beyond that, the 'detailed and meticulously phrased' revisions she made to her work make it seem impossible that she could not write.[69]

The task of refining and recomposing her text was evidently her life's work. She may have been revising it further when she died. At its conclusion she writes, 'This booke is begunne be Gods gift and his grace, but it is not yet performid, as to my syte' ('This book was begun by God's gift and His grace, but it seems to me that it is not yet completed').[70] Although she worked on her text while she was enclosed, she was in no sense intellectually limited by her confinement. Julian's learning is apparent throughout her work, although she never directly cites her source-texts. Her biblical references convey the sense but not the wording of the Scriptures.[71] Her work only contains one direct quotation, but is veined by biblical allusion and imagery and contains many oblique references to other forms of theological writing.[72] This lack of direct citation is intriguing. Did she feel confident enough in the validity of her work that she did not need the intellectual buttressing of citation? Or it may be that she encountered the majority of her source material aurally, through sermons, or discussions with spiritual advisors, and did not have physical texts to cite.[73]

The advisory literature on the enclosed life – such as the *Ancrene Wisse* – gives us a powerful sense of the privations of the anchoritic existence. Yet Julian's 'Long Text', which she appears to have worked on once she was enclosed, is free of references to the realities of her way of life. At one point she writes that 'this place is prison and this life is penance', but she was likely referring to her life on earth, rather than the confines of her cell.[74] She probably saw her life as no more than a way-station on the road to heaven. Given the restrictions in which she chose to live, her text is strikingly hopeful, almost radically so. She insists that 'in al thing I leve as holy church levith, preachith, and teachith' ('in everything I believe what the Holy Church believes, preaches and teaches').[75] Yet her most famous line, 'all shall be well and all shall be well and all manner of thing shall be well', which encapsulates her generous vision of God's love, appears somewhat at odds with some contemporary Church teaching.[76] There is an anonymous text from the same period which may also have been written by an anchoress (although the attribution is not entirely secure).[77] It is provisionally dated to 1422 and entitled *A Revelation of Purgatory*. The text is a description of purgatory that reads like a low-budget horror film, in which sinners are boiled in barrels, pierced with hooks, forced to drink poison and have their lips cut off. Similar tortures are inflicted on a pet cat and dog. If that was purgatory, what was hell like?

Across her two texts, we see Julian refining her theology and altering the way she presents herself. The 'Long Text' is of a very different quality to the 'Short Text' – in it many of the personal references have been removed. The person of Julian recedes, such that the 'shewings' – as she called them – are fore-grounded. The description of her deathbed experience is also rewritten: the domestic, human details are stripped out. In the 'Short Text' there is a striking passage in which Julian defends her authority to write as a woman:

> Botte God forbede that ye schulde saye or take it so that I
> am a techere, for I meene nought soo, no I mente nevere
> so. For I am a woman, leued, febille and freylle, Botte for
> I am a woman, schulde I therfore leve that I schulde

nought telle yowe the goodenes of God, syne that I sawe in that same tyme that it is his wille that it be knawen?[78]

God forbid that you should ever say or take it that I am a teacher, because I do not mean to be, nor did I ever mean to be, for I am a woman – ignorant, weak and frail, but just because I am a woman, must I therefore believe that I should not tell you about the goodness of God, when I saw at the same time both His goodness and His will for it to be known?

In the 'Long Text,' this passage has been removed, as has any reference to her gender. It is hard to know why she made this change. Did she feel more confident in her authority, perhaps by dint of having been enclosed? Or perhaps she was aware that writing as a woman made her a more peripheral voice and, wishing to be read by the widest possible audience, removed references to her gender in order not to alienate readers. Reading the manuscripts of the 'Long Text' today, Julian's gender is announced in an introductory rubric, but the imprecise nature of manuscript transmission means that when texts were copied, they might lose this kind of extra-textual material. Medieval readers could come to a text 'blind', knowing nothing of its authorship or title. Without these rubrics it would be possible to read the 'Long Text' and not know that the author was a woman.

Not all of Julian's changes were deletions. The main change between the 'Short Text' and the 'Long Text' is an expansion of Julian's meditations on her visions. But there are also episodes in the Long Text which do not appear in the 'Short Text.' Perhaps the most striking is her image of Christ as a mother. This is an extraordinary identification. She writes: 'And our saviour is our very mother, in whom we are endlessly borne and never shall come out of him.' Here Julian figures the womb as a safe space, where humankind is held and protected. It is a generous and 'homely' vision of divine love. It also prompts the question, had she been a mother herself? We cannot know – so little survives of her biography. All the information we have on her is derived from some brief references in the 'Short Text' (later removed) and a collection of wills and documents which attest to her being enclosed. A 1394 will bequeathed money to 'Julian ankorite' (Julian the anchoress). There was a further bequest in 1404, and in 1415, John Plumpton, a Norwich citizen, left forty pence to Julian and twelve pence each to her maid Sarah and former maid Alice.[79] Julian seems to have been still alive in 1416 because in that year Isabel Ufforde, the Countess of Suffolk, left twenty shillings to a 'Julian, recluse at Norwich'. Julian would have been seventy-three, and had been enclosed for decades. But for these scant references, nothing else remains of her life, except her text.

Julian's text, in its two versions, has a complex manuscript history. The 'Short Text' survives in a single copy, held at the British Library.[80] The text appears in a collection of Middle English devotional material, which may have been assembled by a Carthusian scribe, whose mysterious monogram 'I.S.' occurs throughout.[81] It appears to have been copied when Julian was still alive. The rubric at the start describes the text as 'a vision' received by 'a devoute woman and hir name es Julyan that is recluse ate Norwyche and ȝitt on lyfe' ('a devout woman and her name is Julian, she is a recluse in Norwich and is still alive'). The rubric dates the manuscript to 1413. The manuscript appears to have been in Carthusian hands during the fifteenth century. There are annotations in it made by James Grenehalgh (born c. 1465/70), a Carthusian monk of Sheen.[82] Thereafter the manuscript passed into the hands of antiquarians in the post-Reformation period.

The 'Long Text' does not survive, complete, in any medieval manuscripts. Some extracts of it appear in a manuscript held in Westminster Cathedral (dated to c. 1500), but the earliest full versions of the text were copied at various points between the end of the sixteenth and eighteenth centuries. Five copies appear to have been made by a community of exiled Benedictine nuns in Europe. In 1670 an early edition of Julian's work, based on a manuscript likely copied by the nuns, was produced by the Catholic convert Father Serenus de Cressy.[83] The work was dismissed in some quarters. Edward Stillingfleet, Bishop of Worcester, called it 'blasphemous and senseless tittle tattle'.[84] Further editions followed in the nineteenth century, but it was only through the work of the scholar Grace Warrack that Julian's text became better known. Warrack's 1901 edition was more accessible than earlier ones – she modernised spelling and punctuation, added paragraphs and translated obscure words.[85] It is appropriate that the *Revelations* – such an important work by a female writer – was preserved by devoted, female scribes and made accessible in the modern era by a female scholar.

The Poetry of Gwerful Mechain

The *Ancrene Wisse* and *Þe Wohunge* articulate a life of severe restriction. But we should not imagine that the only literature produced by female writers from medieval Britain was bound by stricture. The Welsh poet Gwerful Mechain (c. 1460–1502) wrote in a gloriously unrestricted way. Her surviving work is varied. She wrote the kind of religious verse common to her era – the late fifteenth century – but she also wrote about topics that few, if any, medieval women writers discussed: unambiguous sexual desire, bodily functions, domestic violence. Her work circulated in manuscript form for centuries, but upon being rediscovered in the twentieth century, it was long dismissed as profane, and excluded from poetry anthologies and textbooks. It is only recently that it has come to be better known. Like the work of Julian of Norwich or *Þe Wohunge*, the manuscript evidence is sometimes confusing and the voice of the woman in the past is hard to reach.

'Every drunken fool of a poet is quick / In his pompous vanity,' begins one of her poems, 'To sing of the girls of the lands / In fruitless praise all day long.'[86] The poem's tone is raucous, dismissing the fatuousness of fellow poets. But as it unfolds, the text reveals itself as a brilliant, unabashed work about the female body. The poem 'Cywydd y gont' – variously translated as 'Ode to the Vagina' or 'Poem of the Cunt' – continues, stating that poets too often praise a girl's 'hair', 'the eyebrows above the eyes' and the 'bare breasts, soft and smooth', as well as the 'hands'. But, she complains, they leave 'the middle without praise':

> That palace where children are conceived,
> The snug vagina, clear hope,
> Tender and lovely, open circle strong and bright
> The place I love, delicate and healthy.[87]

Mechain goes on to compare the vagina to a page of musical notation with red staves, a 'Dabl y gerdd â'i dwbl o goch' ('Table of song with its double in red'). The association here is clear – musical notation of this kind would have appeared in service books used in church. The image is irreverent, conjoining the sacred and the profane, but Mechain's use of the metaphor is strategic. In the next line she takes aim at the hypocrisy of the contemporary Church, noting that 'bright saintly men of the church / Don't abstain to give it a good feel'. Despite directing a jibe at 'men of the church', she closes the poem with an invocation to God: 'Berth addwyn, Duw'n borth iddo' ('Noble bush, may God save it').

'Cywydd y gont' is Gwerful Mechain's most famous poem, and the evidence of surviving manuscripts suggests that it was also one of her most popular; it survives in thirteen copies.[88] Perhaps part of its shocking, witty, joyous appeal was the way it takes a familiar form and refashions it. The poem is likely a response to Dafydd ap Gwilym's famous 'Cywydd y Gal' ('Ode to the Penis'). Scholars have noted that 'Ode to the Vagina' is 'a challenge both to the established literary tradition and to accepted social mores'.[89] To find a work of medieval British literature which discusses female sexuality so unashamedly is unusual, but to find one written by a woman is highly unusual. When sexuality or sexual desire is discussed by female writers of the period, it is so often sublimated into a desire for Christ, as in Þe Wohunge.

Mechain is the only female medieval Welsh poet from whom a substantial body of work is known to have survived. We know precious little about her biography. She appears to have lived in Mechain in Powys, in north-east Wales, close to the border with England. She was the daughter of Hywel Fychan and appears to have had brothers and sisters. She married John ap Llywelyn Fychan and had at least one daughter, called Mawd.[90]

Although 'Ode to the Vagina' is now her most famous poem, it does not characterise her oeuvre, which 'varies from light-hearted to *angst*-ridden, from biting satire and anger to gentle fun-poking, from the passionate to the devotional.'[91] To modern readers it may seem strange that a poet who wrote so unabashedly about her sexual organs could also be a poet of devotion and admonition. And this is perhaps all the more surprising given the medieval Church's anxiety about human sexuality, an anxiety exemplified by the *Ancrene Wisse*. But the fact that Mechain was a lay woman may have given her more freedom to express herself. Although the details of her biography are scant, it is clear that she was part of a lively coterie of fellow poets who exchanged verse that was combative, profane and sometimes ideological. She was not an isolated figure creating verse for herself, like – say – Emily Dickinson, but an active participant in a dynamic milieu. She was part of a wider poetic network, whose nucleus was a circle of amateur poets clustered around Dafydd Llwyd of Mathafarn (c. 1395–1486). Through her husband, John ap Llywelyn Fychan, she was related to the poet Llywelyn ab y Moel (died 1440).[92]

Welsh poetry has a fiendishly complicated metrical system, which conforms to the conventions of *cynghanedd* (which literally means 'harmony') and comprises the essential component of 'strict-metre'. *Cynghanedd* is 'a stunning edifice of aural architecture', which uses a combination of rhyme and stress in particular patterns.[93] There are twenty-four different forms of metre in the tradition. Understanding *cynghanedd* is near-impossible for a non-Welsh speaker. But it is enough to understand that the system was highly complex and that Mechain's work was a high-wire act with language. Mastering the art was said to take nine years of training.[94] In *cynghanedd* each verse line is broken down into two half-lines (much like Old English poetry), but the 'Welsh tradition makes this patterning even more complex by insisting that the sequence of consonants in one half of the line follows the order in the other'.[95] Unlike Old English poetry, which has no end rhyme, Welsh poets had to find both internal rhymes *and* end rhymes. This mindboggling complexity has advantages, especially for oral performance: *cynghanedd* 'is an excellent mnemonic device. If you can't remember the second half of a given line, all you have to do is fit in the words needed according to the pattern in the first half.'[96]

Strict-metre verse was patronised by and performed for Welsh nobles and gentry in this period. It was part of a professionalised bardic tradition from which women and low-born men were excluded.[97] Thus, poets like Mechain would have learned their craft by hearing strict-metre poetry declaimed by professional poets in formal and informal settings at home. Female poets like her may have learned the craft from their fathers, husbands or other male relatives.[98] Some of her most famous works, like 'Ode to the Vagina', appear to have been composed in response to works by male poets. Works like this are 'in the tradition of adversarial poetry – *canu ymryson* – where one poet challenges the other'.[99] Another of her works, 'I wragedd eiddigus' ('To Jealous Wives'), is, like 'Cwydd y gont' ('Ode to the Vagina'), a refashioning of a familiar form. It accuses wives of being 'too jealous', of being women who would rather

> give away the houses and land
> And mind you, even her own good cunt,
> Than give away her [husband's] penis.[100]

As Mechain drily notes, 'Byd caled yw bod celyn / Yn llwyr yn dwyn synnwyr dyn' ('It's a hard world when a penis / Leaves a woman bereft of her senses'). The poem is 'a response to a male-dominated poetic tradition' where male poets attack 'the jealous husband for guarding his nubile young wife so closely that young men cannot have a share of her'.[101] I read the poem as heavily ironic and feminist in its outlook: the wives' 'ownership' of their husbands' sexual organs is satirical – Mechain is drawing attention to the way *women's* bodies are most often controlled by men in a patriarchal society. The poem ends with the following disclaimer: 'Ni chenais, 'y nychanon,/ I nebo ffurfeidd-deb y ffydd/ A fyn gala fwy no'i gilydd' ('I did not sing my satire to anyone who wants a bigger than average cock').[102] The poem is clearly addressed to women, so the disclaimer is a witty jibe at a male audience.

Mechain's adversarial poetry is not always comic. In 'I ateb Ieuan Dyfi am gywydd Anni Goch' ('A Response to Ieuan Dyfi's poem on Red Annie') she takes Ieuan Dyfi to task for his misogynistic description of his lover, Annie Goch.[103] Ieuan Dyfi's text is a 'highly conventional and a deeply personal complaint against women'.[104] It is in the tradition of '*querelle des femmes*' ('complaints against women'), which present a sequence of examples intended to show that women are dishonest.[105] (Several writers wrote rebuttals to this popular form, which include Christine de Pizan's *Book of the City of Ladies* and Geoffrey Chaucer's *Legend of Good Women*.) Mechain's response combines the personal with the historical. She lists a catalogue of worthy women from history, scripture and mythology, including the legendary queen Gwendolen, who raised an army against her husband after he spurned her in favour of his mistress, and Dido, whom Mechain calls 'graceful and good'.[106] Strikingly, all the women are chosen for their achievements in a 'non-domestic context, not for motherhood or for conventionally feminine, passive virtues'.[107] Some of her examples, however, are women who were scorned or ignored by society. She mentions the wife of Pontius Pilate, who was supposed to have had a prophetic dream and attempted to persuade her husband not to have Christ crucified, but was ignored. She appears alongside the biblical Susanna, in the Apocrypha, who was spied upon by two lecherous judges as she bathed (Susanna 1: 1–64). They attempt to rape her, threatening to accuse her of adultery if she does not acquiesce. She refuses to be blackmailed and is sentenced to death, only to be released after the intervention of the prophet Daniel. Alongside these mythical and biblical stories, Mechain voices direct criticism of Ieuan:

> Dywed Ifan, 'rwy'n d'ofyn
> Yn gywir hardd, ai gwir hyn?
> Ni allodd merch, gordderchwr,
> Diras ei gwaith, dreisio gŵr.

> *Tell me, Ifan, I'm asking you,*
> *Truly and nicely, is this true?*
> *No woman could, fornicator*
> *Ever rape a man, your doings are wicked.*[108]

Later she calls on Ieuan to 'stop your attacks, adulterer, / Calling a lovely woman a whore'. The poem is 'particularly poignant' because records in the Hereford Consistory Court show that Annie alleged Ieuan had raped her.[109] The pair were lovers, but Annie was married; they were summoned to court more than once for the sin of adultery. Ieuan was punished with six lashes, but Annie pleaded not guilty. Later she was accused of plotting to kill her husband and subsequently changed her plea, arguing that her husband had sold her to Ieuan Dyfi.[110]

Many of Mechain's poems are lengthy and make use of the quintessentially bardic device of *dyfalu* (literally 'to compare') – where she layers descriptions on top of one another. But in other places, her work has an elegant economy within a clipped form. Mechain was masterful in her use of the *englyn* – a crisp three- or four-line poem, which uses varying and highly complex metrical patterns. One of the more memorable is 'I'w gŵr am ei churo' ('To her husband for beating her'):

> Dager drwy goler dy galon—ar osgo
> I asgwrn dy ddwyfron;
> Dy lin a dyr, dy law'n don,
> A'th gleddau i'th goluddion.

> *A dagger through yout heart's stone – on a slant*
> *To reach your breast bone;*
> *May your knees break, your hands shrivel*
> *And your sword plunge in your guts to make you snivel.*[111]

Katie Gramich – the poem's translator – has noted the 'physical emphasis' of the poem, which discusses the man's 'heart, breastbones, hands, knees and guts'.[112] Of course, we cannot know if Gwerful was ever a victim of domestic violence, but there's a peculiar force to this work. It conveys the sense of a speaker who has fantasised, in itemised detail, about returning the violence done to them. In another poem, of somewhat uncertain authorship, but likely by Mechain, the use of the *englyn* has something of the quality of the Japanese haiku – brief and elegant with the sensation of transience. In 'Yr eira' ('The Snow') Mechain uses a four-line *englyn* over two stanzas:

> Gwynflawd, daergnawd, du oergnu — mynydd,
> Manod wybren oerddu;

Eira'n blât oer iawn ei blu
Mwthlan a roed i'm methlu

Eira gwyn ar fryn fry—a'm dallodd,
A'm dillad yn gwlychu;
O, Dduw gwyn, nid oedd genny'
Obaith y down byth i dŷ.[113]

White flour, earthflesh, black mountain – with cold fleece
Cold, black, snow-laden horizon;
A plate of snow, feathers frozen,
A soft snare to trip me all of a sudden.

White snow on a high peak blinded me,
And my clothes were soaked;
I really thought I'd never manage,
Oh dear God, to reach the village.[114]

Mechain's work appears to have circulated orally both in her lifetime and long after her death. There is evidence of it still being transmitted in this way as late as the nineteenth century.[115] Crucially, 'very few of her poems appeared in print'.[116] Instead, 'copies were frequently written down from memory' and were 'corrupted by those who copied them'.[117] Scholars differ as to how many poems should be attributed to her.[118] What makes Mechain's verse tricky is that we can't be sure when it made the transition from oral to written text. All the surviving manuscripts of her work date from after her death,[119] so recovering what might have been her original versions is difficult. Authorial attribution is often scattergun and imprecise in manuscript culture, especially in works which were written down after circulating orally, and her work was sometimes misattributed.[120]

In the centuries after her death, Mechain's work spread in the personal manuscripts of generations of readers, but in more visible, printed forms, her work was long marginalised. She has been 'deliberately and consistently excluded from anthologies, scholarly editions and textbooks'.[121] The reasons for this are complex, but from the eighteenth to the twentieth centuries, Christian Nonconformity – so important to the culture of Wales in that period – played a role in her marginalisation. As Katie Gramich notes,

> in the wake of the notorious 'Blue Books Report' of 1848 (a study of state education in Wales commissioned by the Westminster government, which alleged that the Welsh were poor, ignorant, and unchaste) indignant Welsh people took it upon themselves to display to the world that they were a people of the Book: moral, upright, and industrious.[122]

The legacy of this attitude can be seen in the scholarship on Gwerful Mechain, who was long dismissed as profane and artless. The scholar Leslie Harries edited her verse for his MA thesis in 1933, but omitted her work from his subsequent edition of medieval Welsh poets.[123] He wrote that she produced 'pornographic songs' and described her as 'nothing more than a whore'.[124] Even in comparatively recent scholarship she has been described as 'salacious' and 'technically lax'.[125]

In January 2019 I visited one of the few remaining intact anchorholds (anchorites' cells) left in Britain – in the church of St Nicholas, Compton, in Surrey. The space was the size of a large cupboard. There wasn't enough room to lie down. As I'd come late on a winter afternoon, the light was seeping away and it was dim. The only light came through the 'squint' – the small window that looked onto the altar. It was cruciform in shape, and through it I could see a single candle standing on the altar.

I turned on my phone's torch. In front of the squint was an oak shelf, with a dark circle on its edge that had been rubbed away. Above it was a notice which read: *Please put nothing on the ancient sill. This was the prayer-desk of the anchorites for several centuries.* I knelt in front of it. If the floor level had been the same in the medieval period, it would have been too high for an anchorite to rest their elbows there. Perhaps the indentation had been made by pairs of hands gripping the edge of the desk's ledge. I wondered at those pairs of hands. This cell had been a coffin to its inhabitants – once inside it, they were never to come out. They may have been buried beneath my feet.

I came out of the church and into the churchyard in what remained of the light. I could hear cars on the nearby B-road sighing past; the churchyard was empty. Over the graveyard hedge was a care home. It was a Saturday, but there were only one or two cars in the car park. It didn't seem to be a busy time for visiting. But for the indifferent passing cars on the road, I was alone. The anchorites who'd lived in the cell probably rarely felt that. Anchorites withdrew from the world in one sense, but being anchored to their church, they were at the centre of community life. Anchorholds often appeared in prominent places in medieval English towns – in some they were sited along the routes of liturgical processions.[126] In London there were once many cells along the old city walls, forming 'a ring of prayer' encircling the capital.[127] But this anchorhold had now become as lonely as the care-home car park. I wandered back to my car.

I had come to Compton hoping to understand something of the possible author of Þe Wohunge of Ure Lauerd, but felt instead that her life was closed off to me.

I had a similar feeling about Gwerful Mechain, calling up one of the manuscripts of her startling englyn, 'I'w gŵr am ei churo' ('To Her Husband for Beating Her') in the British Library. There are five other manuscripts of this work, and the earliest dates from c. 1600, but BL Add. MS 14990 is a late one. It was copied in the eighteenth century for the Gwyneddigion Society – a London-based Welsh literature and culture society formed in 1770.[128] It is written in a clear eighteenth-century hand, appearing on a page with some other englynion, carefully and neatly ruled. While medieval manuscripts are often economical with space, aware of the preciousness of parchment or paper, the lines of text in this manuscript are generously spread out. Looking at this manuscript, I reflected that the gaps between the lines were apposite. To reach Mechain, we have to search in the spaces between the lines. This manuscript was copied centuries after her death, for an antiquarian society in London. It is several removes from a moment of oral composition in the late fifteenth century, a moment of composition perhaps occasioned by a moment of intense personal pain. So often, medieval manuscripts give us a tangible connection to the past, but this is not always the case with the figures described here. Each is obscured in a different way. For the author of Þe Wohunge we have no name and no secure attribution, but we have a wealth of contextual information that can tell us what kind of person the author may have been, although ironically most of it comes from guidance literature that prescribed the controls imposed on anchoresses. For Julian we have a name, and two versions of a fascinating text, but precious little sense of biography. And for

Gwerful, we have a smattering of evidence, but no manuscripts to connect us directly to her. In each case, the manuscripts get us a little closer, but never quite close enough to the women in question, whose worlds we can only hazard at, in the spaces between the lines or in the glimpse through a window.

Epilogue

The Decline of the Manuscript

On 12 March 1455, Enea Silvio Piccolomini (who would later become Pope Pius II) wrote to Cardinal Juan de Carvajal. His tone was breathless: 'It seems that everything I had been told was true,' he wrote. 'I have not seen entire Bibles, but I have seen signatures of five folded sheets.'[1] It is hard to imagine today how radical those folded sheets must have seemed. Piccolomini was discussing the work of a 'vir mirabilis' ('admirable man'), Johannes Gensfleisch zur Laden zum Gutenberg, and his printed Bible, produced using moveable metal type, which was to become a landmark in European culture.

Printing with moveable type was already taking place in Korea and China before Gutenberg developed his press. But for Europe, Gutenberg's press was a great innovation, enabling the mass production of texts as never before. One hundred and eighty of Gutenberg's Bibles were printed in two years. During that time, a single scribe would have barely dented the work of copying a manuscript Bible. Yet despite this mechanised production, each copy was bespoke. They were printed on parchment, signalling their cost and luxuriousness, and headings in red ink ('rubrication') were added by hand. The Bibles were sold unbound and undecorated, allowing owners to have them customised with hand-painted border decoration. (Around forty-nine Gutenberg Bibles survive, but each is quite different.) This marriage of new technology with individualised design made the Bibles sought-after objects; when Piccolomini wrote to Cardinal Carvajal, there was already a long waiting list for one of the Bibles, and in time the technology would come to be available to ordinary people.

Printing arrived in England in 1476. It was brought by William Caxton – an enterprising merchant who had lived most of his adult life in the Netherlands.[2] Born in Kent at some point between 1415 and 1424, as a young man Caxton was an apprentice in the Mercers' ('cloth merchants') Company in London. He then moved to the Continent and embarked on a successful career trading textiles. He appears to have learned how to print in Cologne, and thereafter began printing books in various locations in the Low Countries. When Caxton returned to England in 1476, he set up shop in Westminster, near to the seat of government and next door to the Benedictine foundation of Westminster Abbey. Westminster was also outside the jurisdiction of the City of London – which gave him freedom from guild restrictions. We might think of Caxton as the fifteenth century's equivalent of a Silicon Valley tech entrepreneur. But it's clear that Caxton's skill lay not simply in the introduction of a technical innovation, but also in his careful engagement with the texts he produced – as an editor, designer and translator. The first book he printed in English, which he produced while he was still on the Continent (in Ghent, specifically), was a translation of *Recueil des Histoires de Troye* by Raoul Lefèvre. This was to be part of a pattern: in his career he produced more than twenty translations of texts himself. His 1485 edition of the *Morte Darthur* (which we encountered in

Chapter One) was printed once he had returned to London. Caxton made changes to the manuscript 'exemplar' (or copy) he worked from to improve the reading experience. He divided the text into books and chapters, to make it easier to navigate, and in places updated the language. Like Gutenberg, Caxton strove to make his editions visually attractive, often having rubrication added by hand. Although he did not print on parchment, as Gutenberg's Bibles had been, he did add decoration. One of the first books he printed, in 1476, was Geoffrey Chaucer's *Canterbury Tales*. The work was evidently popular, and he produced a second edition in 1483. In the 'Prohemye' – or 'Proem', a kind of preface – to this edition he states that after printing his first edition, 'one gentylman cam to me / and said that this book was not accordyng in many places unto the book that Gefferey chaucer had made' ('a gentleman came to me and said that this book did not accord with the book that Geoffrey Chaucer had written'). So he borrowed another copy of the text from this man's father so as to print a new version more 'trewe and correcte'.[3] This charming story may have been marketing speak. The textual differences between the two editions are relatively minor, but the second edition was printed in a smaller type, allowing more words on each page and reducing the cost of production by reducing the number of pages overall.[4] And Caxton added a new feature for aesthetics: a sequence of twenty-six woodcuts of Chaucer's pilgrims on horseback.

What Caxton brought with him from Europe wasn't simply a printing press, it was a new culture and, some have argued, a new way of thinking – in just the same way that when it arrived, the internet radically changed the way we received, transmitted and distributed information. In spite of the huge change that printing heralded, however, this change did not happen overnight. Opening Lambeth Manuscript 265, you'd have little idea that the text in front of you was actually copied in 1477 verbatim from a text printed by William Caxton.[5] This is a sumptuous manuscript, on parchment, with elegant decorated initials in an Italian fashion with white vine stems. One of its opening folios contains a presentation miniature (depicting the moment the manuscript was presented to its recipient). It shows Anthony Woodville, 2nd Earl Rivers, bestowing the book on Edward IV, who is surrounded by his wife Elizabeth and sons Edward and Richard. Woodville was the translator of the text known in English as the *Dictes and Sayings of the Philosophers*. (His work was based on a French translation of an Arabic text by the eleventh-century Syrian scholar al-Mubashshir ibn Fatik. As a text, it reminds us of the importance of Arabic learning in Western Europe in the medieval period.)

Lambeth MS 265 illustrates the way manuscripts retained their value as high-status objects, but it also has the feeling of a doomed technology. It is a potent metaphor for how things were to change irrevocably. This beautiful book – so laborious to produce – would soon be rendered extinct by Caxton's cheaper, quicker and more streamlined production process. It is an irony that this manuscript was copied from one of these printed editions. But this pattern of manuscripts copied from printed editions was actually common.[6] The scholar Curt F. Bühler wrote that 'experience has taught me that every manuscript ascribed to the second half of the fifteenth century is potentially (and often without question) a copy of some incunable' (an 'incunable' being a book printed before 1500).[7] At the end of

Lambeth MS 265, the scribe has dutifully reproduced Caxton's endnote, which reads, 'Here endeth the book namede the dictes and sayenges of Philosophres emprinted by me William Caxton at Westmynst the yere of our lorde m ccc lxxvij'. The words themselves were eventually to sound the death knell of this very kind of book.

In much the same way that e-readers and traditional books are used today in tandem, so the two technologies of manuscript and print culture continued to exist, side by side, long after printing was introduced into England. Manuscripts had uses that printed books did not. Henry VIII read both printed books and manuscripts, expressing a preference for particular kinds of type that were more readable than others in his later years. But for his personal prayer book, now the 'Henry VIII Psalter' (see Chapter Three), he commissioned a sumptuous manuscript, replete with personalised images of himself as the biblical David. And manuscripts were malleable in a way that printed texts were not. The only literary manuscript containing the hand of William Shakespeare – *The Book of Sir Thomas More* – is a playscript partially authored by Shakespeare. It is the acting company's final draft, a kind of backstage copy from which players' parts could be copied. The manuscript contains notes showing that it had been sent to the censor, Edmund Tilney, Master of Revels, who had prevented the play from being performed. Later, probably after the death of Elizabeth I, the manuscript had been taken up again and prepared for performance. Manuscripts had this important malleability, but were also more private – suitable to personal, devotional reading, or the circulation of potentially scandalous material. Manuscripts allowed poets, like John Donne, to circulate their work amongst a coterie of friends and acquaintances. But by Shakespeare's time, while manuscripts still had important uses in particular contexts, they were being produced less and less and medieval manuscripts were increasingly being collected as objects of historical interest.

Afterword

The Use and Misuse of the Past

In 1533, John Leland – who styled himself the king's 'antiquary' – received some sort of commission from Henry VIII 'to serche and peruse the Libraries of hyse realme before their utter destruccyon'.[1] The fruits of Leland's search were not published until 1549, when John Bale (his friend and associate) had Leland's notes published under the title *The Laboryouse Journey*. In the intervening time between the commission and publication, Henry VIII had died, poor John Leland had lost his mind, and the monastic libraries of the realm had been destroyed and their collections dispersed as part of the English Reformation.

The sad figure of Leland on its 'laborious journey' is a harbinger of the end of one age and the start of another. It was in this period that manuscripts began to acquire a different meaning. They began to be valued – by some – as vestiges of an earlier age, rather than simply as repositories of texts. Manuscripts, as we have seen in the case of Henry VIII's Psalter, did not suddenly disappear when William Caxton set up shop in Westminster, but their uses changed and, over time, they came to signify something different.

One of the places that Leland visited while perusing the libraries of Henry's realm was Lincolnshire.[2] But by the time he arrived, the king's agents had already visited. British Library MS Royal Appendix 69 is entitled 'Tabula liborum de historiis antiquitatum ac diuinitate tractancium in librariis et domibus religiosis' ('A list of books treating ancient histories and divinity in libraries and religious houses'). The list contains nearly a hundred titles, with notes in the margins in Henry VIII's own hand. Thirty-six manuscripts have been marked with a small *x*. Most of these marked titles ended up in the Royal Library at Westminster Palace. Three of Henry's palaces – Hampton Court, Greenwich and Westminster – were remodelled and reordered in this period in order to incorporate newly acquired books. MS Royal Appendix 69 was something of a shopping list.

Since 1527 the king had been racked with doubt about the validity of his marriage to Katherine of Aragon. In 1529 he dispatched agents to Europe to search Continental libraries looking for material that might buttress his case for divorce. A similar search was ordered for the libraries of his own realm. He hoped to find in old monastic books the justifications for a divorce from his wife – justifications that would ultimately lead to the destruction of many of those books.

Henry set about weaponising the past for his own agenda. In January 1533 he married Anne Boleyn without papal approval, thereby dissolving his marriage to Katherine of Aragon. In April of that year, Parliament approved the Act in Restraint of Appeals – the legal foundation of the English Reformation which transferred power from the Catholic Church to the king. The wording of this legislation is telling:

> by diverse sundry old authentic histories and chronicles it is manifestly declared and expressed that this realm of England is an empire, and so hath been accepted in the

world, governed by one supreme head and king having the dignity and royal estate of the imperial crown of the same.[3]

Here 'old authentic histories and chronicles' are assembled by Henry to confer power on himself. Anne was crowned on 1 June 1533. The day before, she had participated in an elaborate coronation procession through London, visiting a number of pageant stations where actors spoke laudatory verses composed by the king's antiquary, John Leland, and Nicholas Udall.[4] Further legislation followed, including the Act of Supremacy in 1534, and in 1536 a bill was passed in Parliament which suppressed all religious houses in England with an income of less than £200 (around £94,000 in today's money). This began the Dissolution of the Monasteries and the dispersal of their libraries. The process would continue until 1539. It was 'the largest transfer of power in England since the Norman Conquest'.[5]

The scale of the destructive energy was huge. The intention was to demolish England's monastic buildings so thoroughly that they could never again be sites for the old religion. In 1538 John London – one of the king's agents – wrote that he had so thoroughly 'pullyd down' and 'defacyd' a series of friaries that 'they shuld nott lyghtly be made Fryerys agen'.[6] At Lewes Priory, the work of destruction was concerted. An Italian military engineer – Giovanni Portinari – was sent from London to oversee its demolition.[7] He took with him a team of seventeen men including 'carpenters, smiths, plumbers and a furnace man'.[8] They undermined the foundations, putting in props and firing them.

Of course, the destruction of buildings led to the destruction and dispersal of their contents, including books. Although some books were saved, many were used for ignoble purposes:

stuffing for scarecrows, mending material for wagons or as wrapping paper.[9] John Bale described these various uses in *The Laboryouse Journey*. He condemned the 'horryble infamy' of the destruction, saying that:

> A great nombre of them whych purchased those super-stycyouse mansyons, reserved of those lybrarye bokes, some to serve theyr iakes, some to scoure theyr candel-styckes, & some to rubbe their bootes. Some they solde to the grossers and sope sellers, & some they sent over see to ye bokebynders, not in small nombre, but at tymes whole shyppes full, to the wonderynge of the foren nacyons.[10]

> *A great number of those who purchased those superstitious mansions [i.e. monasteries] used those library books: some for use as toilet paper, some to scour their candlesticks and some to rub their boots. Some they sold to the grocers and soap sellers and some they sent overseas to the bookbinders, not in small number, but at times whole ships full, to the wonderment of foreign nations.*

Here Bale draws attention to the national shame of this destruction, noting how 'foren nacyons' are filled with wonder at the dispersal of these English books.

The only literary manuscript to contain the hand of Shakespeare is called the *Book of Sir Thomas More* – a much-revised script of a play that may never have been performed (BL Harley MS 7368). It is wrapped in the fragments of a late thirteenth-century legal text with a later marginal commentary. We can only wonder which medieval monastic library the leaves likely came from. The disregard for these leaves' original purpose is evident. They are stained and scribbled on and have been turned upside down. In a blank space at the new top of the folio someone has added the title 'The Boke of Sir Thomas More' – the medieval past here upended and repurposed. Sometimes books escaped total destruction and were simply defaced. Royal proclamations on 9 June 1535 and 16 November 1538 decreed that the old religion should be expunged from old books. In the Sherborne Missal, which we met in Chapter Four, the word 'pape' ('Pope') and the name of St Thomas of Canterbury have been erased.[11]

The scale of the bibliographic loss during the Reformation is hard to estimate, but it is clear that what survives of England's 'medieval textual heritage represents a small fraction of the medieval books that existed before 1536'.[12] Of the more than six hundred volumes in the medieval catalogue of the Augustinian Friary in York, only five books have survived, while of the three hundred volumes that the bibliophile benefactor Duke Humphrey gave to the University of Oxford, only two survived the Reformation.[13]

We can only wonder what poor John Leland felt about the dispersal of the monastic libraries. According to a later source, he wrote to Thomas Cromwell – the architect of Henry's break with Rome – in 1536, expressing concern for the fate of the monastic libraries:

> whereas now the Germanes perceiving our desidiousness [indolence] and negligence, do send dayly young Scholars hither, that spoileth them, and cutteth them out of Libraries, returning home and putting them abroad as Monuments of their own Country.[14]

What is striking about this is the way Leland frames this as a national shame: the remnants of the English past are being heralded as German Monuments (and there is an irony in this, as Germany was the cradle of the Reformation that precipitated the destruction of the books of which Leland speaks).

Henry VIII died in 1547 and this was the year that – according to John Bale – John Leland lost his mind. Bale worked on Leland's unpublished notes, and *The Laboryouse Journey* was published in 1549. There are a number of theories about what prompted Leland's mental collapse. There is a sense, surveying his uncompleted work, of a life left unfulfilled. Leland's interests were broad. In 1544 he produced *Assertio inclytissimi Arturii regis Britanniae* (*Assertion of the Most Famous Arthur King of Britain*). This work was an attempt to establish the validity of King Arthur's historical existence – it comprises a study of place names, artefacts, texts and landscape features. It reflects Leland's broad interests in material and textual remains of the past as well as topography. It is important that Arthur is described as the 'King of Britain' – this is evidently an important national story which Leland is determined to upgrade from its status as dubious myth.[15] (Leland was evidently concerned with distilling a national history, which gives a particular edge to his concern for how English books were taken overseas and heralded as German 'Monuments'.) But his interests were not simply antiquarian or literary. Sometime in the second half of 1546, Leland was dispatched to France to gather trees, grafts and seeds, including a hundred pear and apple trees from Rouen.

Leland, however, died leaving a wealth of manuscripts of notes, and only a handful of printed texts. He had envisaged completing a number of vast and ultimately unrealisable scholarly projects. In *The Laboryouse Journey* Bale writes that Leland had promised Henry four volumes on the biographies of great British writers, entitled *De viris illustribus* (*Of Eminent Men*).

This work was divided into four books, and contained almost six hundred entries arranged in chronological order. Leland was still working on it when he collapsed into insanity. Alongside this capacious work, he also envisaged producing an account of Britain's topography, as well as a history of Britain (which he anticipated comprising 'fyfty bokes'), and to make sure that every aspect of Britain's history was to be covered, he also proposed a work on the noble families of the realm. Unsurprisingly, none of these expansive projects were completed when Leland lost his mind. Indeed, their scope and ambition may have contributed to his decline. The death of the king may also have weighed greatly on Leland, since his career was contingent on Henry's patronage. But it's hard not to wonder whether the destruction of the libraries that he witnessed did not also contribute, in part, to his mental deterioration.

The destruction of the monastic libraries had an important effect, however. The iconoclasm of Henry's age, and its desire to erase the past, generated a nostalgia for what had come before. And this nostalgia was a catalyst for the emergence of many antiquarians.[16] Viewed in this way, we might see antiquarianism as something that rose, phoenix-like, from the ruins of destruction. Leland was the first to use the title 'antiquarius', and the word 'antiquary' entered the English language not long after. But it feels as though this epithet grew amid the ruins of his own mind. Leland gives human shape to a tragedy of destruction.

Leland was one of the first of a generation of antiquarians who set about gathering up the scattered remnants of the nation's medieval past in order to preserve and organise them, according to their own vision.[17] These antiquarians collected or investigated the past for all kinds of reasons. John Stow (1524/5–1605) – a London antiquarian – was a young man

when Leland lost his mind. He has been called the 'most prolific historical writer of the sixteenth century'.[18] He was an
avid reader, with a magpie-like desire to collect and preserve
fragments of the past. He said of himself, 'I had bene a serchar
of antiquities of divinite, sorency [astrology] & poetrye'.[19]
His interests were diverse: he collected a wealth of rolls, wills,
indentures, coins and monumental inscriptions, and many
were discussed in his lengthy 1580 *Chronicles* of English history.
His *Survey of London* (1598) is a ward-by-ward picture of the
city, which interweaves classical and medieval literature, civic
records, historical information and personal reflection. It gives
us one of the most complete descriptions of the city to survive
from before the Great Fire of 1666. Stow was also greatly interested in literature, and collected countless literary manuscripts,
some of which he used for editions of Chaucer and Spenser.
Stow's work, however, shows the dangers inherent in the use of
the past in the sixteenth century. His interest in the remains of
the monastic libraries dissolved after the Reformation led to his
being investigated by ecclesiastical authorities in 1569. Whether
or not he was a Catholic sympathiser, as was alleged, is hard to
make out, especially as he was part of a circle of notable Protestant thinkers. Stow's legacy, however, is clear. A monument
to him, dating from 1605 – the year of his death – stands in the
church of Saint Andrew Undershaft in Aldgate in the City of
London. His effigy sits beneath the inscription 'AUT SCRIBENDA
AGERE / AUT LEGENDA SCRIBERE' ('Either perform deeds to
be written about, or write things to be read'). The words were
appropriate for Stow, who performed deeds of lasting significance and wrote much that is still read to this day.

In 1561 John Stow presented Matthew Parker, the Archbishop of Canterbury (1504–1575), with a copy of his new

edition, *The workes of Geffrey Chaucer, newly printed, with divers addicions whiche were never in printe before.* The gift coincided with something of an antiquarian turn in Parker's life, in his declining years, as he increasingly devoted himself to collecting and investigating the existence of Protestantism in the British past. In his life, Parker amassed one of the most important collections of early English manuscripts, mainly gathered from the remnants of monastic libraries. The collection included the St Augustine Gospels (the Gospels brought by St Augustine to Canterbury in 597 when he arrived in England to convert the southern English to Christianity); the so-called 'A-version' of the *Anglo-Saxon Chronicle*; a beautiful copy of Chaucer's *Troilus and Criseyde*; an early copy of the *Ancrene Wisse* (see Chapter Seven); and two giant Bibles made for Bury St Edmunds in the twelfth century (Bibles similar in scope and style to the Winchester Bible, which we met in Chapter Four). Parker left his collection to Corpus Christi College in Cambridge in 1574, with strict instructions that it should be cared for judiciously. It was not the first major gift of a private collection to a non-monastic institution: notably, in the fifteenth century, Humphrey, Duke of Gloucester, had donated 280 manuscripts to Oxford University, many of which reflected his interest in humanism. But Parker's bequest illustrates the way collections that came to shape our modern understanding of the past were shaped by personal biases in earlier ages. His collecting efforts aimed to create a particular narrative about the English Church, which he sought to demonstrate was historically independent from Rome. Parker was a leading proponent of Anglican doctrine; the Thirty-Nine Articles – the defining statements on the doctrines and practices of the Church of England – were produced under his direction. For Parker and his circle, the act of collecting was motivated by political and religious ideologies and aligned with a project of nation-building.[20]

The events of the 1530s remind us that what was saved was sometimes the result of chance. Many of the manuscripts discussed in *Hidden Hands* had an uncertain fate after the Reformation. For a large number of them we simply do not know where they were in the period after the Dissolution – this is true, for example, of the Cuthbert Gospel (Chapter One), the Sherborne Missal (Chapter Four) and Lindisfarne Gospels (Chapter Five). But the events of the Reformation and post-Reformation period also remind us that the past has always been susceptible to misuse. The way we understand history has been shaped by the agendas of kings, collectors, antiquarians and historians. But the past asks us again and again to view it with fresh eyes.

At some point before his death in 1345, Richard de Bury, Bishop of Durham (1287–1345) composed his *Philobiblon* ('*Love of Books*'), in which he set out to 'clear the love we have had for books from the charge of excess'.[21] I love de Bury's treatise: it is a battle-hymn for the value of books and learning: 'in books we climb mountains and scan the deepest gulfs of the abyss'.[22] Undoubtedly it is a product of its time, containing criticisms of contemporary ecclesiastical and scholarly practices, but in spite of this, and in spite of the gap of time that separates de Bury's age from our own, many of his concerns are those of today's bibliophiles, scholars and librarians. The work is veined with a deep love for both texts and the material artefacts that contain them; it touches on many of the themes of *Hidden*

Hands. In Chapter 17, he castigates those who treat books carelessly, criticising the 'headstrong youth lazily lounging over his studies' who, susceptible to the winter's frost, allows his nose to drip onto the book in front of him. This dastardly youth, de Bury continues, does not think to clean his nails, which are 'stuffed with fetid filth' and thereby leaves marks on the book, or if he is wearing gloves, 'his finger clad in long-used leather will hunt line by line through the page'.[23] He also eats fruit or cheese over the open pages, marks his place with straws, keeps pressed flowers between the folios, and thinks nothing of using the open book as a pillow when taking a nap. This youth is the stuff of librarians' and curators' nightmares. But de Bury's horror also reminds us of what is magical about the oldest books – that they have been handled and mishandled by so many people in their history; they are smudged with human stories. Although he is incensed that this youth is wont to mark the pages of his book with annotations, those very annotations are the bread and butter of book historians. If we didn't have the annotations of Aldred in the Lindisfarne Gospels (the incomparable eighth-century Northumbrian manuscript, which we met in Chapter Five), we would not know the names of Eadfrith the scribe, or Æthelwald and Billfrið who made its cover. And we also wouldn't have the little messages Aldred left for us, such as the one on the final folio, where he describes how 'he made a home for himself' amongst the four Gospels, referring to the tiny vernacular glosses he added between the lines of the scriptural text, as if he imagined himself tucked, cosily, in between the lines. On the final folio he added a coda in the margin – 'I am called Aldred, born [son of] Ælfred; I speak as the distinguished son of a good woman' – and we hear him, centuries on.

Richard de Bury's sense of horror at the way books are mistreated extends not only to the individual crimes of careless readers, but also to the assaults of war and other disasters, which he addressed in Chapter 7 of the *Philobiblon*. We need only think of the singed edges of the only manuscript containing *Beowulf*, which nearly perished in the fire at Ashburnham House in 1731, to be reminded of the preciousness of the manuscripts that have survived into the modern day. 'All things are corrupted and decay in time,' he wrote, and 'all the glory of the world would be buried in oblivion',[24] were it not for books, noting the 'feebleness of human memory'.[25] De Bury thought books conferred immortality on figures from the past. He said of authors that, 'so long as the book survives, its author remains immortal and cannot die'. [26] Yet de Bury seems to have known that if authors did find immortality, it was necessarily contingent on the whims of scribes, the biases of collectors and the vagaries of chance. As we have seen, authors are sometimes the constructions of later ages. He condemned the work of 'worthless compilers, translators and transformers', as well as 'treacherous copyists' who 'shamefully mutilate the meaning of the author'.[27] But for all de Bury's ire, this is one of the most intriguing aspects of manuscript study: that texts are malleable and each version is unique. Each new form of an author's work creates a new set of meanings in different ages and cultural contexts.

It was not only authors who de Bury thought were made immortal by books – he cited a host of venerable figures from the past, Julius Caesar and Alexander the Great among them, whose stories would not have survived without them. No 'pope or king', he wrote, could 'find any means of more easily conferring the privilege of perpetuity than by books'. This phrase

– 'the privilege of perpetuity' – is an apt one, and reminds us that the way we understand the past is susceptible to bias: perpetuity is not a privilege that is universally conferred.

Manuscripts hold stories and snapshots of the lives of people whom we otherwise might not encounter – anonymous scribes, artists and writers, stories of people of a lower social status, women, and members of different ethnicities. And it is through manuscripts that we can try to access something of their lives. As de Bury wrote, 'in books I find the dead as if they were alive', and in this I could not agree with him more.[28]

Glossary

This is a brief explanation of some of the more unfamiliar terms you may find in this book. For more extensive explanations, see, for example, the 'Glossary' pages of the British Library's Catalogue of Illuminated Manuscripts, <https://www.bl.uk/catalogues/illuminatedmanuscripts/glossary.asp>, and of the Medieval Manuscripts Manual produced by the Department of Medieval Studies at the Central European University, Budapest, <http://web.ceu.hu/medstud/manual/MMM/>, to both of which I am indebted.

amanuensis – A secretary or scribe employed to transcribe by dictation an author's words.

Apocrypha – Those books of the Old Testament of the Bible later excluded as of doubtful or spurious authenticity during the Reformation, and relegated to an appendix (including the Book of Susanna and the First and Second Book of Maccabees).

ascender – The ascending stroke in those letters (*b, d, f, h* and so on) that extend above the body of the letter. (See **descender**.)

bas-de-page – The French for 'the bottom of the page', a *bas-de-page* is a decorative scene in the space at the bottom of a manuscript **folio**.

Benedictional – A book containing all the episcopal blessings (those said by bishops) to be said during the **Mass** and arranged according to the liturgical year (the Church calendar).

bifolium (*pl.* **bifolia**) – A sheet of paper or parchment folded in two to create two **folios** or **leaves**, and slotted together to form **booklets, gatherings** or **quires**.

booklet – Also called a **quire** or **gathering**: a collection of **bifolia** sewn together.

border – The area around a text which might be decorated with images or patterns or left blank.

Canon table – Tables of information found at the beginning of a Bible or copy of the Gospels, detailing which events in the story of Christ's life are found in which **Gospel** and where there is an overlap in the events described.

carpet page – A dense page of ornamental designs, found in manuscripts of **insular** origin. The pages contain no text and usually appear separating the four **Gospels**.

catchword – A word or phrase written at the bottom of the **folio** on the final **leaf** of a **booklet, quire** or **gathering** that repeats the opening word or words on the following leaf. They were used to ensure that the booklets/quires/gatherings were sewn together in the right order.

chemise binding – A sort of coat for a manuscript, protecting its binding. Often made of leather or textile, it could be a simpler affair, like a parchment wrapper, or something more elaborate, perhaps decorated with beads or jewels.

Chi-Rho – The Greek letters *XP*, which are an ancient symbol for Christ. They are a monogram of the first two letters of ΧΡΙΣΤΟΣ (*Christos*).

codex – The Latin word for a **manuscript** or handwritten book. ('Codicology' is therefore the study of a book, or of the physical structure of a codex.)

collation – Establishing the **collation** means working out how many leaves there are in each **booklet**, and how many booklets there are in the **manuscript**. This tells us how a manuscript was put together, how well-planned it was. When we marry the collation information with what else we know about the text, we can begin to establish a clearer picture about the process of creation. It helps to know, for example, that an artist created a particular image on a separate sheet and then sewed it into a booklet, or that a scribe wished to squeeze one more text into the manuscript and had to resort to sewing single sheets into their booklets to have enough space for that text.

colophon – A note added at the end of a text in a manuscript or a printed book which supplies some information on the author, title or – in the case of printed books – the printer. From the Greek, meaning 'finishing touch'.

Coptic binding – A method of book binding generally found in manuscripts of Egyptian or Eastern origin, but also found in the Cuthbert Gospel (Chapter One). The method, whereby the **booklets, gatherings** or **quires** are sewn together by two needles working in a figure of eight pattern from booklet to booklet, allows the book to open easily.

cords – Horizontal bands onto which **booklets, quires** or **gatherings** were sewn to create the **spine** of a book.

cursive – A handwriting **script** in which the individual letters are linked together, with single words being written in one fluid movement ('joined-up writing' as we may call it), rather than individual letters being formed (or 'printed') as separate entities. (See also **uncial**.)

dampfold – An artistic style, ultimately derived from Byzantine art, in which human figures appear in clothing that sticks to them as if wet. The folds of the drapery are sinuous and stylised. (See discussion of the Winchester Bible in Chapter Four.)

descender – The descending stroke in those letters (g, j, f, p and so on) that extend below the body of the letter. (See **ascender**.)

Divine Office – A cycle of daily devotions performed by members of religious orders and the clergy. The cycle contained eight 'canonical hours', namely (with approximate times): *Matins*

(2.30 a.m.), *Lauds* (5 a.m.), *Prime* (6 a.m.), *Terce* (9 a.m.), *Sext* (12 noon), *None* (3 p.m.), *Vespers* (4.30 p.m.) and *Compline* (6 p.m.).

Evangelist portrait – An image of one of the Evangelists – Matthew, Mark, Luke and John – thought by Christians to be the authors of the Gospels. They often appear with their iconographical symbols (Matthew with a man, Mark with a lion, Luke with a bull, and John with an eagle). They are frequently depicted as scribes.

exemplar – The source model, or 'copy-text', used to create a new manuscript.

explicit – A scribal abbreviation of *explicitus est*, the Latin for 'it is finished/completed', an explicit was often written in a different ink colour and designated the end of a text.

folio – From the Latin for 'leaf' – one half of a **bifolium**. Manuscripts, by and large, do not have pages as we think of them, but **folios** or **leaves**. References are not made to, for example, 'p. 2', but instead to 'fol. 1v': because a folio is a single sheet, one refers to its **recto** (the front of the sheet) and the **verso** (the back of the sheet), abbreviated as 'r' and 'v' respectively. (The Sherborne Missal, discussed in Chapter Four, is an exception and contains pagination, not foliation.)

frontispiece – A decorative image facing a book's title page – generally a feature of printed books, not manuscripts. The term is sometimes used to refer to an image at the opening of a particular book of the Bible, as in the frontispiece for the opening of the First Book of Samuel on the Morgan Leaf of the Winchester Bible, discussed in Chapter Four.

gall – (Also known as a gall-nut.) The round, apple-like growths that grow on oak trees when gall-wasps (from the family *Cynipidae*) lay their eggs in an oak tree's developing leaf buds. The galls were ground and mixed with iron salts and tannic acids to make ink.

gathering – Also called a **quire** or **booklet**: a collection of **bifolia** sewn together.

gesso – A thick, white substance usually made from chalk or plaster mixed with an adhesive. It created a raised surface onto which gold leaf could be applied. Sometimes it was coloured red so that a warm red glow showed through the gold.

girdle book – Small manuscripts attached to a belt by a chain or rope. The format was popular for prayer books made for wealthy women in the fifteenth and sixteenth centuries.

Gospel (Gospel Book) – The **Gospels** are the four accounts of the life of Christ, attributed to the Evangelists, Matthew, Mark, Luke and John (see **Evangelist Portrait**). The Cuthbert Gospel, discussed in Chapter One, is a copy of the Gospel of St John, while the Lindisfarne Gospels (Chapter Five) contains all four accounts. Copies of all four tend to contain **Canon tables** at their start.

Gothic – A period of Western art, c. 1100–1500. Gothic manuscripts are generally characterised by their more naturalistic depiction of the human figure, decorated initials and frames, increased use of gilding, and the appearance of hybrid monsters (sometimes called 'grotesques').

gutter – The groove where two pages meet in the middle of a double-page spread, along the **spine** of a book.

half-uncial – A script used in Antiquity and the early Middle Ages. Similar in appearance to **uncial**, except that it is a minuscule script (i.e. akin to modern lower-case letters).

incipit – From the Latin *incipere* – meaning 'to begin', an **incipit** designated the beginning or outset of text. It might appear in a different colour of ink from the main text, could be elaborately decorated, and might contain a title.

incunable – An early printed book, i.e. one created before 1501, when printing was still a novel technology. From the Latin *in cunabula*, meaning 'in the cradle'.

Glossary

Insular – Refers to the art and culture of Britain and Ireland, c. 550–900, characterised by its mixture of Celtic and Germanic motifs.

interlace – A type of decoration that appears to depict interwoven ribbons or straps – a common feature of **Insular** art, it appears in manuscript decoration as well as jewellery design, such as in the Sutton Hoo belt buckle.

lacuna (*pl.* **lacunae**) – A missing section in a text; a hiatus, a blank.

lay – An adjective describing secular society, as opposed to members of the clergy or a religious order.

liturgy – The ceremonies of Christian public worship. The central parts of the liturgy were the celebration of the **Mass** and the **Divine Office**.

lead point – Also known as a **plummet**, this was a piece of lead alloy used for drawing images, or sometimes for ruling the writing space. Sometimes the lead had a holder, a bit like a modern pencil. Scribes and artists would later fill in the lead lines with ink.

leaf (*pl.* **leaves**) – A single sheet of a manuscript. (See **folio**.)

lection mark – Marks added to a text (often a liturgical text) to aid its recitation or performance.

line-filler – A decorative feature or illustration that fills the remainder of a line that is not occupied by text, and that might enhance the appearance of the page.

manuscript – Any handwritten book (see **codex**), sheet or collection of sheets.

Mass – The central feature of the performance of the Christian **liturgy**.

Middle English – The form of the English language from which Old English evolved, containing a high proportion of French vocabulary, which arrived in Britain after the Norman Conquest in 1066, and lasted to around 1500.

mise-en-page – The layout of a page.

Glossary

Missal – A service book containing the texts used in the Christian celebration of the **Mass**.

Old English – A Germanic language, once known as 'Anglo-Saxon', spoken and written in early medieval, pre-Conquest Britain, brought by Northern European settlers.

palaeography – From the Greek-derived *palaeo* (indicating 'old') and *graphy* (meaning 'writing'), so therefore 'the study of old writing', palaeography is the study of a **script** or handwriting. Script styles are informative about a manuscript's date and place of production.

palimpsest – A parchment or other writing surface that once contained text that has now been erased, and which now contains an overwritten text in place of the original.

paper – Medieval **paper** was made from cotton or linen rags, which were soaked and pulverised into a pulp. This pulp was placed into a vat of water and size (a glutinous substance), into which a sieve-like wooden frame set with wires was placed to bring the pulp fibres to the surface. The film of sodden fibres was lifted out of the vat, and then pressed between sheets of felt. The wires of the frame gave the finished paper ghostly lines in its surface which are only visible when the paper is held up to the light. From around 1300, European paper-makers began twisting patterns into the wire to identify the paper as their own. These little patterns are known as 'watermarks' (as can still be seen in expensive modern paper), and can give scholars clues about the origins of particular paper stocks. Medieval and early modern paper made from rags is pretty durable, unlike modern paper made from wood pulp which tends to wither, discolour and crumble over time.

papyrus – A writing material made from the papyrus plant commonly found in ancient Egypt. It was later replaced by **parchment** and **paper**. (See the Prologue for the mythology of parchment's origins.)

parchment – The prepared skin of an animal, often a sheep, used for making the pages of manuscripts. (See the Prologue for a hands-on description of the process of parchment production.)

patron – A powerful individual responsible for commissioning a text, manuscript or other artwork.

pen trial – The scribbling or doodling, usually made by later owners of manuscripts, to test their pens.

pigment – The colouring agent in paint. Pigments might have vegetable, mineral or animal origin, whether from materials native to the artist who used them, or imported from abroad.

plummet – See **lead point**.

polysemous – Capable of yielding many simultaneous meanings.

pricking – The piercing a **folio** or **bifolium** with tiny holes at even intervals to make it easier to rule lines for the text to be written on. This was done with a knife, a sharpened tool called an awl, or a 'pricking wheel'.

Psalter – A copy of the biblical Book of Psalms, which formed much of the basis of the **Divine Office**.

quire – A **booklet** made from **bifolia** slotted and sewn together. **Booklets**, or **quires**, were then attached to one another in sequence to form a complete **manuscript**.

recto – The front (from the Latin *recto*, or 'right-hand side') of a manuscript **leaf** or **folio**. (See **verso**.)

rubrication – The coloured ink titles, 'rubrics', or headings added to a **manuscript**, often after the text was copied. The word derives from *ruber* (the Latin for 'red'), but rubrication could be in different-coloured inks, with which a **rubricator** was employed to add sections of text in these colours.

running title – A section of text at the top of a **folio** or **leaf** that gives the title of a book or a discrete section within it, as – for instance – a particular book of the Bible.

scribe – A person employed to copy a manuscript, or transcribe it by dictation (see **amanuensis** and *scriptrix*).

script – The type of hand or handwriting used by a particular
    scribe or *scriptrix*.

scriptorium (*pl.* scriptoria) – A dedicated room in a monastery for
    the copying and decorating of manuscripts, later replaced by
    the secular, professional **workshop**.

scriptrix – (Latin) A female scribe.

Service Book – The book used for the performance of the **liturgy**.

sewing stations – The little places in the groove of a **bifolio** where
    a sewing needle attaches thread to the outer edge of the **spine**,
    in order to attach one **booklet, quire** or **gathering** to another,
    or each of these to the **cords**.

spine – The edge of a book, to which the **booklets, quires** or
    gatherings are sewn together.

titulus – Latin for 'title' or 'label'. The *tituli Psalmorum* – the titles
    of the Psalms – are a series of titles that appear at the start of
    each of the Psalms in manuscripts and printed books. They
    summarise the content of each Psalm and appear in different
    forms. The earliest form of the *tituli Psalmorum* dates back to
    the third century.

treasure-binding – An elaborate book cover made from metalwork
    in gold or silver, or from ivory, and often studded with jewels.

uncial – A majuscule handwriting **script** (equivalent to modern
    upper-case or capital letters) used in Antiquity and the
    early Middle Ages. The script's individual letters have large,
    rounded forms, and each is written separately (as we might say,
    'printed'), as opposed to being linked together, or 'joined up'.
    Uncial first appeared around the second century, but reached
    the peak of its popularity between the fifth and the eighth
    centuries. It was brought to Britain by the Christian mission of
    Gregory the Great in the late sixth century. (See also **cursive**
    and **half-uncial**.)

vernacular – The 'native' or 'indigenous' language or dialect
    of a country or district. In Britain, in the medieval period,

there were multiple vernacular languages, including Cornish, Welsh, Gaelic and English (**Old English** and later **Middle English**). Vernacular is a term generally used in this context in opposition to Latin, which was the language of the Church and – at different points in the period – the language of law and government.

verso – The back, or reverse (from the Latin *verso*, or 'turned-over side') of a manuscript **leaf** or **folio**. (See **recto**.)

workshop – A place where manuscripts were made. The term usually designates secular places of manuscript production, to distinguish from monastic **scriptoria**. As the medieval period progressed, book production increasingly moved out of the monastery and into the **lay** world. The rise of universities in England from around the twelfth century created a demand for books outside of religious institutions.

zoomorphic – The term used to describe a design containing animal forms.

A note on unfamiliar letter forms

Æ, æ   The letter 'ash', makes the sound of the 'a' in 'ash'.

Ð, ð   The letter 'eth', makes a 'th' sound.

Þ, þ   The letter 'thorn', originally a runic letter, also makes a 'th' sound.

ʒ, ʒ   The letter 'yogh'. Pronounced in different ways depending on its position in a word. At the start of a word it was pronounced like the 'y' in Modern English 'yet'. In the middle or the end of a word it was pronounced like the 'ch' in Scottish 'loch'.

Timeline

Date	Event
597	Augustine's mission to bring Christianity to the south of England begins
c. 658–80	Cædmon, the illiterate cowherd, composes songs in praise of God
687	St Cuthbert dies
c. 705	Aldhelm dedicates a treatise to the nuns of Barking Abbey whose learning he praises
c. 700–25	St Cuthbert Gospel made
c. 710–22	Eadfrith copies and decorates Lindisfarne Gospels
c. 716	The Codex Amiatinus is made
731	Bede finishes *Ecclesiastical History of the English People*
c. 732	St Boniface receives a letter from Leoba containing a poem she has written. Leoba is the first named English female poet.
735	Bede dies
c. 737	The scribe of the 'Moore Bede' adds Cædmon's *Hymn* to the end of the text of Bede's *Ecclesiastical History of the English People*
c. 776–86	Hugeburc, the 'indigna Saxonica' ('unworthy Saxon woman') composes lives of Saints Wynnebald and Willibald
c. 780–825	The Book of Nunnaminster is made, possibly by a female scribe

Timeline

c. 787 First Viking raids in England

793 Vikings raid Lindisfarne

871–99 Reign of King Alfred. The king commissions vernacular English translations of Bede and Gregory the Great's *Pastoral Care* amongst other texts, in order to promote learning.

875 The monks desert Lindisfarne and travel with Saint Cuthbert's relics for seven years

883 The monks of Lindisfarne settle in Chester-le-Street, where they remain until 995

893 Asser completes *Life of King Alfred*

c. 960–80 The 'Exeter Book' of Old English poetry copied (the manuscript contains 'The Ruin' and two female-voiced elegies, 'The Wife's Lament' and 'Wulf and Eadwacer')

c. 970 Aldred annotates the Lindisfarne Gospels, adding an interlinear translation of the text in Old English

c. 985 Emma of Normandy, later queen of England, is born

c. 1000 *Beowulf* manuscript copied

1002 Emma of Normandy arrives in England to marry Æthelred

1013 King Swein of Denmark invades England

1014 Swein dies

1016 Edmund II dies and Cnut takes throne

1017 King Cnut orders Queen Emma to be 'fetched' so that he can marry her

1035 Death of King Cnut

c. 1040–41 *Encomium Emmae Reginae* composed

1042 Harthacnut dies; Edward the Confessor comes to the throne

1042–49 A charter records the gift of 'Æthelwine the Black' to St Alban's minster

c. 1050–1100 Treasure binding made for Judith of Flanders

1066   Battle of Hastings

c. 1100   The Nunnaminster *scriptrix* copies MS Bodley 451

1104   The St Cuthbert Gospel is discovered in the coffin of St Cuthbert by the monks of Durham Cathedral

c.1130   The Byzantine 'dampfold style' appears in the artwork of English manuscripts for the first time

1139–53   Civil War in England

1154   Accession of Henry II, possible patron of Marie de France

c. 1160   Two artists begin decorating the Winchester Bible; the project lasts for some 15 years and is never completed

c. 1165–80   Marie de France, *Lays*

1169   English conquest of Ireland begins

1170   Murder of Thomas Becket

1171   The death of Henry of Blois, the possible commissioner of the Winchester Bible

c. 1200–25   *Ancrene Wisse* (*Anchoresses' Guide*) is written for three anonymous sisters

c. 1210–40   The Tremulous Hand annotates around 20 manuscripts in with 50,000 glosses

1215   Magna Carta

c. 1225   Þe Wohunge of Ure Lauerd (*The Wooing of Our Lord*) composed

c. 1241   Copy of the *Domesday Abbreviatio*, showing a marginal image of a man of African descent, is made

c. 1261–65   BL Harley MS 978, an important manuscript containing Marie de France's *Lays* and *Fables*, is made

c.1275–90   Meir bin Elijah of Norwich composes haunting poetry

1276   Sir Geoffrey Luttrell, who would later commission the Luttrell Psalter, is born

Timeline

1287 Richard de Bury, author of *Philobiblon* (*Love of Books*) born

1290 Jewish people are expelled from England on the orders of Edward I

c. 1300 The Luttrell Psalter is made

c. 1300–30 A scribe copies Cambridge University Library MS Ee. 6. 11 which contains a modified copy of Marie de France's *Fables*

1337 Start of the Hundred Years War, which ends in 1453

1348 Black Death comes to England

1362 English displaces French in law courts and Parliament

1373 Julian of Norwich experiences 15 revelations on what she believes is her death bed. She lives for around another 40 years, during which time she is enclosed as an anchoress and produces at least two versions of her *Revelations*

c. 1374–85 Geoffrey Chaucer composes *The House of Fame*

1381 Peasants' Revolt

c. 1381 Geoffrey Chaucer composes *The Parliament of Fowls*

1382 The works of John Wycliffe, reformist theologian and overseer of a project to translate the Bible into the vernacular, are condemned

c. 1387–99 Geoffrey Chaucer composes *The Canterbury Tales*

c. 1400 Chaucer dies

c. 1399–1407 The Sherborne Missal is created

c. 1400–05 Christine de Pizan composes *Book of the City of Ladies*

c. 1405–06 Thomas Hoccleve composes *La Male Regle*

c. 1410 Thomas Hoccleve composes *The Regiment of Princes*

c. 1410–30 Margery Kempe at work on her *Book*

c. 1413 The only surviving manuscript of the 'Short Text' of Julian of Norwich's *Revelations* is made

1415	Battle of Agincourt
After 1416	The anchoress and writer Julian of Norwich dies
c. 1420	John Lydgate composes *The Siege of Thebes*, a homage to Chaucer's *Canterbury Tales*
1422	Henry VI comes to the throne at nine months old. He is afflicted by bouts of mental illness and the country is ruled by a powerful regent – Richard, Duke of York
c. 1425–50	John Shirley copies Cambridge, Trinity College MS R. 3.20, which contains the only medieval copy of Chaucer's *Words Unto Adam*
c. 1440–50	The only surviving manuscript of Margery Kempe's *Book* is copied
1441	A pregnant Margaret Paston writes to her husband of eight months requesting a new gown
1450	Johannes Gutenberg's press is in operation
1448	James Gloys enters the Pastons' service as a chaplain; he comes to be resented by Margaret's sons
c. 1455	Richard Calle becomes the bailiff of the Pastons' lands
1459	Civil war breaks out in England
—	Sir John Fastolf dies, plunging the Paston family into a protracted legal dispute
c. 1468	William Ebesham copies the 'Grete Booke' (BL Lansdowne MS 285) for John Paston II
1469	Richard Calle and Margery Paston marry in secret
c. 1469–70	Thomas Malory composes his *Morte Darthur* from prison
c. 1460–1502	Gwerful Mechain active
c. 1470–1500	Robert Reynes records a recipe for ink in his commonplace book, Bodleain MS Tanner 407
1471	Thomas Malory dies

1476   William Caxton prints *The Canterbury Tales* for the first time

1477   Anne Paston marries William Yelverton, having been separated from John Pampyng by her family

—   Using a book printed by William Caxton as an exemplar, the scribe 'Haywarde' copies Lambeth MS 235 – a copy of the *Dictes and Sayings of the Philosophers*

1483   William Caxton prints *The Canterbury Tales* for the second time

1485   William Caxton prints Thomas Malory's *Morte Darthur*

1491   Prince Henry, later Henry VIII, is born

c. 1501   Wynkyn de Worde publishes a heavily abbreviated edition of Margery Kempe's *Book*

1509   Henry VIII comes to the throne; in June he marries Katherine of Aragon

1511   Katherine of Aragon gives birth to a son; he dies after a few days

1516   Princess Mary (later Mary I or 'Bloody Mary') born

c. 1526–36   A tiny girdle book (BL Stowe MS 956) is made, possibly for Anne Boleyn

1527   Henry VIII petitions the Pope to have his marriage to Katherine annulled

1533   Henry VII marries Anne Boleyn

—   John Leland receives a commission from Henry VIII to 'serche [sic] and peruse' the libraries of his realm.

1535–40   The 'Dissolution of the Monasteries'

1536   Anne Boleyn executed

1540   Henry VIII marries Anne of Cleves – shortly after, the marriage is annulled; Thomas Cromwell is executed

1540–41 Henry VIII Psalter is made by Jean Mallard

1547 Henry VIII dies

1552 John Leland dies

1556 Nicholas Brigham pays for the creation of a splendid tomb for Chaucer in Westminster Abbey

1574 Matthew Parker leaves his collection of manuscripts to Corpus Christi College in Cambridge

c. 1580 Paris, Bibliothèque Nationale, MS fonds anglais 40 – a manuscript containing Julian of Norwich's 'Long Text' – is copied

— John Stow's *Chronicles* of English history

1598 John Stow's *Survey of London*

1642 Parliamentarian troops in the English Civil War break open Winchester Cathedral's mortuary chests and use the bones as missiles to destroy the Cathedral's stained-glass windows

c. 1650 BL Sloane MS 2499, a copy of Julian of Norwich's 'Long Text' is copied, possibly by Mother Anne Clementina Cary (d. 1671), an exiled Benedictine nun. Several manuscripts are copied by these nuns in the mid-seventeenth century

1669 The Winchester Bible is returned to Winchester Cathedral after the Restoration of the monarchy

1702 Sir John Cotton, grandson of Robert Cotton, leaves the Cotton collection to the nation

1731 On 23 October a fire breaks out in Ashburnham House, damaging precious manuscripts in the Cotton collection

1769 Reverend Thomas Philips presents the St Cuthbert Gospel to the English Jesuit College in Liège

1786 Grímur Jónsson Thorkelin visits Britain looking for materials relating to Danish history. In October he sees the *Beowulf* manuscript for the first time.

Timeline

1807 British naval forces attack Copenhagen; Thorkelin's library is destroyed

1815 Thorkelin publishes first edition of *Beowulf* (*De Danorum rebus gestis seculi II & IV. Poëma Danicum dialect Anglo-Saxonica*)

1865 A fire breaks out in the British Museum's bindery; some fragments of Cotton MS Otho A xii are burnt a second time

1882 Some leaves from one of Ceolfrith's pandects come to light in Newcastle

1901 Grace Warrack produces the first modern-language edition of Julian of Norwich's *Revelations*

1924 John Manly and Edith Rickert embark on an edition of *The Canterbury Tales*; it takes 16 years to complete

1934 The only surviving manuscript of Margery Kempe's *Book* is discovered

— The only surviving manuscript of Thomas Malory's *Morte Darthur* is discovered

1936 First full edition of Margery Kempe's *Book* is published

— The frescoes at the Royal Monastery of Santa María de Sigena are destroyed in a fire

1976 The Winchester Manuscript of Malory's *Morte Darthur* is exhibited alongside Caxton's print of the text; it becomes clear that the two have been together before

1982 Further leaves from one of Ceolfrith's pandects turn up in Kingston Lacy

2008 An alternative version of the *Encomium Emmae Reginae* comes to light

2012 British Library acquires the Cuthbert Gospel after a huge fundraising campaign

Bibliography

MANUSCRIPTS

Aberystwyth

Llyfgell Genedlaethol Cymru [National Library of Wales] Cwrtmawr
  MS 1491 (late copy of Gwerful Mechain's works)
  MS 3050D (containing Gwerful Mechain's 'I wragedd eiddigus')
  MS 3057D (describing Gwerful Mechain as Hywel Fychan's daughter)

Brussels

Bibliothèque Royale
  MS 7965–73 (3723) (charter describing 'Æthelwine the Black')

Cambridge

Corpus Christi College
  MS 2 (The Bury Bible)
  MS 79 (Pontifical, containing an image of an anchoress being enclosed)

Trinity College
  MS B.3.7 (Pentateuch commentary painted by John Siferwas)
  MS B.15.25 (Jocelin of Furness's *Life of St Patrick*)
  MS R.3.20 (collection of verse compiled by John Shirley)

University Library
  MS Kk.5.16 (the Moore Bede, containing an early copy of Cædmon's
    Hymn)
  MS Ee.6.11 (copy of Marie de Frances's 'Del lu e de la troie')

Dublin

Royal Irish Academy
  MS 23 P 16 (An Leabhar Breac)

Exeter

Exeter Cathedral Library
  MS 3501 (The Exeter Book [of Old English verse])

Bibliography

London
British Library (BL)
Additional (Add.)
    MS 11695 (Beatus's Commentary on the Apocalypse)
    MS 14990 (containing works by Gwerful Mechain)
    MS 27445 (Paston Letters)
    MS 33241 (*Encomium Emmae Reginae*)
    MS 34888 (Paston Letters)
    MS 34889 (Paston Letters)
    MS 37790 (Julian of Norwich's 'Short Text')
    MS 42130 (The Luttrell Psalter)
    MS 43488 (Paston Letters)
    MS 43490 (Paston Letters)
    MS 43491 (Paston Letters)
    MS 46487 (Sherborne Cartulary)
    MS 46513 ('Reading Room Register of MSS., Sep. 1784 to Oct. 24. 1788')
    MS 49598 (Benedictional of St Æthelwold)
    MS 59678 (*The Morte Darthur*)
    MS 61823 (*The Book of Margery Kempe*)
    MS 74236 (The Sherborne Missal)
    MS 89000 (The Cuthbert Gospel)
Cotton
    MS Otho A xii (Asser's *Life of Alfred*)
    MS Nero C iv (The Winchester Psalter)
    MS Nero D iv (The Lindisfarne Gospels)
    MS Nero D vii (Golden Book of St Albans)
    MS Tiberius B v (computistical, historical and astronomical miscellany)
    MS Titus D xviii (Þe Wohunge of Ure Lauerd [*The Wooing of Our Lord*])
    MS Vitellius A xv (*Beowulf*)
    Harley
    MS 978 (*Lais* and *Fables* of Marie de France)
    MS 2346 (*Long Charter of Christ*)
    MS 2382 (partial copy of *The Canterbury Tales*)
    MS 2965 ('Book of Nunnaminster')
    MS 5272 (Lydgate's *Life of Our Lady*, once belonged to Elisabeth Danes)
    MS 7026 (Lovell Lectionary, painted by John Siferwas)
Lansdowne
    MS 7368 (*The Book of Sir Thomas More*)
    MS 285 (John Paston's 'Grete Boke')
Royal
    MS 2 A XVI (Henry VIII's Psalter)

Bibliography

MS 17 D VI (Thomas Hoccleve's *Regiment of Princes*)
MS 18 D II (Lydgate's *Siege of Thebes*, depicting the Canterbury pilgrims)
Appendix 69 ('Tabula librorum': list of books in religious houses compiled before the Dissolution of the Monasteries)
Stowe
MS 956 ('girdle book' made for Anne Boleyn)
The National Archives (TNA)
TNA E 36/284 ('Domesday Abbreviatio', containing a marginal image of a man of African descent)
Lambeth Palace Library
MS 546 (devotional manuscript from Syon Abbey)
MS 265 (*Dictes and Sayings of the Philosophers*)

Munich

Bayerische Staatsbibliothek
MS Clm 1086 (Hugeberc's *Lives of Saints Wynnebald and Willibald*)

New York

Morgan Library
MS M. 619 (The Morgan Leaf)

Oxford

Bodleian Library (Bodl.)
MS Auct. E inf. 2 (Bible commissioned by Henry of Blois)
MS Bodley 451 (copied by the Nunnaminster 'scriptrix')
MS Bodley 883 (Le Chemin de Paradis, created by Jean Mallard)
MS Tanner 407 (Commonplace book of Robert Reynes of Acle)
MSS. Eng. hist. c. 140–182; Eng. misc. c. 96, d. 99–100, f. 35 (Journal of Sir Frederic Madden)

Paris

Bibliothèque nationale de France
MS Français 12420 (Boccaccio, *De Mulieribus Claris* [*Of Famous Women*])

St Petersburg

National Library of Russia
MS lat.Q.v. I.18 (The St Petersburg Bede, containing an early copy of Cædmon's *Hymn*)

San Marino

Huntington Library
MS HM 111 (Autograph of Thomas Hoccleve's *La Male Regle*)
MS HM EL 26 C 9 (Ellesmere Manuscript of *The Canterbury Tales*)

Bibliography

Vatican City
Vatican Library
 MS ebr. 402 (Poems of Meir bin Elijah)

Winchester
 The Winchester Bible

HYPERLINKS

for manuscripts digitised or partially digitised as of April 2021

Cambridge
Corpus Christi College
 MS 2 (The Bury Bible)
 https://parker.stanford.edu/parker/catalog/vb856kp8798
 MS 79 (Pontifical, containing an image of an anchoress being
 enclosed)
 https://parker.stanford.edu/parker/catalog/tx112pf2826
Trinity College
 MS B.3.7 (Pentateuch commentary painted by John Siferwas)
 https://mss-cat.trin.cam.ac.uk/Manuscript/B.3.7
 MS B.15.25 (Jocelin of Furness's *Life of St Patrick*)
 https://mss-cat.trin.cam.ac.uk/Manuscript/B.15.25
 MS R.3.20 (collection of verse compiled by John Shirley)
 https://mss-cat.trin.cam.ac.uk/Manuscript/R.3.20
University Library
 MS Kk.5.16 (the Moore Bede, containing an early copy of
 Cædmon's *Hymn*)
 https://cudl.lib.cam.ac.uk/view/MS-KK-00005-00016/264

Dublin
Royal Irish Academy
 MS 23 P 16 (An Leabhar Breac)
 https://www.isos.dias.ie/english/index.html

London
British Library (BL)
Additional (Add.)
 MS 11695 (Beatus's Commentary on the Apocalypse)
 http://www.bl.uk/manuscripts/FullDisplay.aspx?ref=Add_MS_11695

Bibliography

MS 27445 (Paston Letters)
http://www.bl.uk/manuscripts/FullDisplay.aspx?ref=Add_MS_27445
MS 33241 (*Encomium Emmae Reginae*)
http://www.bl.uk/manuscripts/FullDisplay.aspx?ref=Add_MS_33241
MS 34888 (Paston Letters)
http://www.bl.uk/manuscripts/FullDisplay.aspx?ref=Add_MS_34888
MS 34889 (Paston Letters)
http://www.bl.uk/manuscripts/FullDisplay.aspx?ref=Add_MS_34889
MS 37790 (Julian of Norwich's 'Short Text')
http://www.bl.uk/manuscripts/FullDisplay.aspx?ref=Add_MS_37790
MS 42130 (The Luttrell Psalter)
http://www.bl.uk/manuscripts/FullDisplay.aspx?ref=Add_MS_42130
MS 43488 (Paston Letters)
http://www.bl.uk/manuscripts/FullDisplay.aspx?ref=Add_MS_43488
MS 43490 (Paston Letters)
http://www.bl.uk/manuscripts/FullDisplay.aspx?ref=Add_MS_43490
MS 43491 (Paston Letters)
http://www.bl.uk/manuscripts/FullDisplay.aspx?ref=Add_MS_43491
MS 46487 (Sherborne Cartulary)
http://www.bl.uk/manuscripts/FullDisplay.aspx?ref=Add_MS_46487
MS 49598 (Benedictional of St Æthelwold)
http://www.bl.uk/manuscripts/FullDisplay.aspx?ref=Add_MS_49598
MS 59678 (*The Morte Darthur*)
http://www.bl.uk/manuscripts/FullDisplay.aspx?ref=Add_MS_59678
MS 61823 (*The Book of Margery Kempe*)
http://www.bl.uk/manuscripts/FullDisplay.aspx?ref=Add_MS_61823
MS 74236 (The Sherborne Missal)
http://searcharchives.bl.uk/IAMS_VU2:IAMS032-001968352
MS 89000 (The Cuthbert Gospel)
http://www.bl.uk/manuscripts/FullDisplay.aspx?ref=Add_MS_89000

Cotton

MS Otho A xii/1 (Asser's *Life of Alfred* in a 16th-century copy)
http://www.bl.uk/manuscripts/FullDisplay.aspx?ref=Cotton_MS_
Otho_A_XII/1
MS Nero C iv (The Winchester Psalter)
http://www.bl.uk/manuscripts/FullDisplay.aspx?ref=Cotton_MS_
Nero_C_IV
MS Nero D iv (The Lindisfarne Gospels)
http://www.bl.uk/manuscripts/FullDisplay.aspx?ref=Cotton_MS_
Nero_D_IV

MS Nero D vii (Golden Book of St Albans)
http://www.bl.uk/manuscripts/FullDisplay.aspx?ref=Cotton_MS_Nero_D_VII

MS Tiberius B v (computistical, historical and astronomical miscellany)
http://www.bl.uk/manuscripts/FullDisplay.aspx?ref=Cotton_MS_Tiberius_B_V/1

MS Titus D xviii (*Þe Wohunge of Ure Lauerd* [*The Wooing of Our Lord*])
http://www.bl.uk/manuscripts/FullDisplay.aspx?ref=Cotton_MS_Titus_D_XVIII

MS Vitellius A xv (*Beowulf*)
http://www.bl.uk/manuscripts/FullDisplay.aspx?ref=Cotton_MS_Vitellius_A_XV

Harley

MS 978 (*Lais* and *Fables* of Marie de France)
http://www.bl.uk/manuscripts/FullDisplay.aspx?ref=Harley_MS_978

MS 2382 (partial copy of *The Canterbury Tales*)
http://www.bl.uk/manuscripts/FullDisplay.aspx?ref=Harley_MS_2382

MS 2965 ('Book of Nunnaminster')
http://www.bl.uk/manuscripts/FullDisplay.aspx?ref=Harley_MS_2965

MS 5272 (Lydgate's *Life of Our Lady*, once belonged to Elisabeth Danes)
http://www.bl.uk/manuscripts/FullDisplay.aspx?ref=Harley_MS_5272

MS 7026 (Lovell Lectionary, painted by John Siferwas)
http://www.bl.uk/manuscripts/FullDisplay.aspx?ref=Harley_MS_7026/1

Royal

MS 2 A XVI (Henry VIII's Psalter)
http://www.bl.uk/manuscripts/FullDisplay.aspx?ref=Royal_MS_2_A_XVI

MS 17 D VI (Thomas Hoccleve's *Regiment of Princes*)
http://www.bl.uk/manuscripts/FullDisplay.aspx?ref=Royal_MS_17_D_VI

MS 18 D II (Lydgate's *Siege of Thebes*, depicting the Canterbury pilgrims)
http://www.bl.uk/manuscripts/FullDisplay.aspx?ref=Royal_MS_18_D_II

Stowe

MS 956 ('girdle book' made for Anne Boleyn)
https://www.bl.uk/catalogues/illuminatedmanuscripts/record.asp?MSID=7213&CollID=21&NStart=956

Bibliography

Lambeth Palace Library

    MS 265 (*Dictes and Sayings of the Philosophers*)
    https://images.lambethpalacelibrary.org.uk/luna/servlet/s/5ay237

Munich

Bayerische Staatsbibliothek

    MS Clm 1086 (Hugeberc's *Lives of Saints Wynnebald and Willibald*)
    https://iiif.biblissima.fr/collections/manifest/
    ddbc5b54f8357800d8f433c6311effe54b16e214

New York

Morgan Library

    MS M. 619 (The Morgan Leaf)
    https://www.themorgan.org/manuscript/145640

Oxford

Bodleian Library (Bodl.)

    MS Auct. E inf. 2 (Bible commissioned by Henry of Blois)
    https://digital.bodleian.ox.ac.uk/objects/6c9201e7-755f-4510-ae36-
    92e9b67aab41/
    MS Bodley 451 (copied by the Nunnaminster 'scriptrix')
    https://digital.bodleian.ox.ac.uk/objects/5dbb4f95-5c18-4cef-aa52-
    74b0a1651e86/surfaces/bb814b8a-eb0f-43ec-b2cb-0ad861c8f59f/
    MS Bodley 883 (Le Chemin de Paradis, created by Jean Mallard)
    https://digital.bodleian.ox.ac.uk/objects/03c0ec22-fb0d-4606-b5fc-
    399ac6a71a07/
    MS Tanner 407 (Commonplace book of Robert Reynes of Acle)
    https://digital.bodleian.ox.ac.uk/objects/d54cd0f2-60a3-400f-b1f7-
    3fab3aac42cb/

Paris

Bibliothèque nationale de France

    MS Français 12420 (Boccaccio, *De Mulieribus Claris* [*Of Famous
    Women*])
    https://gallica.bnf.fr/ark:/12148/btv1b10509080f/f181.item.zoom

St Petersburg

National Library of Russia

    MS lat.Q.v. I.18 (The St Petersburg Bede, containing an early copy of
    Cædmon's *Hymn*)
    http://people.uleth.ca/~daniel.odonnell/caedmon/html/htm/
    transcription/l/facsimile.htm

Bibliography

San Marino

Huntington Library

MS HM 111 (Autograph of Thomas Hoccleve's *La Male Regle*)
https://hdl.huntington.org/digital/collection/p15150coll7/id/9873/
MS HM EL 26 C 9 (Ellesmere Manuscript of *The Canterbury Tales*)
https://hdl.huntington.org/digital/collection/p15150coll7/id/2359/
rec/1

Vatican City

Vatican Library

MS ebr. 402 (Poems of Meir bin Elijah)
https://digi.vatlib.it/view/MSS_Vat.ebr.402

PRIMARY SOURCES

Acta Sanctorum Martii Tomus a Joanne Bollando, 6 vols (Antwerp: Jacobum
Meursium, 1668)

Æthelwulf, *De abbatibus*, ed. Alistair Campbell (Oxford: Clarendon Press,
1967)

Aldhelm: *The Prose Works*, trans. Michael Lapidge and Michael Herren
(Cambridge: D. S. Brewer, 1979; repr. 2009)

Alfred the Great: Asser's Life of King Alfred and Other Contemporary Sources,
ed. and trans. Simon Keynes and Michael Lapidge (Harmondsworth:
Penguin, 1983)

Anchoritic Spirituality: 'Ancrene Wisse' and Associated Works, ed. and trans.
Anne Savage and Nicholas Watson (Mahwah, NJ: Paulist Press, 1991)

*'Ancrene Wisse': A Corrected Edition of the Texts in CCCC MS 402, with
Variants from other Manuscripts*, ed. Bella Millett, Early English Text
Society (old series) 325 (Oxford: Oxford University Press, 2005)

Ancrene Wisse: Guide for Anchoresses, ed. and trans. Bella Millet (Exeter:
University of Exeter Press, 2009)

The Anglo-Saxon Chronicle, ed. and trans. Dorothy Whitelock and others
(London: Eyre and Spottiswoode, 1961)

The Anglo-Saxon Chronicle, 6: MS D, ed. G. P. Cubbin (Cambridge: D. S.
Brewer, 1996)

*Anglo-Saxon Remedies, Charms and Prayers from British Library MS Harley
585: The Lacnunga. Vol. 1*, ed. and trans. Edward Pettit, Mellen Critical
Editions and Translations, Volume 6a (Lewiston, NY; Lampeter: Edward
Mellen Press, 2001)

Bibliography

Antiquæ Literaturæ Septemtrionalis liber alter ... Catalogus historico-criticus
(1705); facsimile edition (Menston: Scolar Press, 1970)

Asser's 'Life of King Alfred', together with the Annals of St. Neots, with an article
on recent work by Dorothy Whitelock, ed. William Henry Stevenson
(Oxford: Clarendon Press, 1959)

Asser, *The Medieval Life of King Alfred the Great: A Translation and
Commentary on the Text Attributed to Asser*, ed. and trans. Alfred P.
Smyth (Basingstoke: Palgrave, 2002)

Bede's Ecclesiastical History of the English People, ed. and trans. Bertram
Colgrave and R. A. B. Mynors (Oxford: Clarendon Press, 1969)

Beirdd Ceridwen Blodeugerdd Barddas o Ganu Menywod hyd Tua 1800, ed.
Cathryn Charnell-White (Swansea: Cyhoeddiadau Barddas, 2005)

Beowulf, ed. and trans. Michael Swanton, rev. ed. (Manchester; New York:
Manchester University Press, 1997)

Beowulf, trans. Seamus Heaney (London: Faber and Faber, 1999)

Blomefield, Francis, *An Essay Towards a Topographical History of the County
of Norfolk: Volume Three, Part First: The History of Norwich* (London:
William Miller, 1806)

Boccaccio, Giovanni, *Famous Women*, ed. and trans. Virginia Brown
(Cambridge, MA; London: Harvard University Press, 2001)

Boniface, St, *The Letters of Saint Boniface*, ed. and trans. Ephraim Emerton
(New York: W. W. Norton, 1976)

Cædmon's Hymn: A Multimedia Study, Edition and Archive, ed. Daniel Paul
O'Donnell (Cambridge: D. S. Brewer, 2005), <http://people.uleth.
ca/~daniel.odonnell/caedmon/html/index.htm>

Cassiodorus, Flavius Magnus Aurelius, *Institutiones*, ed. R. A. B. Mynors
(Oxford: Clarendon Press, 1937)

————, *Institutions of Divine and Secular Learning and On the Soul*, ed. and
trans. James W. Halporn, with introduction by Mark Vessey (Liverpool:
Liverpool University Press, 2004)

*Catalogue of Additions to the Manuscripts in the British Museum in the Years
MDCCCXLI–MDCCCXLV* (London: George Woodfall and Son, 1850)

Catalogue of Dated and Datable Manuscripts, c. 435–1600, in Oxford Libraries,
ed. Andrew G. Watson, 2 vols (Oxford: Clarendon Press, 1984)

*Catalogue of the Manuscripts Preserved in the Library of the University of
Cambridge*, 5 vols (Cambridge: Cambridge University Press, 1858)

Chaucer, Geoffrey, *The Canterbury Tales* (London: William Caxton, 1483)

————, *The Text of 'The Canterbury Tales' Studied on the Basis of all Known
Manuscripts*, ed. John Manly and Edith Rickert, 8 vols (Chicago:
University of Chicago Press, 1940)

Bibliography

———, *The Riverside Chaucer*, gen. ed. Larry D. Benson, 3rd edition (Oxford: Oxford University Press, 1988)

———, *The Norton Chaucer*, ed. David Lawton (New York; London: W. W. Norton, 2019)

———, *The Canterbury Tales*, ed. Julia Boffey and A. S. G. Edwards (Cambridge: Cambridge University Press, forthcoming)

de Bury, Richard, *The Philobiblon*, ed. and trans. Ernest C. Thomas (London: Kegan Paul, Trench and Co., 1888)

Documents of the English Reformation, ed. Gerald Bray (Cambridge: James Clarke, 1994)

The Earliest Life of Gregory the Great by an Anonymous Monk of Whitby, ed. and trans. Bertram Colgrave (Lawrence: University of Kansas Press, 1968)

Emmæ Anglorum Reginæ Richardi I. Ducis Normannorum filiæ Encomium, incerto authore, sed coætaneo (London, 1619)

Encomium Emmae Reginae, ed. Alistair Campbell, with a supplementary introduction by Simon Keynes, Camden Classic Reprints 4 (Cambridge: Cambridge University Press, 1998)

Erasmus, Desiderius, *The Correspondence of Erasmus: Letters 1252 to 1355, 1522 to 1523* [Volume 9], trans. R. A. B. Mynors, annotated by James M. Estes (Toronto; Buffalo, NY; London: University of Toronto Press, 1989)

The Exeter Anthology of Old English Poetry: An Edition of Exeter Dean and Chapter MS 3501, ed. Bernard J. Muir, 2nd ed., 2 vols (Exeter: University of Exeter Press, 2000)

Fitzgerald, Thomas, *Poems on Several Occasions by the late Reverend Thomas Fitzgerald* (London and Oxford, 1781)

The Gutenberg Bible of 1454: A Facsimile, ed. Stephan Füssel, 3 vols (Cologne: Taschen, 2018)

Gwaith Huw, Cae Llwyd ac Eraill [*The Works of Huw of Cae Llwyd and Others*], ed. Leslie Harries (Caerdydd: Gwasg Prifysgol, 1953)

Hebrew Manuscripts in the Vatican Library, ed. Benjamin Richler (Vatican: Biblioteca Apostolica Vatican, 2008)

Hoccleve, Thomas, *Hoccleve's Works*, ed. Frederick J. Furnivall, 2 vols (1892; repr. Oxford: Oxford University Press, 1970)

Hoccleve, Thomas, *The Regiment of Princes*, ed. Charles R. Blyth, TEAMS Middle English Texts Series (Kalamazoo, MI: Medieval Institute Publications, 1999), <https://d.lib.rochester.edu/teams/publication/blyth-hoccleve-the-regiment-of-princes>

———, *Thomas Hoccleve: A Facsimile of the Autograph Verse Manuscripts*, ed.

Bibliography

J. A. Burrow and A. I. Doyle, Early English Text Society (supplementary series) 19 (Oxford: Oxford University Press, 2002)

———, *Hoccleve's 'Male Regle'*, trans. Jenni Nuttall, International Hoccleve Society, <https://hocclevesociety.org/texts-and-resources/hoccleves-male-regle/>

The Inventory of King Henry VIII: The Transcript, ed. David Starkey (London: Harvey Miller; Society of Antiquaries, 1998)

James, M. R., and Claude Jenkins, *A Descriptive Catalogue of the Manuscripts in the Library of Lambeth Palace*, 2 parts (Cambridge: Cambridge University Press, 1930), rev. ed. Richard Palmer (2011), <https://archives.lambethpalacelibrary.org.uk/CalmView/Record.aspx?src=CalmView.Catalog&id=MSS%2F265>

Julian of Norwich, *XVI Revelations of Divine Love, shewed to a devout servant of our Lord, called Mother Juliana, an anchorete of Norwich: who lived in the dayes of King Edward the Third*, published by [Hugh] R. F. S. Cressy (n.p., 1670)

———, *Revelations of Divine Love: A Version from the MS in the British Museum*, ed. Grace Warrack (London: Methuen, 1901)

———, *The Shewings of Julian of Norwich*, ed. Georgia Ronan Crampton, TEAMS Middle English Texts Series (Kalamazoo, MI: Medieval Institute Publications, 1994), <https://d.lib.rochester.edu/teams/text/the-shewings-of-julian-of-norwich-introduction>

———, *Revelations of Divine Love (Short Text and Long Text)*, trans. Elizabeth Spearing, ed. A. C. Spearing (London; New York: Penguin, 1998)

———, *Revelations of Divine Love: The Short and the Long Text*, ed. Barry Windeatt (Oxford: Oxford University Press, 2016)

Kempe, Margery, *The Book of Margery Kempe: A Modern Version*, ed. W. Butler-Bowdon, Life and Letters 103 (London: Jonathan Cape, 1936)

———, *The Book of Margery Kempe*, ed. Sanford Brown Meech and Hope Emily Allen, Early English Text Society (old series) 212 (London: Humphrey Milford; Oxford University Press, 1940)

———, *The Book of Margery Kempe*, ed. Barry Windeatt (Cambridge: D. S. Brewer, 2000, repr. 2004)

———, *The Book of Margery Kempe*, trans. Anthony Bale (Oxford: Oxford University Press, 2015)

King Henry's Prayer Book, facsimile edition, with a commentary by James P. Carley (London: Folio Society, 2009)

Leabhar Breac, the Speckled Book, Otherwise Styled Leabhar Mór Dúna Doighre, a Collection of Pieces in Irish and Latin, Compiled about the Close of the

Bibliography

XIV Century . . . Lithograph facsimile, ed. J. Ó Longáin and J. J. Gilbert (Dublin: Royal Irish Academy, 1876)

Leland, John, *The Laboryouse Journey: serche of Johan Leylande, for Englandes antiquitees, geven of hym as a newe yeares gyfte to kynge Henry the viij. in the xxxvij. yeare of his reygne, with declaracyons enlarged: by Johan Bale* (London, 1549)

———, and Nicholas Udall, *Poetry for the Coronation of Anne Boleyn (1533): A Hypertext Critical Edition*, ed. Dana F. Sutton (2006), <http://www.philological.bham.ac.uk/boleyn/>

Lydgate, John, *Lydgate's 'Fall of Princes'*, ed. Henry Bergen (Washington, DC: Carnegie Institute of Washington, 1923)

Malory, Thomas, *The most ancient and famous History of the renowned prince Arthur King of Britaine* (London: printed by William Stansby, for Iacob Bloome, 1634)

———, *Le Morte Darthur*, ed. Stephen A. Shepherd (New York: W. W. Norton, 2004)

Marie de France, *Seven of her Lais Done into English*, trans. Edith Rickert (London: David Nutt, 1901)

———, *Fables of Marie de France*, ed. and trans. Harriet Spiegel, Toronto Medieval Texts and Translations 5 (Toronto: University of Toronto Press, 1987)

———, *Lais*, ed. Alfred Ewert, with introduction and bibliography by Glyn S. Burgess (London: Bristol Classical Press, 1995)

Mechain, Gwerful, *Gwaith Gwerful Mechain ac Eraill* [*The Works of Gwerful Mechain and Others*], ed. Nerys Ann Howells, Cyfres Beirdd yr Uchelwyr (Aberystwyth: Canolfan Uwchefrydiau Cymreig a Cheltaidd Prifysgol Cymru [Aberystwyth: Centre for Advanced Welsh and Celtic Studies], 2001)

———, *The Works of Gwerful Mechain*, ed. and trans. Katie Gramich (Peterborough, Ontario: Broadview Press, 2018)

Meir of Norwich [Meir bin Elijah], *Into the Light: The Medieval Hebrew Poetry of Meir of Norwich*, trans. Ellman Crasnow and Bente Elsworth (Norwich: East Publishing, 2013)

Memorials of Saint Dunstan, Archbishop of Canterbury, ed. William Stubbs (London: Longman & Co., 1874)

Memorials of St Edmund's Abbey, ed. Thomas Arnold, 3 vols (London: Eyre and Spottiswoode, 1890–1896)

The Middle English Charters of Christ, ed. Mary Caroline Spalding (Bryn Mawr, PA: Bryn Mawr College, 1914)

Middle English Religious Prose, ed. N. F. Blake (London: Edward Arnold, 1972)

Bibliography

Morley, Henry, *The Exposition and Declaration of the Psalme, Deus Ultionem Dominus, made by syr Henry Parker night, Lord Morley etc.* (London: Thomas Berthelet, 1539)

Myrc, John, *Instructions for Parish Priests*, ed. Edward Peacock, Early English Text Society (original series) 31 (London: Kegan, Trench, Trübner and Co. 1868)

Old and Middle English, c. 890–1450: An Anthology, ed. Elaine Treharne, 3rd ed. (Oxford: Wiley Blackwell, 2010)

The Old English Heptateuch and Ælfric's 'Libellus de Veteri Testamento et Novo' I, ed. Richard Marsden, Early English Text Society (old series) 330 (Oxford: Oxford University Press, 2008)

Paston Letters and Papers of the Fifteenth Century, ed. Norman Davis, 2 vols (Oxford: Clarendon Press, 1971)

The Paston Women: Selected Letters, ed. and trans. Diane Watt (Woodbridge: Boydell and Brewer, 2004)

Piramus, Denis, *La vie seint Edmund le rei, poème anglo-normand du XIIe siècle*, ed. Hilding Kjellman (Gothenburg, 1935)

Pollard, A. W., and G. R. Redgrave, *A Short Title Catalogue of Books Printed in England, Scotland and Ireland, 1475–1640*, 2nd ed., rev. and enlarged by W. A. Jackson, F. S. Ferguson and Katherine E. Pantzer, 3 vols (London: Bibliographical Society, 1986–91)

Report from the Committee appointed to view the Cottonian Library, A [9 May 1732] (London: R. Williamson, 1732)

A Revelation of Purgatory, ed. Liz Herbert McAvoy (Cambridge: D. S. Brewer, 2017)

Reynes, Robert, *The Commonplace Book of Robert Reynes of Acle: An Edition of Tanner MS 407*, ed. Louis Cameron (New York: Garland, 1980)

Rites of Durham, being a Description or Brief Declaration of all the Ancient Monuments, Rites & Customs belonging or being within the Monastical Church of Durham before the Suppression, written 1593, ed. Joseph T. Fowler, Surtees Society (Durham: Andrews, 1903)

Ryves, Bruno, *Mercurius Rusticus: or, The Countries Complaint of the Barbarous Outrages Committed by the Sectaries of this Late Flourishing Kingdom* (1646)

Shakespeare, William, *Antony and Cleopatra*, ed. John Wilders (Arden Shakespeare; London: Routledge, 1995)

Simeon of Durham, *Symeonis Dunelmensis Opera et Collectanea*, ed. I. Hodgson-Hinde, 2 vols (Durham: Andrews, 1868)

Simeon of Durham's 'History of the Kings of England', in *The Church Historians of England Containing the Historical Works of Simeon of*

Bibliography

Durham, translated from the original Latin with preface and notes, ed. and trans. Joseph Stevenson (London: Seeleys, 1855)

Skelton, John, *Magnyfycence, a Goodly Interlude and a Mery / Deuysed and made by Mayster Skelton/ Poet Laureate Late Deceasyd* (London: J. Rastell, 1533)

Stillingfleet, Edward, *A Discourse Concerning Idolatry Practised in the Church of Rome*, 2nd ed. (London, 1672)

Stuart, Lady Louisa, *Selections from her Manuscripts*, ed. James Home (Edinburgh: David Douglas, 1899)

Two Lives of Saint Cuthbert: A Life by an Anonymous Monk of Lindisfarne and Bede's Prose Life, ed. and trans. Bertram Colgrave (Cambridge: Cambridge University Press, 1940)

William of Malmesbury, *The Deeds of the English Kings* (*Gesta regum Anglorum*), ed. and trans. R. A. B. Mynors, completed by R. M. Thomson and M. Winterbottom (London: Folio Society, 2014)

Þe Wohunge of Ure Lauerd, ed. Meredith W. Thompson, Early English Text Society (old series) 241 (London: Oxford University Press, 1958)

Wood, Anthony, *Athenae Oxonienses: An Exact History of All the Writers and Bishops who Have Had Their Education in the University of Oxford. Volume 1*, ed. Philip Bliss (London: F. C. and J. Rivington, 1813)

SECONDARY SOURCES

Aston, Margaret, 'English Ruins and English History: The Dissolution and the Sense of the Past', *Journal of the Warburg and Courtauld Institutes* 36 (1973), 231–55

Backhouse, Janet, *The Lindisfarne Gospels* (Oxford: Phaidon/British Library, 1981)

——, 'Birds, Beasts and Initials in Lindisfarne's Gospel books', in *St Cuthbert, His Cult and His Community to AD 1200*, ed. Gerald Bonner, David Rollason and Clare Stancliffe (Woodbridge: Boydell, 1989), pp. 165–74

——, *The Luttrell Psalter* (London: British Library, 1989)

——, *The Sherborne Missal* (London: British Library, 1999)

——, *Medieval Birds in the Sherborne Missal* (London: British Library, 2001)

Bale, Anthony, *The Jew in the Medieval Book: English Anti-Semitisms, 1350–1500* (Cambridge: Cambridge University Press, 2006)

——, 'From Translator to Laureate: Imagining the Medieval Author', *Literature Compass* 5 (2008), 918–34

Bibliography

————, 'Poems of Protest: Meir ben Elijah and the Jewish People of Early Britain', 'Our Migration Story', <https://www.ourmigrationstory.org.uk/oms/put-a-curse-on-my-enemies-meir-ben-elijah-and-the-jews-of-early-norwich>

Battiscombe, C. F., ed., *The Relics of Saint Cuthbert: Studies by Various Authors Collected and Edited, with an Historical Introduction* (Oxford: Oxford University Press, 1956)

Beach, Alison I., *Women As Scribes: Book Production and Monastic Reform in Twelfth-Century Bavaria* (Cambridge: Cambridge University Press, 2004)

Beer, Barrett L., 'Stow [Stowe], John (1524/5–1605), historian', *ODNB*, <https://www.oxforddnb.com/view/10.1093/ref:odnb/9780198614128.001.0001/odnb-9780198614128-e-26611>

Bell, David N., *What Nuns Read: Books and Libraries in Medieval English Nunneries*, Cistercian Studies 158 (Kalamazoo, MI: Cistercian Publications, 1995)

Beverley, Tessa, 'Portinari, Sir Giovanni (b. c. 1502x1508, d. in or after 1572), military engineer', *ODNB*, <https://www.oxforddnb.com/view/10.1093/ref:odnb/9780198614128.001.0001/odnb-9780198614128-e-52154>

Binski, Paul, *Gothic Wonder: Art, Artifice and the Decorated Style, 1290–1350* (New Haven, CT: Yale University Press, 2014)

Bjork, Robert E., 'Grímur Jónsson Thorkelin's Preface to the First Edition of Beowulf, 1815', *Scandinavian Studies* 68 (1996), 291–320

Blake, N. F., 'Manuscript to Print', in *Book Production and Publishing in Britain 1375–1475*, ed. Jeremy Griffiths and Derek Pearsall (Cambridge: Cambridge University Press, 1989), pp. 409–32

Bloch, R. Howard, *The Anonymous Marie de France* (Chicago: University of Chicago Press, 2003)

Boffey, Julia, and A. S. G. Edwards, *A New Index of Middle English Verse* (London: British Library, 2005)

Bolton, Timothy, 'A Newly Emergent Mediaeval Manuscript Containing Encomium Emmae Reginae with the Only Known Complete Text of the Recension Prepared for King Edward the Confessor', *Mediaeval Scandinavia* 19 (2009), 205–21

Bowyer, William, *Literary Anecdotes of the Eighteenth Century: Comprizing Biographical Memoirs of William Bowyer, printer, F.S.A.*, 34 vols (London, 1812–15)

Braswell, Laurel, 'Saint Edburga of Winchester: A Study of Her Cult, AD 950–1500, with an Edition of the Fourteenth-Century Middle English and Latin Lives', *Mediaeval Studies* 33 (1971), 292–333

Bibliography

Breay, Claire, and Bernard Meehan, ed., *The St Cuthbert Gospel: Studies on the Insular Manuscript of the Gospel of Saint John (BL, Additional MS 89000)* (London: British Library, 2015)

Brown, Michelle P., 'Female Book Ownership and Production in Anglo-Saxon England: The Evidence of Ninth-Century Prayerbooks', in *Lexis and Text in Early English: Papers in Honour of Jane Roberts*, ed. Christian Kay and Louise Sylvester (Amsterdam: Rodopi, 2001), pp. 45–68

——, *The Lindisfarne Gospels: Society, Spirituality and the Scribe* (London: British Library, 2003)

——, *The Luttrell Psalter: A Facsimile* (London: British Library, 2006)

——, *The World of the Luttrell Psalter* (London: British Library, 2006)

——, *The Lindisfarne Gospels and the Early Medieval World* (London: British Library, 2011)

———, 'Reading the Lindisfarne Gospels: Text, Image, Context', in Gameson, ed., *The Lindisfarne Gospels: New Perspectives* (2017), pp. 84–95

Bugyis, Katie Ann-Marie, *The Care of Nuns: The Ministries of Benedictine Women in England during the Central Middle Ages* (Oxford: Oxford University Press, 2019)

Bühler, Curt F., *The Fifteenth-Century Book: The Scribes, The Printers, The Decorators* (Philadelphia: University of Pennsylvania Press, 1960)

Busby, Keith, 'The Manuscripts of Marie de France', in *A Companion to Marie de France*, ed. Logan E. Whalen (Leiden: Brill, 2011), pp. 302–17

Butterfield, Ardis, 'Mise-en-page in the *Troilus* Manuscripts: Chaucer and French Manuscript Culture', *Huntington Library Quarterly* 58 (1995), 49–80

Camille, Michael, *Image on the Edge: The Margins of Medieval Art* (London: Reaktion Books, 1992)

——, *Mirror in Parchment: The Luttrell Psalter and the Making of Medieval England* (London: Reaktion Books, 1998)

Campbell, Thomas, *Henry VIII and the Art of Majesty: Tapestries at the Tudor Court* (New Haven, CT and London: Yale University Press, 2007)

Carley, James, 'John Leland and the Contents of English Pre-Dissolution Libraries: Lincolnshire', *Transactions of the Cambridge Bibliographical Society* 9 (1989), 330–57

——, *The Libraries of King Henry VIII* (London: British Library in association with the British Academy, 2000)

——, *The Books of King Henry VIII and his Wives* (London: British Library, 2004)

Cartwright, Jane, *Y Forwyn Fair, Santesau a Lleianod. Agweddau ar Wyryfdod*

Bibliography

a Diweirdeb yng Nyghymru'r Oesoedd Canol (Cardiff: University of Wales Press, 1999)

——, 'Women Writers in Wales', in *The History of British Women's Writing, 700–1500: Volume I*, ed. Liz Herbert McAvoy and Diane Watt (New York: Palgrave, 2012), pp. 60–71

Castor, Helen, *Blood and Roses: The Paston Family in the Fifteenth Century* (London: Faber and Faber, 2004)

Chappell, Julie A., *Perilous Passages: 'The Book of Margery Kempe' 1534–1934* (Basingstoke: Palgrave, 2013)

Charnell-White, Cathryn A., 'Problems of Authorship and Attribution: The Welsh-Language Women's Canon Before 1800', *Women's Writing* 24 (2017), 398–417

Christie-Miller, Ian, 'Henry VIII and British Library, Royal MS. 2 A. XVI: Marginalia in King Henry's Psalter', *Electronic British Library Journal* 2015 (article 8): <https://www.bl.uk/eblj/2015articles/pdf/ebljarticle82015.pdf>

Clark, David, 'Race/Ethnicity and the Other in Beowulf: Return to the Shieldlands', in *'Beowulf' in Contemporary Culture*, ed. David Clark (Newcastle: Cambridge Scholars Publishing, 2020)

Crampton, Georgia Ronan, 'The Shewings of Julian of Norwich: Introduction', TEAMS Middle English Texts Series (Kalamazoo, MI: Medieval Institute Publications, 1994), <https://d.lib.rochester.edu/teams/text/the-shewings-of-julian-of-norwich-introduction>

Devereux, E. J., 'Empty Tuns and Unfruitful Grafts: Richard Grafton's Historical Publications', *The Sixteenth Century Journal* 21 (1990), 33–56

Donovan, Claire, *The Winchester Bible* (London and Winchester: British Library and Winchester Cathedral, 1993)

Dowding, Clare M., '"A Certain Tourelle on London Wall . . . Was Granted . . . for Him to Inhabit the Same": London Anchorites and the City Wall', *Journal of Medieval Religious Cultures* 42 (Special Issue: 'Anchoritic Studies and Liminality') (2016), 44–55

Drieshen, Clarck, 'English Nuns as "Anchoritic Intercessors" for Souls in Purgatory: The Employment of A Revelation of Purgatory by Late Medieval English Nunneries for Their Lay Communities', in *Medieval Anchorites in Their Communities*, ed. Cate Gunn and Liz Herbert McAvoy (Woodbridge; Rochester, NY: Boydell & Brewer, 2017), pp. 85–100

Drogin, Marc, *Anathema!: Medieval Scribes and the History of Book Curses* (Totowa, NJ: Allanheld and Schram, 1983)

Duffy, Christina, 'Under the Microscope with the Lindisfarne Gospels', British Library Collection Care Blog (29 July 2013), <https://blogs.

bl.uk/collectioncare/2013/07/under-the-microscope-with-the-
lindisfarne-gospels.html>

Edwards, A. S. G., 'Editing Malory: Eugène Vinaver and the Clarendon
Edition', *Leeds Studies in English*, new series XLI (2010), 76–81

——, 'Chaucer and "Adam Scriveyn"', *Medium Ævum* 82 (2012), 135–38

——, 'To speken short and pleyn', *Times Literary Supplement*, No. 6013
(2018), <https://www.the-tls.co.uk/articles/to-speken-short-and-
pleyn/>

——, 'William Caxton and the Introduction of Printing to England'
('Discovering Literature: Medieval', 2018), <https://www.bl.uk/
medieval-literature/articles/william-caxton-and-the-introduction-of-
printing-to-england>

Einbinder, Susan L. 'Meir b. Elijah of Norwich: Persecution and Poetry
Among Medieval English Jews', *Journal of Medieval History* 26 (2000),
145–62

Fell, Christine E., *Women in Anglo-Saxon England and the Impact of 1066*
(London: British Museum Publications, 1984)

——, 'Some Implications of the Boniface Correspondence', in *New
Readings on Women in Old English Literature*, ed. Helen Damico and
Alexandra Hennessey Olsen (Bloomington: Indiana University Press,
1990), pp. 29–43

Fellows-Jensen, Gillian, 'By-names', in *The Wiley Blackwell Encyclopedia
of Anglo-Saxon England*, ed. Michael Lapidge, and others, 2nd ed.
(Chichester: Wiley Blackwell, 2014)

Ferry, Anne, 'Anonymity: The Literary History of a Word', *New Literary
History* 33 (2000), 193–214

Fox, Adam, *John Mill and Richard Bentley: A Study of the Textual Criticism of
the New Testament 1675–1729* (Oxford: Basil Blackwell, 1954)

Frank, Roberta, 'King Cnut in the Verse of his Skalds', in *The Reign of Cnut:
King of England, Denmark and Norway*, ed. Alexander R. Rumble
(London, New York: Leicester University Press, 1994, repr. 1999),
pp. 106–24

Franzen, Christine, *The Tremulous Hand of Worcester: A Study of Old English
in the Thirteenth Century* (Oxford: Clarendon Press, 1991)

Fryer, Peter, *Staying Power: The History of Black People in Britain* (London:
Pluto, 1984)

Gameson, Richard, 'Material Fabric of Early English Books', in *The Cambridge
History of the Book in Britain: Volume 1: c. 400–1100*, ed. Richard
Gameson (Cambridge: Cambridge University Press, 2011), pp. 13–93

——, 'Materials, Text, Layout and Script', in Breay and Meehan, ed.,
The St Cuthbert Gospel (2015), pp. 13–39

Bibliography

———, ed., *The Lindisfarne Gospels: New Perspectives*. Library of the Written Word 57, The Manuscript World 9 (Leiden, Boston: Brill, 2017)

———, 'Northumbrian Books in the Seventh and Eighth Centuries', in Gameson, ed., *The Lindisfarne Gospels: New Perspectives* (2017), pp. 43–83

Gilchrist, Roberta, *Contemplation and Action: The Other Monasticism* (London: Leicester University Press, 1995)

Gillespie, Alexandra, *Print Culture and the Medieval Author: Chaucer, Lydgate and their Books, 1473–1557* (Oxford: Oxford University Press, 2006)

Gillespie, Vincent, '"[S]he Do the Police in Different Voices": Pastiche, Ventriloquism and Parody in Julian of Norwich', in *A Companion to Julian of Norwich*, ed. Liz Herbert McAvoy (Woodbridge: Boydell and Brewer, 2008), pp. 192–207

———, and Maggie Ross, 'The Apophatic Image: The Poetics of Effacement in Julian of Norwich's Revelation of Love', in *The Medieval Mystical Tradition in England*, ed. Marion Glasscoe, Exeter Symposium 5 (Cambridge: D. S. Brewer, 1992), pp. 53–77

Graham, Timothy, 'Siferwas, John (fl. 1380–1421), manuscript artist', *ODNB* online, <https://www.oxforddnb.com/view/10.1093/ref:odnb/9780198614128.001.0001/odnb-9780198614128-e-37958>, accessed 28 Oct 2019

Gramich, Katie, 'Orality and Morality: Early Welsh Women's Poetry', <http://www2.lingue.unibo.it/acume/acumedvd/Essays%20ACUME/AcumeGramichfinal.pdf>

Green, Richard Firth, *Poets and Princepleasers: Literature and the English Court in the Late Middle Ages* (Toronto: University of Toronto Press, 1980)

Gullick, Michael, 'How Fast did Scribes Write?: Evidence from Romanesque Manuscripts', in *Making the Medieval Book: Techniques of Production (Proceedings of the Fourth Conference of the Seminar in the History of the Book to 1500, Oxford, July 1992)* (Los Altos Hills, CA; London: Anderson-Lovelace; Red Gull Press, 1995), pp. 39–58

———, and Nicholas Hadgraft, 'Bookbindings', in *The Cambridge History of the Book in Britain: Volume 2: c. 1100–1400*, ed. Nigel Morgan and Rodney M. Thomson (Cambridge: Cambridge University Press, 1998), pp. 95–109

Hammond, Eleanor Prescott, 'On the Order of the Canterbury Tales: Caxton's Two Editions', *Modern Philology* 3 (1905), 159–78

Harries, Leslie, 'Barddoniaeth Huw Cae Llwyd, Ieuan ap Huw Cae Llywd, Ieuan Dyfi, a Gwerful Mechain' (unpublished MA thesis, University College of Wales, Swansea, 1933)

Hasenfratz, Robert, 'Ancrene Wisse, Introduction', TEAMS Middle English

Texts Series (Kalamazoo, MI: Medieval Institute Publications, 2001),
<https://d.lib.rochester.edu/teams/text/hasenfratz-ancrene-wisse-
introduction>

Hathaway, Neil, 'Compilatio: From Plagiarism to Compiling', *Viator* 20
(1989), 19–44

Hellinga, Lotte, 'The Malory Manuscript and Caxton', in *Aspects of Malory*,
ed. Derek Brewer and Toshiyuki Takamiya, Arthurian Studies I
(Cambridge: D. S. Brewer, 1981), pp. 127–42

———, *William Caxton and Early Printing in England* (London: British
Library, 2010)

Herbert, J. A., *The Sherborne Missal: Reproduction of Full Pages and Details of
Ornament from the Missal Executed between the years 1396 and 1407 for
Sherborne Abbey Church and now Preserved in the Library of the Duke of
Northumberland at Alnwick Castle* (Oxford: Roxburghe Club, 1920)

Hill, Carole, *Women and Religion in Medieval Norwich* (Woodbridge: Boydell
and Brewer, 2010)

Hirsch, John C., 'Hope Emily Allen (1883–1960): An Independent Scholar',
in *Women Medievalists and the Academy*, ed. Jane Chance (Madison, WI:
University of Wisconsin Press, 2005), pp. 227–38

Hobson, Jacob, 'National-Ethnic Narratives in Eleventh-Century Literary
Representations of Cnut', *Anglo-Saxon England* 43 (2014), 267–95

Honey, Andrew, 'Practice Makes Perfect?: Lessons Learnt from the
Binding of the Winchester Bible', <https://ora.ox.ac.uk/objects/
uuid:776ac48e-4504-4980-ab07-36f14c50abc7/download_file?file_
format=pdf&safe_filename=Honey%2520CC17%2520July%25202019.
pdf&type_of_work=Conference+item>

Houston, Keith, *The Book: A Cover-to-Cover Exploration of the Most Powerful
Object of Our Time* (New York; London: W. W. Norton, 2016)

Hunt, Alice, *The Drama of Coronation: Medieval Ceremony in Early Modern
England* (Cambridge: Cambridge University press, 2008)

Hunt, Arnold, 'Post-Medieval Movements of the Manuscript', in Breay and
Meehan, ed., *The Cuthbert Gospel*, pp. 137–45

Innes-Parker, Catherine, 'Medieval Widowhood and Textual Guidance: The
Corpus Revisions of Ancrene Wisse and the de Braose Anchoresses',
Florilegium 28 (2011), 95–124

Insley, Charles, 'The Family of Wulfric Spotte: An Anglo-Saxon Mercian
Marcher Dynasty?', in *The English and Their Legacy, 900–1200: Essays in
Honour of Ann Williams*, ed. David Roffe (Woodbridge: Boydell Press,
2012), pp. 115–28

Jambeck, Karen, 'Reclaiming the Woman in the Book: Marie de France and
the Fables', in *Women, the Book and the Worldly: Selected Proceedings*

of the St Hilda's Conference, 1993, II, ed. L. Smith and J. H. M. Taylor (Cambridge: D. S. Brewer, 1995), pp. 119–37

Jeffs, Amy, and Mary Wellesley, 'Sexing Up the Cherry', *Apollo* 659 (2017), 76–81

Johnston, D. R., 'The Erotic Poetry of the Cywyddwyr', *Cambridge Medieval Celtic Studies* 22 (1991), 63–94

Johnston, Michael, 'Constantinian Christianity in the London Thornton Manuscript: The Codicological and Linguistic Evidence of Thornton's Intentions', in *Robert Thornton and His Books: Essays on the Lincoln and London Thornton Manuscripts*, ed. Susanna Fein and Michael Thornton (York: York Medieval Press, 2014), pp. 177–204

Jones, E. A., 'Ceremonies of Enclosure', in *Rhetoric of the Anchorhold: Space, Place and Body with the Discourse of Enclosure*, ed. Liz Herbert McAvoy (Cardiff: University of Wales Press, 2008), pp. 34–49

——, 'A Mirror for Recluses: A New Manuscript, New Information and Some New Hypotheses', *The Library* 15 (2014), 424–431

——, *Hermits and Anchorites in England 1200–1550* (Manchester: University of Manchester Press, 2019)

Kane, George, 'Word Games: Glossing Piers Plowman', in *New Perspectives on Middle English Texts: A Festschrift for R. A. Waldron*, ed. Susan Powell and Jeremy J. Smith (Cambridge: D.S. Brewer, 2000), pp. 43–54

Keene, Derek, *Survey of Medieval Winchester: I, II and III* (Winchester Studies 2), 2 vols (Oxford: Clarendon Press, 1985)

Kelliher, Hilton 'The Rediscovery of Margery Kempe: A Footnote', *British Library Journal* 23 (1997), 259–63, <http://www.bl.uk/eblj/1997articles/pdf/article19.pdf>

Ker, Neil R., *Medieval Libraries of Great Britain: A List of Surviving Books* (London: Royal Historical Society, 1941)

Keynes, Simon, 'The Reconstruction of a Burnt Cottonian Manuscript: The Case of Cotton MS Otho A. I', *British Library Journal* 22 (1996), 113–160

——, 'Emma [Ælfgifu] (d. 1052), queen of England, second consort of Æthelred II, and second consort of King Cnut', *ODNB*, <https://www.oxforddnb.com/view/10.1093/ref:odnb/9780198614128>

——, and Rosalind Love, 'Earl Godwine's Ship', *Anglo-Saxon England* 38 (2009), 185–223

Kiernan, Kevin S., *The Thorkelin Transcripts of 'Beowulf'*, Anglistica XXV (Copenhagen: Rosenkilde and Bagger, 1986)

——, 'Reading Cædmon's "Hymn" with Someone Else's Glosses', in Liuzza, ed., *Old English Literature: Critical Essays* (2002), pp. 103–24

Klapish-Zuber, Christiane, 'Women and the Family', in *Medieval Callings*, ed.

Bibliography

Jacques Le Goff, trans. Lydia G. Cochrane (Chicago; London: University of Chicago Press, 1990), pp. 285–311

Knowles, David, *Religious Orders in England*, 3 vols (Cambridge: Cambridge University Press, 1959)

Krakowka, Kathryn, 'Unlocking the Secrets of the Winchester Cathedral Mortuary Chests', *Current Archaeology* (4 July 2019), <https://www.archaeology.co.uk/articles/unlocking-the-secrets-of-the-winchester-cathedral-mortuary-chests.html>

Lapidge, Michael, 'Hadrian (630x37–709), abbot of St Peter's and St Paul's, Canterbury', *ODNB*, <https://www.oxforddnb.com/view/10.1093/ref:odnb/9780198614128.001.0001/odnb-9780198614128-e-39256>

——, 'Theodore of Tarsus [St Theodore of Tarsus] (602–690), archbishop of Canterbury and biblical scholar', *ODNB*, <https://www.oxforddnb.com/view/10.1093/ref:odnb/9780198614128.001.0001/odnb-9780198614128-e-39256>

Larrington, Carolyne, 'Hugeburc [Huneburc] (fl. 760–780), Benedictine nun and hagiographer', *ODNB* online, <https://www.oxforddnb.com/view/10.1093/ref:odnb/9780198614128.001.0001/odnb-9780198614128-e-49413>

Lees, Clare A., and Gillian R. Overing, *Double Agents: Women and Clerical Culture in Anglo-Saxon England* (Cardiff: University of Wales Press, 2009)

Lerer, Seth, *Chaucer and His Readers: Imagining the Author in Late Medieval England* (Princeton, NJ: Princeton University Press, 1993)

Lester, Godfrey Allen, *Sir John Paston's 'Grete Boke': A Descriptive Catalogue, with an Introduction of British Library MS Lansdowne 285* (Woodbridge: Brewer, 1984)

Lévêque, Élodie, and Claire Chahine, 'Liber Pilosus: les reliures cisterciennes de Clairvaux recouvertes de peau de phoque' ['Liber Pilosus: Cistercian bindings from Clairvaux Abbey bound in seal skin'], *Notebook of the Institute For Research and History of Texts* (June 2017); updated January 2018, <https://irht.hypotheses.org/3003>

Lewis, Gwyneth, 'Extreme Welsh Meter', *Poetry Foundation Magazine*, <https://www.poetryfoundation.org/poetrymagazine/articles/70172/extreme-welsh-meter>

Lipman, Vivian David, *The Jews of Medieval Norwich* (Appendix: 'Hebrew Poems of Meir of Norwich', ed. A. M. Habermann) (London: Jewish Historical Society of England, 1967)

Little, Charles T., 'The Making of the Winchester Bible', <https://www.metmuseum.org/exhibitions/listings/2014/winchester-bible/blog/posts/making-of-the-winchester-bible>

Bibliography

Liuzza, Roy M., ed., *Old English Literature: Critical Essays* (New Haven, CT: Yale University Press, 2002)

Lloyd-Morgan, Ceridwen, 'Women and their Poetry in Medieval Wales', in *Women and Literature in Britain 1150–1500*, ed. Carol M. Meale, Cambridge Studies in Medieval Literature 17 (Cambridge: Cambridge University Press, 1993), pp. 183–201

——, 'The "Querelle des Femmes": A Continuing Tradition in Welsh Women's Literature', in *Medieval Women: Texts and Contexts in Late Medieval Britain: Essays for Felicity Riddy*, Medieval Women: Texts and Contexts 3, ed. Jocelyn Wogan-Browne and others (Turnhout: Brepols, 2000), pp. 101–14

Losseff, Nicky, 'Wycombe, W. of (fl. c.1275)', *ODNB* online, <http://www.oxforddnb.com/view/article/60119>

Miller, Edward, *That Noble Cabinet: A History of the British Museum* (London: Andre Deutsch, 1973)

Mills, Robert, 'Gender, Sodomy, Friendship and the Medieval Anchorhold', *Journal of Medieval Religious Cultures* 36 (2010), 1–27

Milner, John, 'Account of an Ancient Manuscript of St. John's Gospel by Rev. John Milner, F.A.S. in a Letter to the Rev. John Brand, Secretary', *Archaeologia* 16 (1812), 12–21

Minnis, Alastair, *Medieval Theory of Authorship: Scholastic Literary Attitudes in the Later Middle Ages* (Aldershot: Scolar Press, 1984; 2nd ed, Philadelphia: University of Pennsylvania Press, 1988)

Moberly, R. W. L., 'Why Did Noah Send out a Raven?', *Vetus Testamentum* 50 (2000), 345–56

Momigliano, Arnaldo, 'Ancient History and the Antiquarian', *Journal of the Warburg and Courtauld Institutes* 13 (1950), 285–315

Mooney, Linne R., 'Chaucer's Scribe', *Speculum* 81 (2006), 91–138

Morgan, Nigel J., 'Winchester Bible', *The Grove Encyclopedia of Medieval Art and Architecture*, ed. Colum P. Hourihane (Oxford: Oxford University Press, 2013), online edition, <https://www.oxfordreference.com/view/10.1093/acref/9780195395365.001.0001/acref-9780195395365-e-2456>

'Mortuary Chests Unlocked', Winchester Cathedral blog: <https://www.winchester-cathedral.org.uk/mortuary-chests-unlocked/>

Mulder-Bakker, Anneke B., 'Foreword', in *Anchorites, Wombs and Tombs: Intersections of Gender and Enclosure in the Middle Ages*, ed. Liz Herbert McAvoy and Mari Hughes-Edwards (Cardiff: University of Wales Press, 2005)

Nubia, Onyeka, 'Who was the Ipswich Man?', 'Our Migration Story' website, <https://www.ourmigrationstory.org.uk/oms/the-ipswich-man>

Bibliography

Oakeshott, Walter, *The Artists of the Winchester Bible* (London: Faber and Faber, 1945)

——, 'The Finding of the Manuscript', in *Essays on Malory*, ed. J. A. W. Bennett (Oxford: Clarendon Press, 1963), pp. 1–6

——, *Sigena Romanesque Paintings in Spain and the Winchester Bible Artists* (London: Harvey Miller and Medcalf, 1972)

——, *The Two Winchester Bibles* (Oxford: Clarendon Press, 1981)

O'Donnell, Daniel Paul, *Cædmon's Hymn: A Multimedia Study, Edition and Archive*

Ohajuru, Michael, 'An African Presence in Thirteenth-century Britain', 'Our Migration Story' website, <https://www.ourmigrationstory.org.uk/oms/an-african-presence-in-the-thirteenth-century>

Olusoga, David, *Black and British: A Forgotten History* (London: Pan Macmillan, 2016)

Orchard, Andy, 'The Literary Background to the Encomium Emmae Reginae', *Journal of Medieval Latin* 11 (2001), 156–83

Owen, Charles, A., *The Manuscripts of 'The Canterbury Tales'* (Woodbridge: D. S. Brewer, 1991)

Painter, George D., *William Caxton: A Quincentenary Biography of England's First Printer* (London: Chatto and Windus, 1976)

Parkes, Malcolm, 'The Palaeography of the Parker Manuscript of the Chronicle, Laws and Sedulius and Historiography at Winchester in the Late Ninth and Tenth Centuries' (1976), repr. in Parkes, *Scribes, Scripts and Readers: Studies in the Communication, Presentation and Dissemination of Medieval Texts* (London: Hambledon Press, 1991), pp. 143–69

——, *The Scriptorium of Wearmouth-Jarrow: Jarrow Lecture, 1982* (Jarrow: St Paul's Church, 1982)

——, 'A Fragment of an Early Tenth-Century Anglo-Saxon Manuscript and its Significance' (1983), repr. in Parkes, *Scribes, Scripts and Readers: Studies in the Communication, Presentation and Dissemination of Medieval Texts* (London: Hambledon Press, 1991), pp. 171–85

Perratore, Julia, 'The Spanish Connection: The Winchester Bible and Spain', <https://www.metmuseum.org/exhibitions/listings/2014/winchester-bible/blog/posts/the-spanish-connection>

Petrie, Flinders, *Seventy Years in Archaeology* (London: Sampson Low, Marston and Co., 1931)

Pickens, Rupert T., 'Reading Harley 978: Marie de France in Context', in *Courtly Arts and the Art of Courtliness: Selected Papers from the Eleventh Triennial Congress of the International Courtly Literature Society: University of Wisconsin-Madison 29 July–4 August*, ed. Keith Busby and Christopher Kleinhenz (Cambridge: D. S. Brewer, 2006), pp. 527–42

Bibliography

Porck, Thijs, 'Anglo-Saxon Cryptography', <https://thijsporck.
com/2017/05/15/anglo-saxon-cryptography/>

Powell, Nia, 'Women and Strict-Metre Poetry in Wales', in *Women and
Gender in Early Modern Wales*, ed. Michael Roberts and Simone Clarke
(Cardiff: University of Wales Press, 2000), pp. 129–58

Prescott, Andrew, 'Their Present Miserable State of Cremation: The
Restoration of the Cotton Library', in *Sir Robert Cotton as Collector:
Essays on an Early Stuart Courtier and His Legacy*, ed. C. J. Wright
(London: British Library, 1997), pp. 391–454

———, 'The Ghost of Asser', in *Anglo-Saxon Manuscripts and Their Heritage*,
ed. Philip Pulsiano and Elaine M. Treharne (Aldershot: Ashgate, 1998),
pp. 255–92

Radini, A., M. Tromp, and others, 'Medieval Women's Early Involvement
in Manuscript Production Suggested by Lapis Lazuli Identification
in Dental Calculus', *Science Advances*, 5 (2019), <https://advances.
sciencemag.org/content/5/1/eaau7126>

Reynolds, Anna Maria, 'Some Literary Influences in the Revelations of Julian
of Norwich (c. 1342–post-1416)', *Leeds Studies in English* 7–8 (1952),
18–28

Rich, Adrienne, *Of Woman Born: Motherhood as Experience and Institution*
(New York; London: W. W. Norton, 1986, repr. 1995)

Richmond, Colin, *The Paston Family in the Fifteenth Century: Endings*
(Manchester: Manchester University Press, 2000)

———, 'Paston family (per. c. 1420–1504), gentry', *ODNB*
online, <https://www.oxforddnb.com/view/10.1093/
ref:odnb/9780198614128.001.0001/odnb-9780198614128-e-52791>

Riddy, Felicity, '"Women Talking about the Things of God": A Late Medieval
Sub-Culture', in *Women and Literature in Britain, 1150–1500*, ed. Carol
M. Meale (Cambridge: Cambridge University Press), pp. 104–27

Ridyard, Susan J., *The Royal Saints of Anglo-Saxon England: A Study of West
Saxon and East Anglian Cults* (Cambridge: Cambridge University Press,
1988)

Riem, Roland, *The Winchester Bible: The First 850 Years* (Stroud: Pitkin, 2014)

Roberts, Jane, 'On Giving Scribe B a Name and a Clutch of London
Manuscripts from c. 1400', *Medium Aevum* 80 (2011), 247–70

Robinson, Pamela R., 'A Twelfth-Century Scriptrix from Nunnaminster', in
*Of the Making of Books: Medieval Manuscripts, Their Scribes and Readers:
Essays presented to M. B. Parkes*, ed. Pamela. R. Robinson and Rivkah
Zim (Aldershot: Scolar Press, 1997), pp. 73–93

Robinson, Peter M. W., 'New Methods of Editing, Exploring, and Reading
The Canterbury Tales', *Le médiéviste et l'ordinateur* 38 (1999), 19–28

Bibliography

Rosenthal, Joel T., *Telling Tales: Sources and Narration in Late Medieval England* (University Park, PA: Pennsylvania State University Press, 2003)

Sanders, Ernest H., 'Wycombe [Wicumbe, Whichbury, Winchecumbe], W. de', Grove Music online, <https://www.oxfordmusiconline.com/grovemusic/view/10.1093/gmo/9781561592630.001.0001/omo-9781561592630-e-0000030632>

Sandler, Lucy Freeman, *A Survey of Manuscripts Illuminated in the British Isles: V: Gothic Manuscripts 1285–1385*, 2 vols (London and Oxford: Harvey Miller and Oxford University Press, 1986)

Scanlon, Larry, *Narrative, Authority and Power: The Medieval Exemplum and the Chaucerian Tradition* (Cambridge: Cambridge University Press, 1994)

Scott, Kathleen, *A Survey of Manuscripts Illuminated in the British Isles VI: Later Gothic Manuscripts 1390–1490*, 2 vols (London: Harvey Miller, 1996)

Sherman, William H., *Used Books: Marking Readers in Renaissance England* (Philadelphia: University of Pennsylvania Press, 2008)

Simpson, James, *Reform and Cultural Revolution: The Oxford English Literary History: 1350–1574, Volume II* (Oxford: Oxford University Press, 2002)

Sisam, Kenneth, *Studies in the History of Old English Literature* (Oxford: Clarendon Press, 1953)

Skemer, Don C., 'Amulet Rolls and Female Devotion in the Late Middle Ages', *Scriptorium* 55 (2001), 197–227

Smith, Llinos B., 'Olrhain Anni Goch', *Llên Cymru* 19 (1993), 107–26

Smyth, Alfred P., *King Alfred the Great* (Oxford: Oxford University Press, 1995)

Snell, William, 'A Woman Medievalist Much Maligned: A Note in Defense of Edith Rickert (1871–1938)', *Philologie im Netz*, Supplement 4 (2009), 41–54

Stafford, Pauline, 'Emma: The Powers of the Queen in the Eleventh Century', in *Queens and Queenship in Medieval Europe: Proceedings of a Conference Held at King's College, London April 1995*, ed. Anne J. Duggan (Woodbridge: Boydell Press, 1997)

——, *Queen Emma and Queen Edith: Queenship and Women's Power in Eleventh-Century England* (Oxford: Blackwell, 1997)

Stephens, Meic, *The Oxford Companion to the Literature of Wales* (Oxford: Oxford University Press, 1986)

——, *A New Companion to the Literature of Wales* (Cardiff: University of Wales Press, 1998)

Bibliography

Summit, Jennifer, *Memory's Library: Medieval Books in Early Modern England* (Chicago; London: University of Chicago Press, 2008)

Taylor, Andrew, *Textual Situations: Three Medieval Manuscripts and their Readers* (Philadelphia: University of Pennsylvania Press, 2002)

Thacker, Alan, 'Eadfrith [Eadfrid] (d. 721?), bishop of Lindisfarne', *ODNB* online, <https://www.oxforddnb.com/view/10.1093/ref:odnb/9780198614128.001.0001/odnb-9780198614128-e-8381>

Thomas, M. Wynn, 'Foreword', in Mererid Hopwood, *Singing in Chains: Listening to Welsh Verse* (Ceredigion: Gomer Press, 2004, repr. 2016)

Tite, Colin, *The Manuscript Library of Sir Robert Cotton: The Panizzi Lectures, 1993* (London: British Library, 1994)

Tyler, Elizabeth M., 'Fictions of Family: The Encomium Emmae Reginae and Virgil's Aeneid', *Viator* 36 (2005), 149–80

Walker, Greg, *Persuasive Fictions: Faction, Faith and Political Culture in the Reign of Henry VIII* (Aldershot: Scolar Press, 1996)

——, *Writing Under Tyranny: English Literature and the Henrician Reformation* (Oxford: Oxford University Press, 2005)

Warner, Lawrence, 'Scribes, Misattributed: Hoccleve and Pinkhurst', *Studies in the Age of Chaucer* 37 (2015), 55–100

——, *Chaucer's Scribes: London Textual Production, 1384–1432* (Cambridge: Cambridge University Press, 2018)

Warren, Ann K., *Anchorites and their Patrons in Medieval England* (Berkeley: University of California Press, 1985)

Watt, Diane, *Women, Writing and Religion in England and Beyond, 650–1100: Studies in Early Medieval History* (London: Bloomsbury Academic, 2020)

Weiskott, Eric, '"Adam Scriveyn" and Chaucer's Metrical Practice', *Medium Ævum* 86 (2017), 147–51

Weitzmann, Kurt, *Age of Spirituality: Late Antique and Early Christian Art, Third to Seventh Century* (New York: Metropolitan Museum of Art in association with Princeton University Press, 1979)

Wellesley, Mary 'Lydgate's Life of Our Lady: Form and Transmission' (unpublished doctoral thesis, University College London, 2017)

Yapp, Brunsdon, *Birds in Medieval Manuscripts* (London: British Library, 1981)

Yorke, Barbara, 'Eadburh [Eadburga] (fl. c. 716–c. 746), abbess (probably of Wimborne)', *ODNB* online, <https://www.oxforddnb.com/view/10.1093/ref:odnb/9780198614128.001.0001/odnb-9780198614128-e-50659>

Acknowledgements

A lot of people have not laughed at me when I said I wanted to write a book about medieval manuscripts (or if they did, they did so kindly). I am so grateful to all of those people, beginning with Henry Hitchings, who chose not to laugh about a decade ago. Consequently, I carried the germ of an idea around for years. Inigo Thomas also chose not to laugh and chose to be encouraging and interested and always keen for sushi at lunchtime. Dan Jones has mainly distracted me with stupid stuff in texts, but he also suggested I meet George Capel. Thank you, George, for helping this idea about why material books are so precious become an actual, material book. I can't believe it. Thank you also to Irene Baldolini and Rachel Conway.

I am indebted to my editors at Quercus and Basic Books. Jon Riley has quietly piloted this book through the choppy waters of a global pandemic and a rather monumentally distracting life-change. I could not have asked for a kinder and more thoughtful hand at the tiller. He read multiple drafts of chapters with patience and precision. I placed my book-baby into the hands of Nick de Somogyi as I waited for my human-baby. I cannot thank him enough for his care. Huge thanks also to Jasmine Palmer for many kindnesses, to Wilf Dickie for beautiful designs and Cathie Arrington for picture help. Thank you, Claire Potter, for understanding what this book is about and knowing exactly when I needed to hear words of encouragement.

Acknowledgements

Many other people have helped in direct and indirect ways. Several people read sections of this book, made wise suggestions and gently pointed out examples of my idiocy. Kathleen Doyle read two different versions of a chapter, which is quite beyond the call of duty. Julian Harrison kindly read two chapters, for which I am so grateful. I lost track of the different drafts my mother so graciously agreed to read. The others – Andrea Clarke, Alison Hudson, Amy Jeffs, Cathryn Charnel-White and Amia Srinivasan – only had to endure the torture of one chapter. Tony Edwards is the harshest of critics, but also a great ally. Thank you for reading such a big chunk of this book. Any remaining errors are entirely my own. As the (probably female) author(s) of the *Earliest Life of St Gregory* wrote, '[Do not] nibble with critical teeth at this work of ours which has been diligently twisted into shape by love rather than knowledge.'[1]

Other people answered queries and talked over points with me. Thank you so much to Clarck Drieshen, Claire Breay, Anne Marie D'Arcy, Lloyd de Beer, Emilia Henderson, Matthew Lampitt, Hussein Omar, Alison Ray and Roly Riem. Colleen Curran shared PDFs of two much-needed resources. Ellie Jackson sent images. Andy O'Hagan cheered from the sidelines.

Most of this book was written in the reading rooms of the British Library. I'm so grateful to all the staff on the reference and issue desks of the rooms I haunted daily. And grateful to my library-wife, Amina, for a thousand unnecessary coffees and Tupperware lunches and stupid jokes. It has been an endless pleasure to talk about so many of the manuscripts in this book with students I have taught on the British Library's adult learning courses. Working in the Department of Ancient, Medieval and Early Modern Manuscripts at the British Library furnished me with dear friends and so much invaluable experience. Thank you to everyone in the section and in the Learning department for the opportunity to

Acknowledgements

work on the Discovering Literature webspace. Working as a writer on that project and writing posts for the section blog was excellent training and I thank Julian Harrison, in particular, for editing so many blog posts.

Tom Jones, editor of the LRB blog, has been Marie Kondo-ing my prose for a while and every time he makes me realise what needs to be there and what doesn't. Without knowing it, he also made me think I could write a book. I'm incredibly sorry about all the horrid adjectives in this book.

Kate Rundell is my writing partner in crime. I'll never write as well as you, but I am so grateful to be able to write toe-to-toe with you. I could not have survived without you and Mirra and Alice and Kathryn and Amia and Molly. Amy Jeffs is the best reader and an unfailing friend and she never thinks anything is too weird and medieval.

A global pandemic made the completion of this book tougher than normal and I called in a lot of favours. Amanda Herries provided WiFi and lunch in the Scottish wilds over several days. Thank you for those days of peace and seamless internet surfing. Mirra and Alice both collected and posted books for me when I wasn't able to get them for myself. Richard Espley and a kind receptionist whose name I did not catch opened up the Senate House 'Click and Collect' office when I turned up late and fretful. Amy Plewis helped me to check references when time in the library was severely restricted: thank you so much.

To my brothers and sisters: you are the only people I ever want to hang out with. None of you give a toss about manuscripts, and that is just fine by me. Thank you also to everyone at Crofts for tolerating me over many months of lockdown and for looking after me when I was so green about the gills.

Acknowledgements

Huge thanks to my mother, who took me to see the Ruthwell Cross when I was a teenager and so made me the monster I am today. Nobody writes or talks the way you do, with such a sense of the anarchic possibility of words. What a thrill to have learnt words and the love of them from you. And also to learn new words all the time which you appear to have invented. Thank you for reading so much of this book and pointing out where I was abusing my reader's goodwill. (I fear there are many instances we did not catch.) Thank you to my father, who somehow pronounces it 'manna-scripts', and I agree: they are manna from heaven. What a good day we had going to visit the Winchester Bible.

Thank you to Fred, who laughs always, mainly at me. You remind me daily that there is more to life than manuscripts, but have helped me create a life where I get to think about them a lot of the time. Thank you for the jokes, but also the peace that makes writing possible. And thank you to my tiny Elfrieda, who gestated alongside the final chapters and gurgled through the copy-edit. I hope one day you will read this book and find something in it that you like.

Notes

All hyperlinks are correct as of December 2020. All quotations from the Bible are from the Douay-Rheims translation (made directly from the Latin Vulgate – the version which would have been used by medieval readers); the numbering of the Psalms in the Vulgate Bible differs from those of later editions.

Page v

1 BL MS Tiberius B v, fol. 19r.
2 Lambeth Palace MS 546, fol. 56r, quoted in Bell, *What Nuns Read*, pp. 191–2.
3 Margaret Atwood, *The Testaments* (London: Vintage, 2019), p. 5.

Introduction

1 Franzen, *The Tremulous Hand of Worcester*, p. 1.
2 See Ohajuru, 'An African Presence in Thirteenth-century Britain'.
3 For a Roman example, the 'Beachy Head Lady', see Olusoga, *Black and British*, p. 33. An African girl was buried in North Elmham, near Norwich, in c. 1000 (see Fryer, *Staying Power*, pp. 1–2; Olusoga, *Black and British*, pp. 18, 29–32). For the 'Ipswich Man' (a man of North African origin buried in Ipswich in the thirteenth century), see Nubia, 'Who was the Ipswich Man?'. For more general discussion, see Clark, 'Race/Ethnicity and the Other', pp. 44–5.
4 The charter only survives in later copies, some only in Latin. The vernacular text is from Brussels, Bibliothèque Royale, 7965-73 (3723), fols 165r–v, the translation from <https://esawyer.lib.cam.ac.uk/charter/1228.html>.

5 In a similar vein, it is hard to know what to make of the name 'Maurus', which sometimes turns up in documents of the period. It can mean 'Moor' or might also be a reference to St Maurice. Examples include Wulfsige Maurus, who was a Mercian 'thegn', or lord (see Insley, 'The Family of Wulfric Spotte', pp. 122–3). On 'golden' or 'red', see Fellows-Jensen, 'By-names', pp. 80–1.

6 We know that there was trade and travel between Britain and the wider world in the medieval period, both from archaeological evidence and written sources. Bede tells us, for example, that Hadrian (630/637–709), Abbot of St Peter's and St Paul's in Canterbury, was 'a man of the African race' (*Bede's Ecclesiastical History*, p. 25; and see Lapidge, 'Hadrian', *Oxford Dictionary of National Biography* [hereafter *ODNB*]). Bede also tells us that Archbishop Theodore of Kent was not from Kent, but Cilicia in modern-day Turkey (*Bede's Ecclesiastical History*, pp. 330–1; see also Lapidge, 'Theodore of Tarsus', *ODNB*).

7 It is thought that Strayler depicts himself on fol. 108r.

8 The history of people of colour in medieval England is gaining increasing attention, but still relatively little has been written on the subject (see Fryer, *Staying Power*, pp. 2–3; and Olusoga, *Black and British*, esp. pp. 33–40).

9 *Hebrew Manuscripts*, ed. Richler, pp. 348–50.

10 Translation by Susan Einbinder, in Bale, 'Poems of Protest'. An alternative edition and translation appears in Meir of Norwich, *Into the Light*, ed. and trans. Crasnow and Elsworth, pp. 30–7.

11 For further context, see Lipman, *The Jews of Medieval Norwich*, pp. 157–9 and Appendix ('Hebrew Poems of Meir of Norwich', ed. A. M. Habermann); and Einbinder, 'Meir b. Elijah of Norwich'.

12 Meir of Norwich, *Into the Light*, ed. and trans. Crasnow and Elsworth, p. 10.

13 Blomefield, *An Essay Towards a Topographical History of the County of Norfolk*, p. 64; Lipman, *The Jews of Medieval Norwich*, p. 177.

14 Camille, *Mirror in Parchment*, p. 9.

15 Beatus's Commentary on the Apocalypse (c. 1091–1109), BL Add. MS 11695, fol. 278r; translation from Marc Drogin, *Anathema!*, p. 19.

16 In the twelfth century, Hervey, the sacristan of Bury St Edmund's Abbey commissioned a spectacular Bible (now Corpus Christi College MS 2) for his brother. The right materials were hard to come by, and the artist and bookmaker, one Master Hugo, 'was unable to find any suitable calf-hide in these parts' and had to purchase parchment from Scotland ('Gesta sacristarum', *Memorials of St Edmund's Abbey*, ed. Arnold, 2, 289–96).

Notes

17 Reynes, *Commonplace Book*, ed. Cameron, pp. 29–30 (fols 15v–16r).

18 See Gullick, 'How Fast did Scribes Write?'.

19 Manuscript scholars become very exercised about 'collation', which means working out how many folded pieces there are in each booklet and how many booklets there are in the manuscript. This tells us how a manuscript was put together, how well planned it was. When we marry the collation information with what we know about the text we can begin to establish a clearer picture about the process of creation. It helps to know, for example, that an artist created a particular image on a separate sheet and then sewed it into a booklet, or that a scribe wished to squeeze one more text into the manuscript and had to resort to sewing single sheets into their booklets to gain enough space to include it.

20 Lévêque and Chahine, 'Liber Pilosus'.

21 Gameson, 'Material Fabric of Early English Books', pp. 13–14; Gullick and Hadgraft, 'Bookbindings', pp. 105–6.

22 'Chemise Binding', in 'Glossary', British Library Catalogue of Illuminated Manuscripts, <https://www.bl.uk/catalogues/illuminatedmanuscripts/GlossC.asp>.

23 Liuzza, 'Introduction', *Old English Literature*, p. xi.

Prologue

1 Houston, *The Book*, p. 19.

2 Fol. 52r. *Middle English Charters of Christ*, ed. Spalding, p. 27.

3 De Mure and Langland both quoted in Kane, 'Word Games: Glossing *Piers Plowman*', pp. 50–1.

Chapter One

1 Francis Bacon, *The tvvoo bookes of Francis Bacon. Of the proficience and aduancement of learning, diuine and humane* (London, 1605), p. 27.

2 Petrie, *Seventy Years in Archaeology*, p. 36.

3 Walter Oakeshott, 'The Finding of the Manuscript', pp. 5–6

4 The following description of the discovery of the Cuthbert Gospel is taken from *Relics of Saint Cuthbert*, ed. Battiscombe, p. 101. The original Latin can be found as cap. xvii in the *Historia Translationum Sancti Cuthberti auctore anonymo*, in Simeon of Durham, *Symeonis Dunelmensis Opera*, ed. Hodgson-Hinde, 1, 188–97. An alternative edition made from

Notes

different manuscript sources appears in the Bollandist *Acta Sanctorum Martii Tomus* (1668), 3, 138–42.

5 Simeon of Durham's 'History of the Kings of England', in *The Church Historians of England*, ed. Stevenson, 3, 457.

6 Symeon of Durham's 'History of the Church of Durham', in ibid., 3, 671.

7 A church made 'of boughs of trees' was built, to be followed by a stone church which was subsequently replaced by the Romanesque cathedral, begun in 1093 (ibid., 3, 671–3).

8 See Arnold Hunt, 'Post-Medieval Movements of the Manuscript'.

9 *Rites of Durham*, ed. Fowler, p. 61.

10 *Lady Louisa Stuart*, ed. Home, pp. 26–7.

11 Milner, 'Account of an Ancient Manuscript', pp. 19–20.

12 Hunt, 'Post-Medieval Movements of the Manuscript', p. 142.

13 For the library's Digitised Manuscripts, see <http://www.bl.uk/manuscripts/Default.aspx>, and the permanent URL <http://searcharchives.bl.uk/IAMS_VU2:IAMS032-002226193>.

14 Weitzmann, *Age of Spirituality*, no. 495 (pp. 550–1).

15 Gameson, 'Materials, Text, Layout and Script', p. 22.

16 The great palaeographer Malcolm Parkes describes the Wearmouth-Jarrow script as one characterised by 'concern for calligraphy, increased discipline in the writing and the control of variant forms' (*Scriptorium of Wearmouth-Jarrow*, p. 11).

17 Bede was commissioned to write a life of St Cuthbert in c. 720.

18 'Bede's Life of Saint Cuthbert', in *Two Lives of Saint Cuthbert*, ed. and trans. Colgrave, p. 215.

19 Ibid., p. 217.

20 A slightly different account of the manuscript's discovery is given by Lt-Col. Butler-Bowden in *The Times*, 30 September 1936. He writes that 'the manuscript has lain on a bookshelf in the library of Pleasington Old Hall, Lancashire, next to a missal of 1340 in the rite of York, ever since I can remember' (p. 13). Both properties were owned by the family and it is unclear which account – that of the father, or the son – is most trustworthy. The father's was written closer to the time of the event, but he might not have wanted to admit to the fact that he nearly threw the book on the bonfire.

21 The letter was written in 1970, to a friend, Mrs D. Winifred Tuck. See Kelliher, 'The Rediscovery of Margery Kempe' (p. 260). All subsequent quotations from the letter are from this article.

22 A slightly modernised version of the original text may be found in *The Book of Margery Kempe*, ed. Windeatt (2000). For an excellent recent translation, see *The Book of Margery Kempe*, trans. Bale (2015).

Notes

A transcription of the original manuscript appears in *The Book of Margery Kempe*, ed. Meech and Allen (1940), from which all quotations from Kempe's *Book* are taken. The translations are my own.

23 *Book of Margery Kempe*, ed. Meech and Allen, p. 7.

24 Ibid., p. 8.

25 Ibid.

26 Ibid.

27 *The Book of Margery Kempe: A Modern Version*, ed. Butler-Bowdon.

28 *Book of Margery Kempe*, ed. Meech and Allen, p. 19.

29 Ibid., pp. 177–8.

30 Ibid., p. 178.

31 Ibid., p. 181.

32 Ibid., p. 4.

33 *Book of Margery Kempe*, ed. Meech and Allen, p. 1.

34 *Book of Margery Kempe*, ed. Meech and Allen, p. xxxiv.

35 It is possible that it was made earlier but remained unbound, but in that case we might expect the first and last pages or the outer leaves of each booklet within it to look grubby, which they do not.

36 It appears on fol. iv verso. The manuscript may have been acquired by the Carthusian author, prior and mystic, John Norton (died 1521/22), since there are two references to him in red ink in the margins (fols 33v and 51v).

37 Chappell, *Perilous Passages*, pp. 65–7.

38 Technically she took her PhD from Radcliffe College – attached to, but not part of, Harvard. Radcliffe women were forbidden from attending lectures with Harvard men, and had to wait for the same lecture to be repeated by graduate students or younger members of the faculty.

39 Hirsch, 'Hope Emily Allen (1883–1960)', p. 235.

40 *The Times*, 27 December 1934, p. 15.

41 Hirsch, 'Hope Emily Allen (1883–1960)' p. 235.

42 BL Add. MS 61823, fol. 1r.

43 Adrienne Rich, *Of Woman Born*, p. 16.

44 Oakeshott, 'The Finding of the Manuscript', p. 1.

45 Ibid., pp. 2–3.

46 Ibid., p. 3.

47 'Malory Find at Winchester', *Daily Telegraph*, 25 June 1934. See also 'A "Morte Darthur" Manuscript', *The Times*, 26 June 1934, which suggests that the find was made as the library's contents were in 'the process of being rehoused'. It does not mention Oakeshott, who wrote a longer piece describing the manuscript and its divergences from Caxton's

printed edition in *The Times Literary Supplement*, 27 September 1935, issue 1704, p. 650.

48 On the history of this edition, see Edwards, 'Editing Malory: Eugène Vinaver and the Clarendon Edition'.

49 *Le Morte Darthur*, ed. Shepherd, p. 819.

50 'Explicit' is a scribal abbreviation of '*explicitus est*': 'it is finished/ completed'.

51 *Le Morte Darthur*, ed. Shepherd, p. 112.

52 Oakeshott, 'The Finding of the Manuscript', pp. 5–6.

53 *Le Morte Darthur*, ed. Shepherd, p. 62.

54 Hellinga, 'The Malory Manuscript and Caxton', expanded from an original article in the Autumn 1977 issue of the *British Library Journal*.

55 Ibid., p. 128.

56 See <http://www.bl.uk/manuscripts/Viewer.aspx?ref=Add._ ms_59678_fs001r>. On fol. 314v, in the top left-hand corner of the page, there is an obvious smudge. Elsewhere to the trained eye, you can see on fol. 159r, line 13, a capital *F*; on fol. 186v line 7 a capital *B*; on fol.187v, line 6, capital *I*; on fol. 407r, line 4, a lower-case *y*.

57 Oakeshott, 'The Finding of the Manuscript', p. 6.

58 The Winchester College library catalogue made reference to a 1634 version of the *Morte* (*The most ancient and famous history of prince Arthur*).

59 Oakeshott, 'The Finding of the Manuscript', p. 6.

60 *The Times*, 30 September 1936, p. 13.

Chapter Two

1 Richard de Bury, *The Philobiblon*, ed. Thomas, p. 196.

2 From *Almansor* (1823): *The Concise Oxford Dictionary of Quotations*, ed. Elizabeth Knowles, fourth edition (Oxford: Oxford University Press, 2001), p. 155.

3 First published in *New Library: The People's Network*, a report by the Library and Information Commission, <https://journals.sagepub.com/ doi/pdf/10.1080/03064229908536539>.

4 Miller, *That Noble Cabinet*, p. 32.

5 *A Report from the Committee* [9 May 1732], p. 4.

6 Keynes, 'The Reconstruction of a Burnt Cottonian Manuscript', p. 113.

7 The two collections had been housed together since 1707; see Miller, *That Noble Cabinet*, p. 32.

Notes

8 William Bogdani to Maurice Johnson (30 October 1731), in Fox, *John Mill and Richard Bentley*, p. 150.

9 *Report from the Committee*, Appendix, p. 11.

10 This account of the library describes the collection as it was in Cotton House, but it is likely that the furniture was reinstalled at Ashburnham House: see Tite, *The Manuscript Library of Sir Robert Cotton*, p. 95.

11 I am indebted to Rosemary Hill for the observation that the moon-phase is important in understanding the events of that night.

12 Tite, *The Manuscript Library of Sir Robert Cotton*, p. 95.

13 Bogdani to Johnson, in Fox, *John Mill and Richard Bentley*, p. 150.

14 Keynes, 'The Reconstruction of a Burnt Cottonian Manuscript', p. 143, n.14.

15 Prescott, 'Their Present Miserable State of Cremation', p. 392.

16 *Alfred the Great*, ed. Keynes and Lapidge, p. 225.

17 Prescott, 'Their Present Miserable State of Cremation', p. 393.

18 Bowyer, *Literary Anecdotes of the Eighteenth Century*, 9, 592. It should be noted that this account refers to Ashburnham House as 'Abingdon House', so its authority may not stand on rock-solid foundations.

19 Fitzgerald, *Poems on Several Occasions*, p. 72.

20 The manuscript, in its original condition, is described in a letter written by Humfrey Wanley in 1721, printed in Sisam, *Studies in the History of Old English Literature*, p. 148, n. 3.

21 These included John Leland, Matthew Parker and William Camden. The work of these early antiquarians is briefly explored in the Afterword.

22 By William Camden and Francis Wise respectively. For a summary of the textual history, see *Asser's 'Life of King Alfred'*, ed. Stevenson, pp. xi–xxxii.

23 All quotations are from *Alfred the Great*, ed. Keynes and Lapidge, pp. 66–110.

24 Ibid., p. 75.

25 Ibid., p. 91.

26 Ibid., p. 92.

27 Ibid., p. 74.

28 Smyth, *King Alfred the Great* (1995) and also *The Medieval Life of King Alfred*, ed. and trans. Smyth (2002).

29 On the problems caused by lost manuscripts, see Prescott, 'The Ghost of Asser'.

30 *Beowulf*, ed. and trans. Swanton, p. 186 (lines 3178–82). (Translation my own.)

31 *Beowulf*, trans. Heaney, pp. xiii–xiv.

32 Ibid., p. xiii.

Notes

33 Kiernan, *The Thorkelin Transcripts of 'Beowulf'*, p. 4.

34 BL Add. MS 46513 fols. 120v–121v ('Reading Room Register of MSS., Sep. 1784 to Oct. 24. 1788').

35 'In hoc libro, qui Poesos Anglo-Saxonicæ egregium est exemplum, descripta videntur bella quæ Beowulfus quidam Danus, ex Regio Scyldingorum stirpe Ortus, gessit contra Sueciæ Regulos' (*Antiquæ Literaturæ Septemtrionalis liber alter*, p. 219).

36 Bjork, 'Grímur Jónsson Thorkelin's Preface to . . . *Beowulf*, p. 311.

37 Ibid., pp. 300–3.

38 Ibid., p. 303.

39 Ibid., p. 297.

40 *Exeter Anthology*, ed. Muir, 1, 2.

41 Ibid., 1, 357 (lines 1–11).

42 Ibid. (lines. 12–20).

43 Ibid., 1, 320 (lines 1–6).

44 Unpublished journal of Sir Frederic Madden (10 July 1865). Photocopies of Madden's journal are available on open shelf in the Manuscripts Reading Room of the British Library. The originals are held by the Bodleian Library in Oxford. Further information on the extent of the damage in the bindery fire can be found in Prescott, 'Their Present Miserable State of Cremation', p. 450, n. 236.

45 Prescott, 'The Ghost of Asser', p. 270.

Chapter Three

1 *Encomium*, ed. Campbell, p. 5. Translation modified.

2 BL Royal MS 17 D VI, fol. 40r.

3 Ibid. For a modern edition, see Hoccleve, *The Regiment of Princes*, ed. Blyth, lines 2017–23.

4 'Gesta Cnutonis' was the usual name in the late Middle Ages for what we now refer to as the *Encomium*, which wasn't called that until Duchesne's 1619 *Emmæ Anglorum Reginæ Richardi I . . . Encomium* (Stafford, 'Emma: The Powers of the Queen in the Eleventh Century', p. 44, n. 7).

5 See Stafford, *Queen Emma and Queen Edith*, p. 29.

6 *Encomium Emmae Reginae*, ed. Campbell, p. xiv. I have Latinised that edition's Norse spellings (such as 'Knútr') for the sake of clarity.

7 Discussion of her age at the time of marriage can be found in Stafford, *Queen Emma and Queen Edith*, p. 211.

8 *Anglo-Saxon Chronicle*, ed. Cubbin, p. 51.

9 William of Malmesbury, *Deeds of the English Kings*, ed. Mynors, p. 169.

10 Keynes, 'Emma [Ælfgifu] (d. 1052), queen of England, second consort of Æthelred II, and second consort of King Cnut', *ODNB*.
11 Stafford, *Queen Emma and Queen Edith*, p. 221.
12 Keynes, 'Emma [Ælfgifu] (d. 1052)'.
13 Whitelock translates it as 'widow', but the word 'widuwe' is not used (*The Anglo-Saxon Chronicle*, ed. and trans. Whitelock and others, p. 97).
14 Frank, 'King Cnut in the Verse of his Skalds', p. 122.
15 Tyler, 'Fictions of Family', p. 149.
16 *Encomium*, ed. Campbell, p. 5. Translation modified.
17 Ibid.
18 Ibid., p. 37.
19 For a full account of the literary analogues, see Orchard, 'The Literary Background to the *Encomium Emmae Reginae*'.
20 Hobson, 'National–Ethnic Narratives', p. 283.
21 The following discussion is indebted to Tyler, 'Fictions of Family', esp. pp. 175–9.
22 *Encomium*, ed. Campbell, p. 13.
23 *Antony and Cleopatra*, ed. Wilders (2.2.205–7).
24 *Encomium*, ed. Campbell, p. 33.
25 Ibid., esp. pp. 33–5.
26 Ibid., p. 5.
27 Ibid., p. 25.
28 Ibid., p. 53.
29 Bolton, 'A Newly Emergent Mediaeval Manuscript'.
30 Keynes and Love, 'Earl Godwine's Ship', pp. 195–6.
31 The following discussion is indebted to Krakowka, 'Unlocking the Secrets', and the Winchester Cathedral blog, 'Mortuary Chests Unlocked'.
32 Ryves, *Mercurius Rusticus*, pp. 211–12.
33 There has been some debate as to whether the image is an intentionally unflattering portrait; see Walker, *Persuasive Fictions*, p. 80.
34 *Inventory of King Henry VIII*, ed. Starkey, no. 9042.
35 Not only does the Psalter reflect Henry's tastes and fears in its images and annotation, but it may, like the *Encomium Emmae Reginae*, also contain some tactical omissions. Psalm 77, for example, is missing a substantial section. For an argument that this is intentional, see Christie-Miller, 'Henry VIII and British Library'.
36 As in *Le Chemin de Paradis*: Oxford, MS Bodley 883.
37 From the preface to an edition of selected parts of the Bible (see *King Henry's Prayer Book*, ed. Carley, p. 70).
38 Fol. 97r.

Notes

39 Fols 24r, 22r, 46r, 43r, 126v and 82v.

40 *King Henry's Prayer Book*, ed. Carley, p. 74.

41 On the annotation of books in this period, see Sherman, *Used Books*.

42 *King Henry's Prayer Book*, ed. Carley, p. 74.

43 Erasmus to Adrian VI, 1 August 1522 (*The Correspondence of Erasmus*, 9, 152).

44 The Act of Supremacy, 1534 (26 Henry VIII c. 1), in *Documents of the English Reformation*, ed. Bray, p. 114.

45 Campbell, *Henry VIII and the Art of Majesty*, pp. 177–87.

46 In Henry Morley's 1539 *Exposition and Declaration of the Psalme*, for example, Henry is described as 'the royall king David . . . [who] woll not cesse to resist with all his power, the obstinate wylle & vsurped authorite of the proude byshop of Rome (sig. A.7r–v). Similarly, in a tract by Sir Richard Morison, Henry is compared to David, who – Morison contends – was protected above all others by God (*King Henry's Prayer Book*, ed. Carley, p. 72). Thomas Wyatt drew unflattering comparisons (Walker, *Writing Under Tyranny*, pp. 351–76).

47 Fol. 30r.

48 Fols. 33v; 13r; 19v.

49 Fols. 4v; 107v.

50 Fol. 48r.

51 Fol. 63r.

52 See *The Family of Henry VIII* (c. 1545), Royal Collection Inventory Number 405796, <https://www.rct.uk/collection/405796/the-family-of-henry-viii>, where Somers can be seen in the far-right doorway.

53 Fol. 79r.

54 Fol. 118r.

55 He wrote, for example, 'nota de idolatria' ('note: concerning idolatry') next to Psalm 43 (fol. 55r), and 'de confessione' ('on confession') next to Psalm 94: 2 (fol. 115r).

56 Fol. 48v.

57 Fol. 136v.

58 See Carley, *The Libraries of King Henry VIII*, p. 277. The inventory is in two parts; the entry for the Psalter may be found in BL MS Harley 1419, fol. 206r.

Notes

Chapter Four

1 Oakeshott, *Artists of the Winchester Bible*, p. 8.
2 Michael Camille notes the 'socially marginal position of many medieval artists' (*Image on the Edge*, p. 147).
3 Radini et al., 'Medieval Women's Early Involvement in Manuscript Production'.
4 In researching the Winchester Bible, I have been hugely helped by the blog which accompanied the Metropolitan Museum of Art's 2015 exhibition, 'The Winchester Bible: A Masterpiece of Medieval Art': <https://www.metmuseum.org/exhibitions/listings/2014/winchester-bible/blog>. Also useful, on the Bible's conservation, is Andrew Honey, 'Practice Makes Perfect?'.
5 He used rather an old-fashioned script and ruling format, suggesting seniority. See Donovan, *Winchester Bible*, p. 18.
6 Ibid., p. 20.
7 Oakeshott, *Two Winchester Bibles*, p. 15.
8 Donovan, *Winchester Bible*, p. 17.
9 Cited in 'The Winchester Bible: Conservation in Action', <https://www.winchester-cathedral.org.uk/conservation-action/the-winchester-bible/>.
10 Donovan, *Winchester Bible*, p. 5; and Oakeshott, *The Artists of the Winchester Bible*, p. 1.
11 Oakeshott, *Artists of the Winchester Bible*, pp. 3–4.
12 These include the early medieval Benedictional of St Aethelwold (BL, Add. MS 49598), produced between 963 and 984, which contains twenty-eight magnificent images, depicting figures in mauve, gold, blue and emerald green. The Winchester Bible's immediate predecessor is the Winchester Psalter (BL, Cotton MS Nero C. iv), which contains thirty-eight full-page images illuminating the Old and New Testaments.
13 Riem, *Winchester Bible*, p. 5. On the Bodleian manuscript, see <https://medieval.bodleian.ox.ac.uk/catalog/manuscript_520>.
14 See, for example, a marginal note on p. 33 of An Leabhar Breac ('The Speckled Book': Royal Irish Academy MS 23 P 16) – made in Duniry c. 1408–11– in which the scribe writes, 'fiche oidche ondiu co luan cásc, is am fuar toirsech, cen tene, cen tugaid' ('twenty nights from today till Easter Monday , and I am cold and weary, without fire or covering'): see *Leabhar Breac, the Speckled Book*, ed. Ó Longáin and Gilbert, p. 30. See also Gullick, 'How Fast did Scribes Write?', p. 43.
15 Donovan, *Winchester Bible*, p. 5.
16 Fol. 303.

17 Fol. 316; Donovan, *Winchester Bible*, p. 56. A later hand sought to overrule this instruction, this later note, in different ink, beginning 'Fac' ('make'), followed by some illegible words and then 'in templo . . . et cum impetu' ('in the temple . . . and with assault'): Oakeshott, *Two Winchester Bibles*, p. 14.

18 Oakeshott, *Two Winchester Bibles*, p. 37.

19 These included vermilion for the reds, red lead for the oranges, copper-based verdigris or malachite for the greens, iron oxide for the yellows, carbon for the black, and white lead for the whites. (See Little, 'The Making of the Winchester Bible'.)

20 It is possible that the pigment used in the Winchester Bible may be azurite or woad, but as far as I am aware, such tests have yet to be carried out.

21 Donovan, *Winchester Bible*, p. 28.

22 Morgan, 'Winchester Bible' (2013).

23 Oakeshott, *Two Winchester Bibles*, p. 45.

24 Donovan, *Winchester Bible*, p. 24.

25 Ibid., p. 15.

26 Oakeshott, *Sigena Romanesque Paintings*, p. 142.

27 Ibid., p. 116.

28 Some other leaves were removed from the Bible when it was rebound in 1820. (Other leaves may have been removed at the same time and could still come to light.)

29 See <https://www.metmuseum.org/art/collection/search/656524>.

30 Donovan, *Winchester Bible*, p. 27.

31 Oakeshott suggests 'two perhaps three' of the Winchester artists worked there (*Sigena Romanesque Paintings*, p. 113).

32 Perratore, 'The Spanish Connection'.

33 Oakeshott argued that the frescoes came after the Bible (*Sigena Romanesque Paintings*, p. 112).

34 Moberly, 'Why Did Noah Send out a Raven?', p. 346.

35 Oakeshott, *Artists of the Winchester Bible*, p. 3.

36 Riem, *Winchester Bible*, p. 24.

37 Ibid.

38 See <https://www.bl.uk/collection-items/the-luttrell-psalter> and the digitised surrogate, <http://www.bl.uk/manuscripts/FullDisplay. aspx?ref=Add._MS_42130>.

39 In his will Geoffrey Luttrell made provision for twenty chaplains to recite masses for his soul over a five-year period (Brown, *World of the Luttrell Psalter*, p. 24).

40 Fols. 70v, 79v, 84v and 176r.

Notes

41 For a discussion of the origin and development of these kinds of border images, see Binski, *Gothic Wonder*, pp. 293–8.

42 Fol. 54v.

43 This legend is from Osbern's late-eleventh-century *Life and Miracles of St Dunstan*. See *Memorials of Saint Dunstan*, ed. Stubbs, p. 329.

44 Binski, *Gothic Wonder*, p. 286 and discussion pp. 299–305.

45 Camille, *Mirror in Parchment*, p. 318. Lucy Freeman Sandler notes that the calendar and litany have 'a Lincoln "flavour"' (Sandler, *Survey of Manuscripts*, 2, 119).

46 Camille, *Image on the Edge*, p. 156.

47 Camille, *Mirror in Parchment*, p. 316.

48 Camille says 'at least six' (ibid., p. 52), while Sandler says 'at least five individuals' (Sandler, *Survey of Manuscripts*, 2, 120).

49 Backhouse, *Luttrell Psalter*, p. 13.

50 Camille, *Mirror in Parchment*, p. 232. Camille argued that the image of a man's face next to an illuminated initial on fol. 177v was a self-portrait by this artist.

51 Backhouse, *Luttrell Psalter*, p. 14.

52 Camille, *Mirror in Parchment*, p. 232.

53 Sandler, *Survey of Manuscripts*, 2, 120.

54 Fol. 181r.

55 Fols 181v–182r.

56 Fol. 173v.

57 Fol. 170v.

58 Fol. 158v.

59 Fols 172v–173r.

60 Fol. 202v.

61 Brown, *Luttrell Psalter: A Facsimile*, p. 4.

62 Backhouse, *Luttrell Psalter*, p. 57.

63 Fols 207v–208r.

64 Camille, *Mirror in Parchment*, p. 327.

65 Backhouse, *Luttrell Psalter*, p. 14.

66 Fols 23r and 196v. On the symbolism of the cherry, from medieval art to the present day, see Jeffs and Wellesley, 'Sexing Up the Cherry', pp. 76–8.

67 Fol. 157v.

68 Fol. 162r.

69 Fol. 185r.

70 Fol. 59v.

71 Fols 170v–171r.

72 Fol. 172v.

73 Fol. 158v.

74 Scott, *Survey of Manuscripts*, 2, 52.

75 BL Add. MS 74236. The manuscript is digitised at <http://access.bl.uk/item/viewer/ark:/81055/vdc_100104060212.0x000001>; see also Herbert, *The Sherborne Missal: Reproduction of Full Pages*.

76 We cannot be sure because specific records for the the Sherborne Missal do not survive, but the book is very similar in size and scope to the Litlyngton Missal, which took two years just for the text to be copied, let alone decorated (Backhouse, *The Sherborne Missal*, pp. 9–12).

77 Scott, *Survey of Manuscripts*, 2, 52 (no. 9).

78 It must have been produced before Richard Mitford, Bishop of Salisbury, died in 1407 (se below), and after 1399, when Henry V became Prince of Wales (since his arms appear on p. 81). On the different artists, see Scott, ibid., pp. 53–5.

79 Ibid., pp. 53–6.

80 Ibid., p. 55.

81 Scott, *Survey of Manuscripts*, 2, 53.

82 Brunyng and Mitford appear side by side in eight places, including the four major festivals of Christmas, Easter, Pentecost and Trinity Sunday.

83 P. 81.

84 P. 225.

85 A Pentateuch commentary from Glastonbury Abbey, at Trinity College, Cambridge (MS B.3.7); and the fragmentary Lovell Lectionary (BL Harley MS 7026).

86 Graham, 'Siferwas, John', *ODNB*.

87 Ibid.

88 Scott summarises the arguments in *Survey of Manuscripts*, 2, 54.

89 This independent bifolio may have been unintentional, Siferwas meaning to add another image onto the opposite page, or simply preferring to work on an independent sheet, but this feels unlikely for such a meticulously planned manuscript.

90 P. 573.

91 Scott, *Survey of Manuscripts*, 2, 55.

92 Scott believes it may have been Siferwas (ibid.)

93 Backhouse, *Medieval Birds in the Sherborne Missal*, p. 5.

94 P. 382.

95 Backhouse, *Medieval Birds in the Sherborne Missal*, p. 33.

96 P. 364.

97 P. 369.

98 Yapp, *Birds in Medieval Manuscripts*, p. 152.

99 Pp. 373 and 393.

100 Backhouse, *Medieval Birds in the Sherborne Missal*, p. 33.

Notes

101 As on, for example, p. 364, where the goldfinch in the lower left-hand side of the folio sits on top of the decorative devices of the border, unlike the dragon on the lower right-hand side which is plaited into the border design.

102 Boccaccio, *De Mulieribus Claris*, Bibliothèque nationale de France, MS Français 12420, fol. 86r, <https://gallica.bnf.fr/ark:/12148/btv1b10509080f/f181.item>.

103 Boccaccio, *On Famous Women*, ed. and trans. Brown, p. 231.

Chapter Five

1 'An Leabhar Braec': Royal Irish Academy MS 23 P 16, p. 33 (*Leabhar Breac, the Speckled Book*, ed. Ó Longáin and Gilbert, p. 30).

2 Cassiodorus, *Institutiones*, ed. Mynors, p. 75.

3 *Cassiodorus: Institutions*, ed. and trans. Halporn, p. 163.

4 The case for Pinkhurst as Chaucer's scribe was laid out by Mooney, 'Chaucer's Scribe', but has since been disputed, most notably by Warner, *Chaucer's Scribes*.

5 *Riverside Chaucer*, p. 650; corrected against Cambridge, Trinity College, MS R.3.20, p. 367 (my translation).

6 Fol. 259r.

7 Ibid., pp. 67, 35.

8 Some have argued that Eadfrith merely commissioned the book (see Backhouse, *Lindisfarne Gospels*, p. 13).

9 It was at this point that Cuthbert's coffin was opened and his body found miraculously incorrupt.

10 Aldred's note is treated with a degree of scepticism by some scholars, but the rough date-range it proposes tallies with the stylistic and historical context. It is clear that the manuscript was made by one scribe-artist, and it is reasonable to assume that that scribe was Eadfrith, who took a strong interest in the promotion of Cuthbert's cult. The debate is partly summarised in Gameson, 'Northumbrian Books in the Seventh and Eighth Centuries', pp. 61–3, n. 118.

11 See *Two Lives of Saint Cuthbert*, ed. and trans. Colgrave, esp. pp. 302–5.

12 Æthelwulf, *De abbatibus*, p. 18.

13 Brown, *The Lindisfarne Gospels and the Early Medieval World*, p. 38.

14 Thacker, 'Eadfrith [Eadfrid] (d. 721?), bishop of Lindisfarne', *ODNB*.

15 Brown, 'Reading the Lindisfarne Gospels', p. 84.

16 Brown, *The Lindisfarne Gospels and the Early Medieval World*, p. 38.

17 There are a further four 'carpet pages' after this one (fol. 2v), at fols 26v, 94v, 138v and 210v.

18 There are a further four 'incipit pages' after this one (fol. 3r), at fols 27r, 95r, 139r and 211r.

19 Fols 10r–17v.

20 Backhouse, *Lindisfarne Gospels*, p. 44.

21 Fol. 29r.

22 Backhouse, 'Birds, Beasts and Initials in Lindisfarne's Gospel books', p. 166.

23 The Evangelist images appear on fols 25v, 93v, 137v and 209v.

24 Brown, *The Lindisfarne Gospels and the Early Medieval World*, p. 37.

25 Backhouse, *Lindisfarne Gospels*, p. 22.

26 Ibid., p. 28.

27 The orpiment can be identified because it contains arsenic trisulfide (As_2S_3). See Duffy, 'Under the Microscope with the Lindisfarne Gospels'.

28 Ibid.

29 'The Lindisfarne Gospels Tour: Chemistry', British Library website, <http://www.bl.uk/onlinegallery/features/lindisfarne/chemistry.html>. See also Brown, *The Lindisfarne Gospels: Society, Spirituality and the Scribe*, pp. 430–51.

30 Backhouse, *Lindisfarne Gospels*, p. 28.

31 *Letters of Saint Boniface*, ed. and trans. Emerton, p. 60. The manuscript containing this letter is a later copy from the second half of the ninth century, so – as is so often the case with women's writing from the period – we are left with later texts, reports of work, traces, and suggestions. I discuss this at length in my final chapter. See also Watt, *Women, Writing and Religion*, p. 69.

32 Although most scholars identify her as Abbess of Thanet, Barbara Yorke makes a case for her being Abbess of Wimborne (Yorke, 'Eadburh', *ODNB*).

33 There was a decline in learning amongst nuns in England during the Benedictine Reform (Watt, *Women, Writing and Religion*, p. 13), but it is clear that the level of literacy amongst nuns throughout the medieval period was good (Bell, *What Nuns Read*).

34 Christine Fell summarises the evidence in *Women in Anglo-Saxon England*, pp. 113–14.

35 *The Letters of Saint Boniface*, pp. 64–5.

36 Pamela Robinson, 'A Twelfth-Century *Scriptrix* from Nunnaminster', p. 83.

Notes

37 Fell, 'Some Implications of the Boniface Correspondence', p. 29. On the Continental evidence see, for example, Beach, *Women As Scribes*.

38 See the catalogue entry for BL Harley MS 2965 on Digitised Manuscripts, <http://www.bl.uk/manuscripts/FullDisplay. aspx?ref=Harley_MS_2965&index=0>.

39 Fol. 37r.

40 Fols 37v–38r.

41 An edition and translation of a different manuscript version can be found in *Anglo-Saxon Remedies*, ed. and trans. Pettit, pp. 40–57.

42 As in 'peccatrice' (ablative singular of 'peccatrix', meaning 'female sinner' – literally translated as 'with/by/from female sinner') (fol. 41r). Another, possibly contemporary hand also added some masculine forms (fol. 41r).

43 Fol. 40v. On the importance of recording land grants for institutional memory, see Watt, *Women, Writing and Religion*, pp. 58–67.

44 *Alfred the Great*, ed. Keynes and Lapidge, p. 91 (Chapter 75).

45 Pamela Robinson, 'A Twelfth-Century *Scriptrix* from Nunnaminster', p. 74.

46 Malcolm Parkes identified a group of early tenth-century manuscripts copied there ('The Palaeography of the Parker Manuscript' and 'A Fragment of an Early Tenth-Century Anglo-Saxon Manuscript').

47 Bugyis, *The Care of Nuns*, p. 120.

48 Ibid., pp. 123–4.

49 Fol. ii.

50 Bugyis, *The Care of Nuns*, pp. 120–1. See also Ridyard, *Royal Saints*, pp. 28–9, and Braswell, 'Saint Edburga of Winchester', p. 304.

51 These include (on fol. 119v) the famous motto, 'Amor vincit omnia' ('Love conquers all'), which appears on the brooch of Chaucer's Prioress in the 'General Prologue' of *The Canterbury Tales*.

52 Pamela Robinson, 'A Twelfth-Century *Scriptrix* from Nunnaminster', p. 92.

53 Richmond, 'Paston family', *ODNB*.

54 *Paston Letters*, ed. Davis, 1, 226–77 [no. 130]; BL Add. MS 34888, fol. 29 (my translations).

55 The dispute over Gresham is eloquently explained in Castor, *Blood and Roses*, pp. 42–9.

56 *Paston Letters*, ed. Davis, 1, 662–3 [no. 415]; BL Add. MS 43490, fol. 23.

57 This has been disputed by Colin Richmond (*Paston Family*, p. 52, n. 135); but see the counterclaim by Diane Watt (*Paston Women: Selected Letters*, ed. and trans. Watt, p. 137).

58 Rosenthal, *Telling Tales*, p. 100; *Paston Women: Selected Letters*, ed. and trans. Watt, p. 134.

59 *Paston Letters*, ed. Davis, 1, 170 [no. 93]; BL Add. MS 34889, fol. 215.

60 Ibid., 2, 387 [no. 751]; BL Add. MS 43491, fol. 12.

61 Lester, *Sir John Paston's 'Grete Boke'*, p. 7.

62 Gullick, 'How Fast did Scribes Write?', p. 41.

63 *Paston Letters*, ed. Davis, 1, 26 [no. 13]; BL Add. MS 43488, fol. 4.

64 As Castor notes, she was educated, but 'education did not necessarily imply literacy' (*Blood and Roses*, p. 28).

65 Klapish-Zuber, 'Women and the Family', p. 302.

66 John Myrc, *Instructions for Parish Priests*, pp. 3–4.

67 *Paston Letters*, ed. Davis, 1, 216–17 [no. 125]; BL Add. MS 43490, fol. 34.

68 Skemer, 'Amulet Rolls and Female Devotion in the Late Middle Ages', pp. 201–5.

69 *Paston Letters*, ed. Davis, 1, lxxix.

70 Ibid., 1, 576 [no. 353]; BL Add. MS. 27445, fol. 59.

71 Ibid., 1, 582 [no. 355]; BL Add. MS. 27445, fol. 60.

72 He did not write the entirety of all six (ibid., 1, lxxv).

73 Ibid., 1, 322 [no. 193]; BL Add. MS 27445, fol. 9.

74 Ibid., 1, 392 [no. 56]; BL Add. MS 34888, fol. 150.

75 Ibid., 1, 339 [no. 201]; BL Add. MS 34889, fol. 74.

76 Ibid., 1, 541 [no. 332]; BL Add. MS 34889, fol. 77.

77 On this technicality, see Castor, *Blood and Roses*, pp. 216–17.

78 Ibid., pp. 220–4.

79 *Paston Letters*, ed. Davis, 1, 33–4 [no. 203]; BL Add. MS 34889, fols 83v–84r.

80 'brethel (n.)' *Middle English Dictionary* online, <https://quod.lib.umich.edu/m/middle-english-dictionary/dictionary/MED5962/track?counter=2&search_id=2918056>. See also *Oxford English Dictionary*, '**brethel** *Obs.*'.

81 *Paston Letters*, ed. Davis, 2, 498–500 [no. 861]; BL Add. MS 34889, fols. 78–9.

82 Ibid., 1, lxxvi.

83 Richmond, 'Paston family', *ODNB*.

84 *Paston Letters*, ed. Davis, 1, 472 [no. 282]; BL Add. MS 27445, fol. 73.

85 Ibid., 1, lxxvii.

86 Ibid., 1, 473 [no. 283]; BL Add. MS 27445, fol. 74.

87 BL Cotton MS Nero D IV, fol. 89v.

88 Fol. 295r; Brown, *The Lindisfarne Gospels and the Early Medieval World*, p. 66.

Notes

Chapter Six

1 Ælfric, 'On the Old and New Testaments', *The Old English Heptateuch*, ed. Marsden, p. 227.

2 *Hoccleve's Works*, ed. Furnivall, 1, 29–30 (lines 121–8; 161–8).

3 Hoccleve's *'Male Regle'*, trans. Nuttall.

4 See *Thomas Hoccleve: A Facsimile*, ed. Burrow and Doyle; and the digital facsimile, <https://hdl.huntington.org/digital/collection/p15150coll7/id/9873/rec/1>.

5 As Butterfield notes, recent decades have seen 'an effort by a number of scholars to reconstitute the page of the scribal manuscript as an authentic object in its own right' (*'Mise-en-page* in the *Troilus* Manuscripts', p. 49).

6 Cambridge University Library, MS Kk.5.16, fol. 128r.

7 It shoud be noted that almost all Old English verse looks like prose in its manuscript examples (or 'witnesses').

8 See, for example, the *Norton Anthology of English Literature*, ed. M. H. Abrams, sixth edition (New York; London: W. W. Norton and Co., 1993), p. 17. For a brilliant account of the disparities between the medieval and modern texts, see Kiernan, 'Reading Cædmon's "Hymn" with Someone Else's Glosses'.

9 Bede describes him as a lay brother, but the story makes clear that he was responsible for caring for the livestock.

10 *Bede's Ecclesiastical History*, ed. and trans. Colgrave and Mynors, p. 417.

11 For a productive discussion of Hild's role in the Cædmon story, see Lees and Overing, *Double Agents*, pp. 19–45 (esp. pp. 30, 32, 35). On how Bede overwrote female-authored sources, see Watt, *Women, Writing and Religion*, pp. 14–18, 21–39.

12 *Bede's Ecclesiastical History*, ed. and trans. Colgrave and Mynors, p. 415.

13 The idea of the 'clean animal' is from Leviticus 11: 3 and Deuteronomy 14: 6.

14 Lees and Overing, *Double Agents*, p. 22.

15 For a full explanation, see *Cædmon's Hymn: A Multimedia Study*, ed. O'Donnell Chapter 5 ('Filiation and Transmission'). The text was given further currency around 150 years after Bede's death, when – under the rule of King Alfred (reigned 886–899) – a large number of Latin texts were translated into Old English, as part of a programme to promote learning. Alfred wrote that he wished to render books 'ða ðe niedbeðearfosta sien eallum monnum to wiotonne, ðæt we ða on ðæt geðiode wenden ðe we ealle gecnawan mægen' ('most needful for all men to know, into that language that we all can understand'): Alfred,

Notes

Preface to the Translation of Gregory the Great's 'Pastoral Care', in *Old and Middle English*, ed. Treharne, pp. 12–13. One of these books 'most needful for all men to know' was Bede's *Ecclesiastical History*. When the translator came to Bede's description of the cattle byre, he inserted a version of the *Hymn* that was very similar to that which appears in the edges of early copies of the *Ecclesiastical History*, rather than providing a new translation from Bede's Latin version of the text. (The translator also removed Bede's reference to translating from the original.)

16 Kiernan, 'Reading Cædmon's "Hymn" with Someone Else's Glosses', pp. 108, 122–3 (n. 18).

17 A list of contents and folio references for each text can be found on the British Library's Digitised Manuscripts website: <http://www.bl.uk/manuscripts/FullDisplay.aspx?ref=Harley_MS_978>.

18 Fol. 40r.

19 Fol. 67r. Marie de France, *Fables*, ed. and trans. Spiegel, p. 256 (my translation).

20 Bloch, *The Anonymous Marie de France*, pp. 25–50.

21 'E compassa les vers de lais / Ke ne sunt pas del tut verais' (Piramus, *La vie seint Edmund*, ed. Kjellman, p. 4).

22 Marie de France, *Lais*, ed. Ewert, p. 2.

23 Examples include Phaedrus's first-century collection, as well as the *Romulus* and the so-called *Romuli Anglici Cunctis* (see Jambeck, 'Reclaiming the Woman in the Book', p. 122; my discussion is indebted to Jambeck's fascinating work).

24 Ibid., p. 121.

25 *Fables of Marie de France*, ed. and trans. Spiegel, pp. 82–5.

26 Ibid., p. 84.

27 Cambridge University Library MS Ee.6.11. See *Catalogue of the Manuscripts Preserved in the Library of the University of Cambridge*, 2, 260–1; and Jambeck, 'Reclaiming the Woman in the Book', p. 135.

28 See Jambeck, 'Reclaiming the Woman in the Book'.

29 *Fables*, ed. and trans. Spiegel, p. 256 (my translation).

30 This was the suggestion of Andrew Taylor (*Textual Situations*, pp. 76–136, esp. p. 99), but Rupert T. Pickens suggests it originated in Herefordshire ('Reading Harley 978: Marie de France in Context').

31 BL Harley 978, fol. 160r.

32 Namely Abbot Simon (d. 1226) on 13 February, and Abbot John de Fornsett (d. 1261) on 19 January (fols 15v–16r).

33 Sanders, 'Wycombe . . . , W. de', *Grove Music Online*.

34 See Taylor, *Textual Situations*, esp. pp. 76–136, figs 8, 11–14; and Losseff, 'Wycombe, W. of', *ODNB*.

35 Busby, 'The Manuscripts of Marie de France', p. 305–6.

36 Marie de France, *Lais*, ed. Ewert, p. 1 (my translation).

37 Lerer, *Chaucer and His Readers*, p. 23. On Lydgate's central role in the installation of Chaucer's pre-eminence, see Scanlon, *Narrative, Authority and Power*, p. 322.

38 Some scholars believe, however, that three early manuscripts may have been started before Chaucer's death (see *The Norton Chaucer*, ed. Lawton, p. 31).

39 Lerer, *Chaucer and His Readers*, p. 8.

40 Green, *Poets and Princepleasers*, p. 6.

41 His *House of Fame* (a dream-vision), the *Legend of Good Women* and, most probably, *The Canterbury Tales* are all unfinished (but see note 45 below), and it seems likely that Chaucer also wrote texts that are now lost.

42 Gillespie, *Print Culture and the Medieval Author*, p. 35.

43 Ferry, 'Anonymity: The Literary History of a Word'.

44 Two scholars have recently suggested that the poem was left intentionally, jokily, in this state – as the number of tales that would be required for each pilgrim to tell one there and one on the way back would make a vast and cumbersome poem (see Edwards, 'To speken short and pleyn' (2018), and the forthcoming edition of *The Canterbury Tales*, ed. Boffey and Edwards).

45 Boffey and Edwards, *New Index of Middle English Verse*, no. 4019.

46 It has been claimed that this manuscript was written by a particular scribe who was personally known to Chaucer (Mooney, 'Chaucer's Scribe'), but this has been disputed (notably in Warner, *Chaucer's Scribes*).

47 *Marie de France: Seven of her Lais*, trans. Rickert.

48 See 'John M. Manly & Edith Rickert', <https://www.lib.uchicago.edu/projects/centcat/centcats/fac/facch16_01.html>.

49 Peter Robinson, 'New Methods of Editing', p. 19.

50 *The Text of 'The Canterbury Tales'*, ed. Manly and Rickert, 1, viii; Snell, 'A Woman Medievalist Much Maligned'.

51 Anthony Bale suggests the texts were intentionally split up, contending that the Prioress's Tale was 'reformatted as part of Lydgate's *Testament*', noting that Chaucer's text 'interrupts the *Testament* at the point at which "Lydgate", the narrator, has detailed his youthful excesses' (*The Jew in the Medieval Book*, p. 96).

52 *The Text of 'The Canterbury Tales'*, ed. Manly and Rickert, 1, 248.

53 Owen, *The Manuscripts of 'The Canterbury Tales'*, p. 115.

54 BL Harley MS 2382, fol. 97r ('Prioress') and fol. 100 ('Second Nun').

Notes

55 While the non-attribution to Chaucer is not in itself unusual, it is my view that in this case it was strategic and deliberate (Wellesley, 'Lydgate's *Life of Our Lady*', pp. 193–203).

56 *Riverside Chaucer*, gen. ed. Benson, p. 210 (line 559).

57 From the thirteenth century onwards, the compilation (and glossing) of textual material was seen as a literary activity in itself (see Hathaway, '*Compilatio*: From Plagiarism to Compiling', pp. 19–22).

58 Michael Johnston, 'Constantinian Christianity in the London Thornton Manuscript', p. 177.

59 *Riverside Chaucer*, gen. ed. Benson, p. 650, corrected against Cambridge, Trinity College MS R.3.20, p. 367.

60 I take the 'a' to be a contracted form of the pronoun 'he': see *Oxford English Dictionary*, '**he**. *pers. pron., 3rd sing. masc. nom.*' (**A.** Forms 1η).

61 Doubt has been cast on the poem's authenticity by two scholars, looking at the manuscript evidence and the metre respectively (see Edwards, 'Chaucer and "Adam Scriveyn"', and Weiskott, '"Adam Scriveyn" and Chaucer's Metrical Practice').

62 *Riverside Chaucer*, gen. ed. Benson, p. 356 (lines 652–60).

63 Ibid., p. 362 (line 1146).

64 *Lydgate's Fall of Princes*, ed. Bergen, pp. 7–8 (lines 246–7, 279–80).

Chapter Seven

1 Kundera, *The Book of Laughter and Forgetting*, trans. Aaron Asher (London: Faber and Faber, 1996), p. 4.

2 *Aldhelm: The Prose Works*, trans. Lapidge and Herren, pp. 61–2.

3 I am indebted to Thijs Porck's excellent blog post 'Anglo-Saxon Cryptography'.

4 Christine Fell argues that the fact that this manuscript is held in a German collection may be a reason it has survived, while most 'equivalent material in England either failed to survive Viking raids, the Norman Conquest, or the Dissolution of the Monasteries and related hazards' (Fell, 'Some Implications of the Boniface Correspondence', p. 29).

5 Watt, *Women, Writing and Religion*, pp. 2–3.

6 Minnis, *Medieval Theory of Authorship*, p. 10. See, more generally, Bale, 'From Translator to Laureate'.

7 Larrington, 'Hugeburc [Huneburc]', *ODNB*.

8 *Exeter Anthology of Old English Poetry*, ed. Muir, 1, 284 and 328–30.

9 *Þe Wohunge of Ure Lauerd* (*The Wooing of Our Lord*), BL Cotton MS Titus D xviii, fols 127r–133r (*Middle English Religious Prose*, ed. Blake,

pp. 61–2); translations are from or based on *Anchoritic Spirituality*, ed. and trans. Savage and Watson, pp. 247–8. (All subsequent references are to these editors.)

10 Blake, p. 62; Savage and Watson, p. 248.

11 Blake, p. 66; Savage and Watson, p. 251.

12 Blake, p. 63; Savage and Watson, p. 249.

13 Blake, p. 71.

14 Savage and Watson, p. 255.

15 Blake, p. 67; Savage and Watson, pp. 252–3.

16 Blake, p. 70; Savage and Watson, p. 255.

17 Blake, p. 71.

18 Savage and Watson, p. 256.

19 Blake, pp. 71–2.

20 Savage and Watson, p. 256.

21 Warren, *Anchorites and their Patrons in Medieval England*, p. 20.

22 *Ancrene Wisse: A Corrected Edition*, ed. Millett (2005). The work is translated in *Ancrene Wisse: Guide for Anchoresses*, ed. and trans. Millett (2009). (The pages of both the edition and translation of the text by Millett correspond, so all subsequent references will be to a single page reference for both works by this editor, differentiated by date where appropriate.)

23 'Muche word is of ou, hu gentile wummen ȝe beoð, vor godleic and for ureoleic iȝirned of monie, and sustren of one ueder and of one moder, ine blostme of ower ȝuweðe uorheten alle wor[l]des blissen and bicomen ancren' (Millett, p. 73).

24 Description drawn from Jones, 'Ceremonies of Enclosure', pp. 40–1.

25 Jones, *Hermits and Anchorites in England*, p. 57.

26 Millett, p. 46 ('schrapien euche dei þe eorðe up of hare put þet ha schulen rotien in').

27 Ibid., p. 43 (translation modified).

28 Gilchrist, *Contemplation and Action*, p. 192.

29 See Warren, *Anchorites and Their Patrons in Medieval England*.

30 E. A. Jones, *Hermits and Anchorites in England*, p. 62.

31 Ibid.

32 Ibid., p. 81.

33 Ibid., p. 83.

34 Millett, p. 158.

35 Millett (2009), p. ix.

36 Millett, p. 48.

37 Ibid., p. 56.

38 Ibid., p. 48.

39 Ibid., pp. 76–9.

40 Ibid., p 46 (modified translation).

41 For example, Blake, p. 63, and Savage and Watson, p. 249.

42 Millett, p. 147.

43 Þe Wohunge of Ure Lauerd, ed. Thompson, pp. xxi–xxii.

44 Savage and Watson, pp. 418–19.

45 Jones, *Hermits and Anchorites in England*, p. 77.

46 Jones, 'A Mirror for Recluses: A New Manuscript', p. 427.

47 Millett, p. 73.

48 Innes-Parker, 'Medieval Widowhood and Textual Guidance'.

49 Millett, p. 96.

50 Ibid., p. 160. Two women shared a cell at Worcester Priory, and Christina of Markyate dwelt with a female recluse called Alfwen and then Roger the hermit. See Mills, 'Gender, Sodomy, Friendship and the Medieval Anchorhold', p. 6.

51 Mulder-Bakker, 'Foreword', p. 1.

52 St Julian's Church in Conesford, where Julian was enclosed, was destroyed by bombing in the Second World War. Its exact original layout is unclear. Margery may have been able to eat with Julian in a parlour adjoining the cell or she may simply have sought her counsel at a window. On the architecture of cells, see Hasenfratz, 'Ancrene Wisse, Introduction'.

53 Some manuscripts say 13 May.

54 Julian, *Revelations*, ed. Windeatt, p. 31.

55 The title of the text is a matter of scholarly debate: some term it *A Revelation of Love*, some the *Shewings*, but most modern editions call it the *Revelations of Divine Love*.

56 Julian, *Revelations of Divine Love*, trans. Spearing, ed. Spearing, p. xii.

57 Julian, *Revelations*, ed. Windeatt, p. 10.

58 Vincent Gillespie, '"[S]he Do the Police in Different Voices"', p. 196.

59 The first bequest made to her as an anchoress is from 1394, but she may have been enclosed for a long time before this.

60 Julian, *Revelations*, ed. Windeatt, p. 39.

61 Ibid., p. 137.

62 Hill, *Women and Religion*, p. 14.

63 Julian, *Revelations*, ed. Windeatt, p. 35.

64 Ibid. (quotation from Long Text).

65 Riddy, '"Women Talking about the Things of God"', p. 114.

66 See Gillespie and Ross, 'The Apophatic Image'.

67 Julian, *Revelations*, ed. Windeatt, p. 29.

68 Ibid., p. 110.

69 Ibid., p. xv.

70 Ibid., p. 164.

71 Ibid., p. xv.

72 See Reynolds, 'Some Literary Influences in the *Revelations*'.

73 Julian, *Revelations*, ed. Windeatt, p. xv.

74 Ibid., p. 154.

75 Ibid., p. 44.

76 The Short Text version is slightly different (see ibid., p. 73).

77 *A Revelation of Purgatory*, ed. McAvoy. For a discussion of the problems of attribution, see Drieshen, 'English Nuns as "Anchoritic Intercessors"'.

78 Julian, *Revelations*, ed. Windeatt, p. 7.

79 Crampton, 'The Shewings of Julian of Norwich: Introduction'.

80 BL Add. MS 37790, digitised at <http://www.bl.uk/manuscripts/FullDisplay.aspx?ref=Add._MS_37790>.

81 Fols 96v and 226r, and repeated in black ink on fols 1r and 226r.

82 Fols 23r, 33r, 110v and 114r.

83 *XVI Revelations of Divine Love* (1670).

84 Stillingfleet, *A Discourse Concerning Idolatry*, p. 226.

85 Julian, *Revelations of Divine Love*, ed. Warrack.

86 Mechain, *Works*, ed. and trans. Gramich, p. 41. Gramich's work contains both literal and free translations. With a few exceptions, I have mainly chosen the literal ones for quotation.

87 She refers here to the *descriptio pulcritudinis* – the bardic convention of praising a woman systematically. Mechain, *Works*, ed. and trans. Gramich, p. 43; *Gwaith Gwerful Mechain*, ed. Howells, pp. 103–5. (All subsequent references are to these two editions, by Howells and Gramich.)

88 Howells, p. 104. It is not her *most* popular, however; her *cywydd* to Christ appears in sixty-nine manuscripts (ibid., p. 51).

89 D. R. Johnston, 'The Erotic Poetry of the *Cywyddwyr*', p. 82.

90 Howells, p. 2. She is described as Hywel Fychan's daughter in Aberystwyth, Llyfrgell Genedlaethol Cymru [National Library of Wales] MS 3057D, and this is supported by other evidence elsewhere (see Gramich, p. 7).

91 Lloyd-Morgan, 'Women and their Poetry in Medieval Wales', p. 198.

92 Howells, p. 4.

93 M. Wynn Thomas, 'Foreword', p. ix.

94 Ibid., p. xiv.

95 Lewis, 'Extreme Welsh Meter'. This is slightly easier to achieve in Welsh than English because in Welsh the first letter of a word changes according to gender, place and function.

96 Ibid.

Notes

97 This bardic tradition was 'the preserve of Wales's professional medieval poetic guild and its elite patrons: the indigenous princes of Wales (c. 1137–1282) in the first instance and, in its latter stages, the Welsh nobility and clerics (1282–c. 1650). Rules surrounding membership of the guild were strict: like its Gaelic counterpart in Ireland, the guild also had a hereditary dimension and poetic families have been identified' (Charnell-White, 'Problems of Authorship and Attribution', p. 402).

98 Powell, 'Women and Strict-Metre Poetry in Wales', pp. 134–5.

99 Ibid., p. 132.

100 Gramich, pp. 46–53; Howells, pp. 106–7.

101 D. R. Johnston, 'The Erotic Poetry of the *Cywyddwyr*', p. 83.

102 Aberystwyth, Llyfrgell Genedlaethol Cymru [National Library of Wales] MS 3050D (*olim* Mostyn Hall MS 147), p. 360.

103 Gramich, pp. 64–73; Howells, pp. 80–3.

104 Gramich, p. 111.

105 See Lloyd-Morgan, 'The "Querelle des Femmes": A Continuing Tradition'.

106 Gramich, p. 67.

107 Lloyd-Morgan, 'The "Querelle des Femmes": A Continuing Tradition', p. 107, citing Cartwright, *Y Forwyn Fair*, pp. 33–4.

108 Gramich, pp. 71–3.

109 Cartwright, 'Women Writers in Wales', p. 67, citing Smith, 'Olrhain Anni Goch'.

110 Gramich, p. 111.

111 Ibid., p. 88. (This is one of Gramich's freer translations.)

112 Ibid., p. 89.

113 Howells, p. 123.

114 Gramich, pp. 104–5. Cathryn Charnell-White ascribes this poem to Gwerful Fychan in her anthology, *Beirdd Ceridwen Blodeugerdd Barddas*.

115 Cartwright, 'Women Writers in Wales', p. 60. The manuscript is Aberystwyth, Llyfrgell Genedlaethol Cymru [National Library of Wales], Cwrtmawr MS 1491 (Llyfr Dolwar Fach).

116 Lloyd-Morgan, 'Women and their Poetry in Medieval Wales', p. 190.

117 Harries, 'Barddoniaeth', p. 26; English translation from Gramich, 'Orality and Morality: Early Welsh Women's Poetry'.

118 Howells ascribed nineteen out of a possible forty poems to Gwerful Mechain (p.31).

119 The earliest manuscript, BL Add. MS 14967, is dated to the second quarter of the sixteenth century. See Howells, p. 25.

120 Charnell-White, 'Problems of Authorship and Attribution', p. 401.

121 Lloyd-Morgan, 'Women and their Poetry in Medieval Wales', p. 190.

Notes

122 Mechain, *Works*, ed. and trans. Gramich, p. 9.

123 Harries, *Gwaith Huw, Cae Llwyd ac Eraill* [*The Works of Huw of Cae Llwyd and Others*].

124 Howells wittily called her 2001 edition of Gwerful's works *Gwaith Gwerful Mechain ac Eraill* [*The Works of Gwerful Mechain and Others*] as a rebuttal to Leslie Harries.

125 Stephens, *The Oxford Companion to the Literature of Wales*, p. 238. Stephens did soften his criticism in *A New Companion to the Literature of Wales*, praising her devotional poetry and her 'spirited response' to domestic violence (p. 294).

126 Keene, *Survey of Medieval Winchester*, 2, 128.

127 Dowding, '"A Certain Tourelle on London Wall"', p. 44.

128 It was copied by Hugh Maurice under the direction of Owen Jones (1741–1814), a Welsh antiquary and the president of the society. The library's nineteenth-century catalogue reports that the manuscript contains verse 'complimentary and abusive in regard to young women' (*Catalogue of Additions*, p. 59).

Epilogue

1 *The Gutenberg Bible*, ed. Füssel, 3 vols, commentary vol, p. 9.

2 See, for example, Edwards, 'William Caxton and the Introduction of Printing'; Hellinga, *William Caxton and Early Printing*; and Painter, *William Caxton*.

3 Chaucer, *Canterbury Tales* (1483), sig. A2v (Pollard and Redgrave, *Short Title Catalogue*, no. 5083).

4 See Hammond, 'On the Order of the Canterbury Tales'.

5 James and Jenkins, *Descriptive Catalogue*, pp. 412–14; see also Blake, 'Manuscript to Print', pp. 413–14.

6 An AHRC-funded research project on 'Manuscripts after Print c.1450–1550: Producing and Reading Books during Technological Change' is currently underway at the University of Newcastle: <https://research.ncl.ac.uk/mssafterprint/about/>.

7 Bühler, *The Fifteenth-Century Book*, p. 16.

Afterword

1 On the self-styled title 'Antiquarius', see Momigliano, 'Ancient History and the Antiquarian', pp. 313–14; Leland, *Laboryouse Journey*, sig. C1v.

Notes

2 He seems to have made two or three trips there before the Dissolution of the Monasteries, and one or two afterwards (Carley, 'John Leland and the Contents of English Pre-Dissolution Libraries', p. 331).

3 Carley, *Books of King Henry VIII*, pp. 93–4.

4 See Alice Hunt, *Drama of Coronation*, pp. 39–76; and *John Leland and Nicholas Udall*, ed. Sutton.

5 Simpson, *Reform and Cultural Revolution*, p. 9.

6 Knowles, *Religious Orders in England*, 3, 363.

7 Beverley, 'Portinari, Sir Giovanni', *ODNB*.

8 Aston, 'English Ruins', p. 239.

9 Ibid., p. 245.

10 Leland, *Laboryouse Journey*, sig. B1r.

11 See Herbert, *Sherborne Missal*, p. 9.

12 Summit, *Memory's Library*, p. 102.

13 Ker, *Medieval Libraries of Great Britain*, pp. xi–xii; *Catalogue of Dated and Datable Manuscripts*, ed. Watson, 1, xi.

14 Wood, *Athenae Oxonienses*, ed. Bliss, pp. 197–8.

15 The presentation copy for Henry VIII, printed on parchment and containing a correction in Leland's own hand, is held by the British Library (C.20.b.3).

16 Aston, 'English Ruins', p. 255; Simpson, *Reform and Cultural Revolution*, p. 14.

17 For more on the collectors of this period, see Summit, *Memory's Library*.

18 Beer, 'Stow [Stowe], John', *ODNB*.

19 On 'sorency', see Devereux, 'Empty Tuns and Unfruitful Grafts', p. 44, n. 47.

20 Summit, *Memory's Library*, p. 103.

21 De Bury, *Philobiblon*, ed. and trans. Thomas, p. 159.

22 Ibid., p. 229.

23 Ibid., p. 237–39.

24 Ibid., pp. 161–2.

25 Ibid., p. 226.

26 Ibid., p. 162.

27 Ibid., pp. 179–80.

28 Ibid., p. 161.

Acknowledgements

1 *The Earliest Life of Gregory*, p. 129

Index

Index

Index

Index

Index

Index

Index